NEGOTIATING THE HIEROPHANT
WALT WHITMAN AND OTHER GURUS

ALSO BY MIKE KING:

Luminous: The Spiritual Life on Film
(Stochastic Press, 2018 / McFarland & Company, 2014)

Mountain Calls
(Stochastic Press, 2017)

The Beauty of Judaism on Film
(Stochastic Press, 2017)

Enigma's Coda
(Stochastic Press, 2016)

The American Cinema of Excess: Extremes of the National Mind on Film
(Stochastic Press, 2016 / McFarland & Company, 2009)

Quakernomics: An Ethical Capitalism
(Anthem Press, 2014)

The Angel of Har Megiddo: A novel of the US-Israel-Palestine conflict
(Stochastic Press, 2012)

Postsecularism: The Hidden Challenge to Religious Extremism
(James Clarke & Co., 2009)

Secularism: The Hidden Origins of Disbelief
(James Clarke & Co., 2007)

Other writings are archived at www.jnani.org/mrking/writings and
www.stochasticpress.com/papers.html

NEGOTIATING THE HIEROPHANT

WALT WHITMAN AND OTHER GURUS

Mike King

Text copyright © 2019 Mike King

All rights reserved. No part of this book may be reproduced or transmitted in any form or by any means, electronic or mechanical, including photocopying, recording, or by an information storage and retrieval system – except by a reviewer who may quote brief passages in a review – without permission in writing from the author.

mike@jnani.org

Version 1.0 © 2019

This book is also available in Kindle format.

ISBN-13: 978-0-9956480-5-0
ISBN-10: 0-9956480-5-0

London: Stochastic Press
www.stochasticpress.com

The cover is based on the Tarot card "The Hierophant," illustrated below. Walt Whitman is placed centrally and holds a walking stick, symbolic of the open road. He is flanked by two Greek columns to suggest that his religious outlook has more in common with ancient Greece than with the Abrahamic traditions. To Whitman's left is Anne Gilchrist and to his right is Edward Carpenter, two key disciples. They face away from the teacher to show their individuality and independence from him, unlike the disciples in the Tarot card who face towards the hierophant.

CONTENTS

Introduction	1
1. The role of the spiritual teacher	**5**
Western Counterparts to the Guru	6
A note on my own experience	7
The spiritual teacher through texts	12
The teacher-pupil relationship in the spiritual life	13
2. Introducing Whitman as guru	**15**
Religious interpretations of *Leaves*	16
The life of Whitman	20
Evidence from Richard Maurice Bucke	24
3. Whitman's system	**27**
A first look: "Song of Myself"	29
Whitman's system and the East	46
The unchristian Whitman	52
The American Transcendentalists	55
Whitman and Nature Mysticism	58
Traherne and Blake: "Poets of the *via positiva*"	64
Gaps in Whitman's system	71
4. Gurus in the West	**74**
Romanticism, Neoplatonism and the New Age	78
Non-Christian Western Spiritual Teachers	79
Rabbis, priests and imams as Western spiritual teachers	81
Eastern Gurus in the West	83
Modern Western teachers	95
5. Cult catastrophes	**97**
The terrible: Waco, Heaven's Gate, Jonestown	98
The debacle: Rajneesh in America	99
The embarrassing: Scientology	103
The resented: Cohen	106
6. Instructive negotiations	**112**
Socrates / Alcibiades	112

	Marpa / Milarepa	117
	Shams-e Tabrizi / Rumi	119
	Gurdjieff / Ouspensky	123
	Ramana Maharshi / Paul Brunton	128
	Radha Mohan Lal / Irina Tweedie	132
	Krishnamurti / Bohm and U.G.	138
	Good Lance / Crow Dog	143
	Andrew Cohen / Michael Wombacher	147
	Maharishi Mahesh Yogi / Robert Forman	152
	Mother Meera / Andrew Harvey	156
	A comparison of systems	160
7.	**The hierophancy of Walt Whitman**	**161**
	Eros and *agape*	161
	Whitman as teacher	164
	Horace Traubel	172
	John Burroughs	178
	John Addington Symonds	183
	Edward Carpenter	187
	Anne Gilchrist	191
	Richard Maurice Bucke	194
8.	**Negotiating the hierophant**	**199**
	Spiritual materialism	201
	Discipleship heavy, discipleship light	208
	Negotiating the Hierophant	210
	The hierophancy of Walt Whitman	212
	Go, seeker, go	215
Bibliography		**216**
References		**219**
Index		**226**

INTRODUCTION

What on earth *is* a spiritual teacher? What is a guru, a master, a hierophant? And why on earth should we see the nineteenth century poet Walt Whitman as guru, master, or hierophant relevant to the twenty-first century? And if we do, what does his case tell us about gurus in general? This book answers those questions and offers some thoughts, partly based on personal experience, as to how to negotiate the spiritual teacher today. I have chosen the word "negotiate" to suggest that this is no easy matter and I have chosen the word "hierophant" to suggest a possible counterpart, the sycophant. For many it seems that one of the most difficult parts of negotiating the guru, master, or hierophant is the apparent sycophancy required of the pupil.

The word "hierophant" in ancient Greek simply means priest, but its etymology is significant: its two parts mean in turn the holy and to show. The priest, guru, master, or hierophant is one who shows us the holy. I prefer "spiritual teacher" but whatever term we use we have to recognize that for Westerners with a belief in progressive democratic values there lies a problem with the very idea. If there is a "holy" then why do we need a teacher of it? Does not placing yourself as pupil to a spiritual teacher open yourself to the worst kinds of sycophancy, meaning unquestioning obedience? I have been negotiating this question for some forty years and Walt Whitman has been a significant figure in this process. On the subject of etymology, the word "guru" in Sanskrit apparently means to make an effort, to raise up, and is related to the Latin word *gravis* meaning grave, weighty or serious. I do take the whole issue of the guru seriously; there certainly can be hard work involved; it is about raising up; and it can be heavy, man.

In this book I will use the term "hierophancy" as a shorthand for the teacher-pupil relationship in the spiritual life. The term is intended to include all such relationships for a particular master and also the spiritual system in which they operate, whether inherited or constructed *de novo*. This book can then be summed up as a comparison between a selection of historical hierophancies and that of Walt Whitman.

We can introduce the idea of Whitman as a spiritual teacher firstly through the opinion of an Indian scholar and secondly through a Whitman poem. O. K. Nambiar has called Whitman a "Maha Yogi" meaning great adept at the yoga system. Though technically inaccurate – Whitman was not trained in yoga or any Indian system – the term was meant to convey both the universal nature of Whitman's teachings and his accomplishments in the field. Furthermore Nambiar commented with regard to one of Whitman's friends that "Whitman was Traubel's Guru."

Whitman himself wrote:

> No dainty dolce affettuoso I,
> Bearded, sun-burnt, gray-neck'd, forbidding, I have arrived,
> To be wrestled with as I pass for the solid prizes of the universe,
> For such I afford whoever can persevere to win them.
> (Starting from Paumanok, v. 15)

Any master of a profession, skill or trade might talk like this regarding the novice but the phrasing of it would be odd in all cases other than just one kind of discipline: the spiritual. A Zen master would more likely express such sentiments, the "solid prizes of the universe" being spiritual enlightenment. These two hints, one from a Hindu, and one from Whitman himself, will be greatly amplified through this book as Whitman's hidden nature as spiritual teacher is revealed.

Many years ago I bought a small volume from a second-hand bookshop in Oxford with the title "Cosmic Consciousness." It was written by a self-confessed spiritual disciple of Walt Whitman called Richard Maurice Bucke, and it was a key part in my process of eclectic spiritual searching that had just previously taken me to India and the ashram of the guru then known as Bhagwan Shree Rajneesh. This guru – later utterly discredited – made much of his eclecticism and Bucke's book marked a continuation of that eclecticism, as it prompted me to search for a spirituality that was specifically Western but not necessarily Christian. What Rajneesh and Whitman have in common is a spiritual world view or system that is intensely world-curious as opposed to world-denying; what separates them is that Rajneesh as a teacher of an Eastern tradition seems to have crashed spectacularly in the West, while Whitman, whose teachings are possibly much better suited to the West, has been almost entirely forgotten as a spiritual teacher.

Rajneesh, for all his faults, was amongst a group of Eastern gurus who understood that modernity had changed everything and that spirituality was no exception. Rajneesh thought that Freud in particular had unleashed changes that meant the renunciative forms of spirituality no longer made any sense. Although he did not discover Whitman as a spiritual teacher Rajneesh's celebration of sexuality fits well with Whitman's worldview. If we think of spiritual teachers operating within existing worldviews or constructing new ones then their teachings become "systems" varying in how explicit or comprehensive they are. Indeed, crucial to negotiating the hierophant is the understanding of their system, whether explicit or implicit. My search for spiritual systems, initiated by Rajneesh's eclecticism and bolstered by Bucke's, has led me to discover many figures not normally considered spiritual teachers, including Whitman of course. If Whitman is lost to us as poet instead of a spiritual teacher then others, such as Plotinus, Descartes and Spinoza, each with important spiritual systems, are lost to us as philosophers. However this book is not so much about spiritual systems as the relationship between spiritual seeker and spiritual teacher. At the same time negotiating the hierophant must also involve negotiating their system, particularly as their system will very often be both counter-intuitive and counter-cultural.

While the hierophant in various guises and using various terms is at least present in Western consciousness – though mostly ignored – the spiritual seeker is usually a figure of ridicule if acknowledged at all. Yet this is what I found myself to be in my mid-twenties as I plunged into a rather early mid-life crisis. The resolution of this involved negotiating many hierophants and their systems, not just in the world of spiritual teachings but also in the world of psychotherapy. I'll bring in this personal detail here and there where relevant.

Was Rajneesh right that Freud had changed everything for the spiritual life, for the religious life? I think so. Most commentators on recent Western history accept that a key phenomenon since the Western Enlightenment is the rise of individualism. It took perhaps a Russian filmmaker, Andrei Tarkovsky – living between East and West – to make the best comment on it:

> The East was closer to the truth than the West; but Western civilization devoured the East with its materialist demands on life.
>
> Compare Eastern and Western music. The West is forever shouting, "This is me! Look at me! Listen to me suffering, loving! How unhappy I am! How happy! I! Mine! Me!" In the Eastern tradition they never utter a word about themselves. The person is totally absorbed into God, Nature, Time; finding himself in everything; discovering everything in himself. [1]

Tarkovsky was writing in the 1980s before the collapse of the Soviet Union and before the liberalization of the Russian and Chinese economies. I would suggest that since then Western materialism and Western individualist culture have gained much ground in the East. Western individualism grows apace as increased material wealth – however badly skewed across rich and poor – gives increased leisure. Above all popular culture increasingly emphasizes the individual over the collective. The East has absorbed both Western capitalism and Western culture and as it does so the rise of individualism, already very noticeable in Eastern cultural production, will inevitably progress further. While there remain some people everywhere who are perhaps attracted to the life of poverty, chastity and obedience – as demanded in the Catholic monastic tradition for example – they swim against the tide. If we are urged in mainstream culture to be "authentic" to our unique selves in all other spheres then how can the spiritual life resist? Why, indeed, should it? If that is the case, modernity demands a radical rethink of the relationship between spiritual teacher and pupil.

1
THE ROLE OF THE SPIRITUAL TEACHER

In the classic eighth-century Indian text *The Crest-Jewel of Discrimination* Shankara says: "Only through God's grace may we obtain those three rarest advantages – human birth, the longing for liberation, and discipleship to an illumined teacher."[2] Leaving aside the probable mistranslation of "God" it is clear that the "illumined teacher" is crucial, not only to Shankara, but to his entire culture. For India the guru – the illumined teacher – has always been a revered part of religious life, and seekers would travel far to find one. India has probably devoted more effort than any other region of the world to understanding what passes between guru and disciple, and Sanskrit is reputed to be the best-equipped language in the world for embodying that understanding. Shankara's idea is remote from twenty-first century Western thought however. To be grateful to exist in a human body is a sentiment rarely expressed today. It is a commonplace in Western thought that the human body is not in any essential way different to that of an animal; at the same time it brings obligations many of us find burdensome. The longing for liberation if encountered is mostly an expression of political thought; for those on the left it is liberation from capitalism, for those on the right liberation from the state. One does not see a situation provoking such longings – the situation of being human – as a rare advantage at all, quite the converse, one sees the continued existence of our unfulfilled longings in political form as confirmation of the dire state of the world. To see discipleship to an "illumined teacher" as anything but a sure path to sycophancy is to court, again, ridicule. And, as stated at the outset, to regard Whitman as such a teacher is surely odd.

While Whitman holds the animals in great regard it is clear that he considers the human realm of infinite significance; certainly an advantage. He clearly understands the longing for spiritual liberation and considers those who seek it from him lucky to some extent at least. For myself in my late twenties I had little insight as to what exactly separates us from the animals but I knew with considerable desperation that "liberation" in the Indian spiritual sense was what I was looking for and I was determined to find any and all spiritual teachers that could deliver it. I was in fact the classic disciple, placing learning at the feet of the master above all other facets of my life.

What I appreciated in examining Indian systems was that the East appears to operate a "discipleship light" as opposed to the "discipleship heavy" of Western tradition. India had no habit, for example, of burning people at the stake for holding the wrong beliefs or following the wrong guru, not, that is, until Christianity and Islam turned up. I also learned that the Buddha, then known as Siddhartha Gautama, became a seeker who had several spiritual teachers. The first was Alara Kalama who taught him meditation, and, when Gautama reached the same level as his teacher, was asked to teach in his place. Gotama refused and went on to another teacher called Uddaka Rāmaputta and learned all he could from him. I call this "discipleship light" because firstly the teacher is candid when the pupil has attained to the same level, and secondly because in this system the pupil is free to move from one guru to another. Three factors seem to operate here: firstly whether the hierophant is inclined to the heavy or light approach; secondly whether the system they teach in is heavy or light – for example a system of eternal damnation can make it heavy – and finally whether the seeker himself or herself negotiates the whole thing in a heavy or light manner.

Western Counterparts to the Guru

The Christian world has plenty of charismatic teachers, Billy Graham being a famous one in the late twentieth century, even having audiences with Queen Elizabeth II. Nothing in the West quite matches the role or status

1. The Role of the Spiritual Teacher

of the Indian guru however because of the position of Jesus in Christianity as both unique and of a stature by definition unattainable by the rest of us. However promising a disciple of Christ you may be, you cannot in turn attain "Christhood." In contrast any pupil of a guru in India can potentially become a guru in their own right and not only match but exceed their master. Christianity's centralized organization, personified for centuries in the Pope, ensured that there was orthodoxy of belief and to stray too far or to innovate too quickly met with disapproval. In my book *Secularism: The Hidden Origins of Disbelief* I chart everything that is inevitably absolutist in monotheism, and posit that modern atheism is largely a reaction to that absolutism. Christian mystics sometimes operate like gurus but could, like Teresa of Avila or St John of the Cross, meet opposition in their lifetime or even persecution, torture and execution. The closest I have found to a culturally sanctioned spiritual teacher in the West is perhaps what is known as the "spiritual advisor" in the Catholic tradition.

In the researches prompted by Rajneesh and Bucke I uncovered a swathe of philosophers, as mentioned, who also operated like spiritual teachers and who clearly had disciples. These include Pythagoras, Socrates and Plotinus in the early period and Descartes and Spinoza in the period of the European Enlightenment. I have called these teachers the "lost buddhas of the West"[3] because, going back to Shankara, it seems that they taught a system of "liberation," also known as *moksha*, or spiritual enlightenment, that is not so removed from that taught by the Buddha. Descartes' *Meditations* reads in places like the thinking of the Buddha, and he had a following in the relatively liberal Holland in his day. The essential difference between the Christian system and that of the Indian teachers – and my lost buddhas – as pointed out above, is that the state of Christ is always unattainable. It is worth adding that my lost buddhas of the later period, although ostensibly Christian, were in fact more in tune with the ancient Greek spiritual tradition, a feature also relevant to Whitman.

A note on my own experience

I had no sense as a child or young adult of being religious, but I did have a spiritual sensibility best described as animistic. In my twenties I gravitated to the yoga made popular in the West by B. K. S. Ayengar and was taught his hatha yoga system by an African, the son of a Ghanaian prime minister. I landed up living in a yoga household enthusiastic for all kinds of Eastern teachings, and knew when I went on an intensive course to study yoga with Ayengar in Pune, India, that I would also visit the ashram of the controversial guru Bhagwan Shree Rajneesh. I was by this time a seeker, but I was utterly unprepared for the culture shock of India and for the psychological shock of the Rajneesh ashram and its mixture of meditation and psychotherapeutic techniques. I broke down.

Though I was enormously grateful to escape India, on return to my familiar England I had the strange experience of observing the typical academics and students and other residents of home-town Oxford from a new perspective. Compared to the peaceful visages of the Indians I had met, Oxford's people all looked like axe-murderers. They looked tense, that is. I began to understand that cultural differences are profound and that as a citizen of the world I could shape myself by drawing on far wider sources than I had previously thought, and particularly in the spiritual life. I was already the son of a double refugee on one side and a sculptor who died young on the other side, a background rather different to most of my school- and college-mates. I didn't find it too big a step therefore to dress in orange, wear the beads with a picture of Rajneesh on them and instruct my mother to call me "Swami Yogananda." In other words I took initiation in a cult.

I found my discipleship to Rajneesh was as "heavy" or "light" as I made it, mostly because the following was so large by then that Rajneesh had no time for personal interventions beyond his inner circle. Instead I joined meditations and therapy groups and was instructed by minor figures in the organization, though mostly I got on with daily life of earning a living – in orange mind you. Rajneesh was gloriously varied in his lectures, ranging from Zen to Sufism to the Gospel of Thomas, and also encouraged his followers to learn from other gurus he approved of, including in my case Jiddu Krishnamurti, and Douglas Harding. It was with the latter that I had a fully-fledged master-disciple relationship and out of which I learned the typical contours of this deeply misunderstood but profoundly vital exchange.

It is hard to put dates on things now but I would estimate that I was a seeker for around twenty years. However from early on I was also a finder, in that, for example, I had an "enlightenment experience" at the Rajneesh ashram. At an experiential level, therefore, I was coming to recognize from my own experience what the spiritual teachers were describing and at the same time I was triangulating across the various system I came across. As an academic that was natural. I couldn't say however that my enquiry has ever finished because I still find the persons and the writings of the spiritual teachers to be an existential challenge. While I might admire skills in all kinds of fields I don't find that I am challenged by them or those that practice them. To give an example at random, I read a "road" novel by the German-born writer W. G. Sebald recently and found much to enjoy in it. However there is nothing in Sebald that challenges me in the way that the "road" poetry of Whitman does. I am not concerned to find out more about Sebald – no offence intended – but Whitman exercises me, as does the Buddha, and as does Rajneesh still to the point that I re-read his discourses after thirty years and ponder on them. Something *happened* to these individuals which remains of immense significance to me.

Although Rajneesh was my first guru, Harding my real teacher, and Krishnamurti a great influence, I made a point of encountering other gurus when I could, in particular Andrew Cohen, Tony Parsons and Mother Meera, having visited the latter three times in Germany and once in London. The journey was not smooth, as from time to time I built up resentments to the idea of teacher; at the same time I kept a critical distance which may have made me a poor student, I cannot tell. I had a brief period in the 1980s of writing poetry as a response to my intense spiritual experiences with Rajneesh, Harding and others. I neither know nor care whether the poems have merit as poetry but will reproduce two here. The first reflects both the intensity of that period and also the sense of just beginning to come out of a very dark place.

> THE PETALS OF ME
>
> The petals of me: far from the swamp?
> The petals of me: from roots in the frozen soil.
> How I ache in my groin and heart,
> One growth: from frozen swamp to unblemished petal.
>
> Oh yes, its cold here, don't kid yourself.
> This Lord mixes no comfort with love:

> Your choice he says: swampy comforts,
> Or the agonies of aerial couplings.
>
> The petals of me: squirted up from the swamp,
> Hang in the cold dawn with the sun's
> Promised brilliance glimpsed but not warming.
> One growth: yet gossamer-stitched, articulated.
>
> Silver thread of grace runs downwards
> Physical nerves eviscerated from stalk-sheaths,
> Carry the petal-strength in molten
> Silver streams that crush me.
>
> The sombre petals of me: composted,
> Life's *danse macabre* mulched for my roots.
> Crushed bones and crushed dreams make
> Black food-fluids for my pink petals.
>
> Stamen and pistil in the sex-pink petals
> Of me: God-pure sexual organs; not
> Down and covered, but up and shamelessly free
> Reaching to him; he breathes lust on my petals.
>
> Aerial couplings! With tender parts high
> Roots twist and stem twists: the lover is here,
> The petals of me: have summoned the Lord,
> And he services me.
>
> Am I lower that I am swamp-rooted?
> Am I lesser that I am fixed, he is free?
> The petals of me: must wait for the lover,
> Must shiver in cold. Then the fire.

I was shocked on reading this again, perhaps for the first time in thirty-five years, at the strength of feeling in it, the rawness. It is also pertinent perhaps to our examination of Whitman because the imagery of it is so sexual.

The second poem from that period is about my feelings for the guru.

1. The Role of the Spiritual Teacher

MASTERS ARE DISRESPECTFUL
Masters are disrespectful to their
Disciples, on the whole.
I suppose it is in the nature of things,
Some disciples
Suffer more than others, and,
The master may find that he
Comes to make amends,

When I look with my master's eyes,
When I walk with my master's gait,
When I speak with my master's tongue
When I know what my master knows.

Don't you dare now, cries the disciple,
I have had enough of you all.
Why could you not respect me more?
Even a cat, a dog, or a bird, you
Allow it to be;
To follow its nature and its desires, but,
The master may yet repent,

When I go where you have been,
When I crumble and fade like you have done,
When I burst forth in light like you all,
When I am crowned the peasant's king.

In your name has come much harm,
You have fed many empty minds.
You have fuelled their jealousy
Your victory has left many defeated, and now,
The master must come to regret,

When the all flows through my veins,
When I am no longer afraid,
When my time comes,
When I speak to you all.

When you have reached the last boundary,
And you would dissolve into the mist,

> Then to linger here takes a fine thread,
> To hang by.
> For many of you it is the desire to teach,
> Oh calamitous desire! So few of you
> Are really gifted for it, and this you will
> Finally see,
>
> When in time each apple ripens,
> When in time each soul grows tired,
> When in time the Whole inhales,
> When in time each knows what you know.

I must have been very angry then, though I cannot bring back the context for it at all. I don't know if I would have then responded positively to Shankara's three marks of good fortune; I simply cannot recapture the mood. I certainly don't think now that the hierophant's desire to teach is calamitous. But my point is this: if someone as determinedly positive as I *now* am about the guru could have at one point been so adamant in my criticism of them then there must indeed be a great deal to negotiate with the hierophant.

The spiritual teacher through texts

Rajneesh used to say that without some anchor in the world the enlightened person would disappear (as I express in the poem). For Ramakrishna (a Bengali saint and approximate contemporary of Whitman) Rajneesh said it was the pleasure of eating, while for himself it was the pleasure of reading. I also read continuously, and mostly to encounter spiritual teachers I cannot meet in the flesh. I have met enough enlightened teachers, I believe, to make it possible to do so through texts. This idea partly comes from Whitman:

> Comrade, this is no book,
> Who touches this touches a man,
> (Is it night? are we alone?),
> It is I you hold and who holds you.
>   (So Long)

1. The Role of the Spiritual Teacher

Elmer O'Brien, translator of selected *Enneads* of Plotinus, repeats the idea in his notes at the start of his book: "Walt Whitman (after a fashion) comes to mind. 'Comrade, this is no book, Who touches this touches a man ...'"[4] Translators are crucial of course when it comes to spiritual texts in foreign languages and it so happens I find that the Plotinus of O'Brien touches me more than the Plotinus of other translators; both of us, it seems, resonate with Whitman and his feeling that you can *meet* a person through their writings.

It was Bucke's book *Cosmic Consciousness* that led me to Whitman, as I mentioned above, and which also led me to a slew of other writers. The two historical gurus I have come closest to through texts are perhaps Socrates – a key "lost buddha" in my thinking – and Ramakrishna, both of course only approachable through their translators. However it is hard to quite remember the experience of it, as the feeling of being with and walking alongside these figures is intense at the time but naturally fades. In writing this book I have come close again to Whitman after a gap of perhaps twenty years, and at the same time have revisited many other spiritual teachers in re-reading them or checking references; Gurdjieff in particular has loomed large in my thoughts again.

We will see that many of Whitman's followers came to him through reading *Leaves of Grass*, and some, having never met him in person, became disciples entirely based on the text and exchanges of letters.

The teacher-pupil relationship in the spiritual life

It is some thirty or thirty-five years since my encounter with Douglas Harding and the brief but memorable relationship between us as teacher and pupil in the spiritual life. I came to him as "Yogananda," that is as a follower of Rajneesh and therefore with a background more receptive to the idea of the master-disciple relationship than Harding was necessarily used to. I recall two occasions on which I "felt" his presence over and above the impact of his teachings on me; once when he was asleep on his couch in the house he had built and which had become something of an ashram for his pupils, and another as he arrived in a former Zen monastery in the south of France where he was running a week's retreat. In the first case I had a sense of infinite peace and in the second of the arrival of an energetic source that I visualized as something like a fountain or volcano. As in the Indian system of sitting with the master – *darshan* – I found his presence at least as important as the direct teachings. Crucially in this master-disciple relationship Harding acknowledged at one point that "something had passed between us," – his words. From this I came to realize that the master-disciple relationship is a two-way exchange, giving the master a feeling as much valued in the giving as the one experienced by the pupil in receiving.

It was Harding who first introduced me to the sentiment that the corruption of the best produces the worst. I think he may have put it that the more beautiful the thing the more ugly its perversion, but the meaning is the same. Rajneesh often insisted that the master-disciple relationship is the greatest of all human relationships, so we have to ask, what happens when the master-disciple relationship goes wrong, or when the master is a fake, or when the master who is otherwise genuine succumbs to the desire for power? For Harding it was clearly important to him to have followers and more than that, he was fulfilled by the relationship. Can this become a craving that warps the relationship? Because of these possibilities we must certainly negotiate our course around the hierophant with care.

I have written elsewhere about the similarities and differences between Whitman and Harding.[5] In brief, Harding had an extensive system, the subject of his first book and which received an enthusiastic endorsement from C. S. Lewis. It is systematic in a way that Whitman's could never be, but oddly, it is also far less world-curious and world-celebratory, leading me to suggest that Harding is as *via negativa* as, say, the Buddha, or as the Indian sage Ramana Maharshi, who we consider later on. In discussion once with Harding over the question of reincarnation I seem to recall him saying something to the effect that if reincarnation is true then he did not want to come back. It is a telling remark and for me on a spectrum with those who go further and are certain they never wanted to be here in the first place. I have met enough individuals who live on this spectrum to have respect for it, but it is not my path or Whitman's. He and I would be content to visit here – as he hints in his poem "To the Garden the World" – an infinity of times, though perhaps for slightly different reasons.

2

INTRODUCING WHITMAN AS GURU

It is time to present more extensive evidence for Whitman as guru or religious teacher. In the first instance we look at his writings and then at how some recent interpretations also lean to this view. I'll postpone the longer discussion of Whitman and his disciples after we look at other hierophancies.

Whitman has been mostly received in the period since his death as a poet whose imagery of the open road inspired the beat generation writers such as Jack Kerouac, Allen Ginsberg and William Burroughs. In addition his alleged homosexuality has received much comment. Whitman in popular culture has received little hostility or negative criticism and so the epithet "good gray poet" stands, though this was originally the title of an 1866 pamphlet by one of Whitman's defenders, William Douglas O'Connor.[6] The images of Whitman as an older man also stand in popular imagination, so "gray" is appropriate but trivial, while "gay" remains largely unchallenged. We can sum this up with "good gay poet" perhaps. Whitman may have offended the morals of his age and so "good" was radical in his day. But "religious"? "Founder of a religion?" "Guru?" Such terms are put forward by only a minority of recent Whitman scholars as serious evaluations of his legacy, though as we shall see later on it was not so rare in Whitman's day and in the period immediately following his death.

Religious interpretations of *Leaves*

Recent appreciation of Whitman as a religious figure begins perhaps with the introduction by Malcolm Cowley to the 1961 Penguin edition of *Leaves of Grass*, followed by *The Ecstatic Whitman: Literary Shamanism and the Crisis of the Union* by George Hutchinson, in 1988. 1990 saw the publication of *Minor Prophecy: Walt Whitman's New American Religion* by David Kuebrich, while the twenty-first century saw two more offerings: *Worshipping Walt: The Whitman Disciples*, by Michael Robertson (2010) and *Mysticism in American Literature: Thoreau's Quest and Whitman's Self* by Paul Hourihan (2011). This is probably not a complete list but they present an interesting range of religious, spiritual or mystical perspectives on Whitman, couched in language much nearer to us today than that of Whitman's immediate admirers.

Let us start with Malcolm Cowley. He writes in his introduction to *Leaves of Grass* that it "should be considered in relation to quite another list of works, even though Whitman had probably read none of them in 1855."[7] These include the *Bhagavad Gita*, the *Upanishads*, Blake's prophetic books, Nietzsche's *Thus Spake Zarathustra*, and *The Gospel of Sri Ramakrishna*. I find this list interesting because of a book I wrote twenty years ago with the title *Krishna, Whitman, Nietzsche, Sartre* where I compare four texts I characterize as ecstatic: the *Bhagavad-Gita*, *Leaves of Grass*, *Thus Spake Zarathustra*, and Sartre's *Nausea* (though the latter embodies only a pathological inversion of the ecstatic). I am re-writing that book as focusing on the systems of the four authors, while this volume on Whitman as guru focuses more on teachers.

When it comes to the religious or spiritual ideas put forward by Whitman in "Song of Myself" Cowley says "... the system of doctrine suggested by the poem is more Eastern than Western, it includes notions like metempsychosis [reincarnation] and karma, ..."[8] However Cowley shows that Whitman was unlikely to have read the Eastern religious texts, despite appearing to approve of them, but more likely "breathed" them in from the American Transcendentalists. Also he follows Bucke – "the most acute of Whitman's immediate disciples" as Cowley puts it[9] – in regarding Whitman's religious ideas as having their source in a mystical experience

2. Introducing Whitman as Guru

possibly dated to 1853 or 1854. Cowley was writing in a period where mysticism still retained some cultural credibility in the West and mystical experience could be usefully discussed by Aldous Huxley as central to the "perennial philosophy." However Cowley says that Whitman could not be classed with the Christian mystics "for the simple reason that he was not a Christian at any stage of his career, early or late."[10]

I have not read *The Ecstatic Whitman: Literary Shamanism and the Crisis of the Union* by George Hutchinson but want to make some comments based on a review of it by David Kuebrich. If Kuebrich is right and Hutchinson was keen to make Whitman out to be a modern shaman, then I would have to disagree with Hutchinson, not because one cannot use "shaman" as a metaphor or to extract some features from Whitman's system, but because I want to show later on that Whitman's system, while of tremendous importance to me, lacks precisely what is *properly* called shamanic or animist. Kuebrich writes: "According to Hutchinson, the type of religious experience that inspires Whitman's poetic production and informs many of his major poems is the ritualistic role playing and ecstatic experience of the religious shaman."[11] Along with Kuebrich I am inclined to say that this is a bad fit, partly because of the work by the British academic Mike Tucker who has interpreted a wide range of cultural productions from an exclusively shamanic perspective.[12] For those unfamiliar with the sheer variety of religious experience "shamanic" might be a useful introductory term devoid of conventional religious baggage, but for my own systematization, involving careful delineation between and categorization of these experiences, it does not work at all. The shaman in hunter-gatherer societies may have something of the role that Hutchinson suggests for Whitman, but his or her religious system is utterly different.

I think Kuebrich's insight about Hutchinson is correct, so let us now look at his own book *Minor Prophecy: Walt Whitman's New American Religion*. Published in 1990, Kuebrich has to write in a more skeptical context than Cowley in the late 1950s; a skepticism that continues to harden in my opinion. Yet the title "Minor Prophecy" probably reflects Kuebrich's considered opinion, in opposition to those who saw Whitman as far from minor in the religious sense. Kuebrich usefully detects three phases in Whitman scholarship. Firstly, he suggests, scholars in the period after Whitman's enthusiastic disciples had passed away were keen to distance themselves from the religious nature of this enthusiasm. This approach – present most emphatically in the twenty-first century I would add – "assumes than an author's religious language is really something other: namely, the symbolic manifestation of the distorted desires of the id."[13] In my own writings I refer to this as the *psychologizing* of religious themes. In the second approach Kuebrich tells us that scholars assume the religious elements to be "the prophetic self-image ... a fabrication and posturing on an older, chastened and complacent poet."[14]

Kuebrich then continues:

> The third approach to Whitman acknowledges the presence of a religious theme in various editions but unwittingly misinterprets it in two important respects. It distorts the character of Whitman's spirituality by treating it as a set of intellectual convictions rather than a *special transhistorical mode of consciousness* that gives rise to certain recurring religious values and beliefs; it also depreciates the importance of Whitman's religious faith by presenting it as just one of several themes in the *Leaves* rather than seeing it as constituting an emotional substratum and integrates the various themes into a unified symbolic vision. (My emphasis.)

I like Kuebrich's term "special transhistorical mode of consciousness." It suggests the discovery of something universal to all people and all ages, a term that is of course intended to convey something similar to Huxley's "perennial philosophy." Hence I find myself aligned to Kuebrich's analysis. Despite his rejection of Hutchinson's shamanic approach to Whitman which is based on the work of scholar Mircea Eliade, Kuebrich adopts Eliade's wider definition of religion as the pursuit of the *more real*.[15] I like that too.

Michael Robertson's *Worshipping Walt: The Whitman Disciples* appears to roughly follow Kuebrich's approach though it does not seem to reference it. It is a contemporary book which explicitly puts forward the idea of Whitman as guru, though not using that word and not without a considerable dose of the skepticism so normal to our age. That aside Robertson is clearly an enthusiast for Whitman and concludes his Introduction with this:

> "Stop this day and night with me and you shall possess the origin of all poems," Walt Whitman promised; he believed that reading *Leaves of*

2. Introducing Whitman as Guru

Grass could change your life. Here are the stories of some people who prove that.[16]

I will draw on Robertson's book later on to flesh out my own perception of Whitman's immediate disciples. While Robertson selects nine he states: "A comprehensive history of the Whitman disciples would include hundreds of figures across several continents."[17]

In 2004 I wrote reviews of two of Paul Hourihan's books, sent to me by his widow.[18] One was on Ramakrishna and Christ while the other was on Thoreau and Whitman. What is interesting about Hourihan's approach is that he is in no doubt that Whitman was a mystic of the highest order, but nevertheless reserves much criticism for him. Unlike the books so far mentioned Hourihan comments on Whitman from the knowledge of many other mystics and their lives, saying for example:

> It is striking then, that the backgrounds and family life of mystics almost invariably give us the sensation of the loner amidst the tribe, the speckled bird, the person alienated by his environment – perhaps generating in him a lasting hunger so that he will feel at home only in his true milieu. My kingdom is not of this world, says Christ – the mystic's cry also.[19]

Having said that mystics are often persons alienated from their environment – a generalization that I would anyway dispute – Hourihan then goes on to characterize Whitman most accurately when he says "Specifically his – more than that of any other mystic of whom we have record – was a nature intensely identified with the everyday life of men and women: a warm, exuberant, outgoing, democratic, compassionating humanitarian personality."[20] I would add that this is why the study of Whitman's system and also his modus operandi as a spiritual teacher are important. Hourihan's criticisms of Whitman are also important, because, unlike most criticism, they are from the perspective of what a mystic is and does. Firstly he points out that Whitman appears to have no regular practice such as meditation, spiritual exercises or prayer. Hourihan seems to believe that a powerful mystical insight such as Whitman seems to have had and recorded in "Song of Myself" needs integrating into the personality, giving as an example of this St Paul's retreat into solitude for three years after his Damascene conversion. Crucially he criticizes Whitman:

> With his attractive personality to begin with, made more wonderful by his knowledge of superconscious truth, he carries on as before. No changes are initiated. What he had been before, he continues to be. He acts as though the mystical moment was an aspect of the personality he had known from birth. Hence there was no incentive to amend his ways.[21]

This is an insightful criticism, but perhaps a bit harsh. What "ways" should Whitman have amended? Certainly there was no monastic or other religious context for Whitman's spiritual development as there was for example with St John of the Cross and Teresa of Avila, or for pupils in the Zen tradition. In all such cases the discipline of the religious life set out a ready-made context for the consolidation of religious insight. However perhaps the lack of that context makes Whitman more important to contemporary spirituality rather than less.

In another useful insight from Hourihan he writes of Whitman: "He was in love with the manifestations of the Divine more than the Divine itself, the source of those manifestations."[22] I think this is crucial to our discussion. Almost all spiritual-religious systems emphasize a renunciative stance to the world, a turning away from ordinary life and this perhaps more than anything has made them increasingly irrelevant to the modern world. Whitman is important, I shall argue, precisely because he seeks a spirituality of the everyday, of the marketplace, or in the language used by some Buddhists in revolt against their own tradition, an "engaged" spirituality.

The life of Whitman

If Whitman's spirituality is deeply about everyday life we need to say a little here about Whitman's approach to living. Central to it was the rejection of social strata and the conventions by which judgments are made about others, indeed the suspension of that judgment is core to his system. Whitman's habit of mixing with the ordinary folk of Long Island, Manhattan, or wherever he was, gave him the subject matter and broad appeal that the more literary-circle types lacked. He mingled with workmen and took pleasure in doing their work with or for them, in a way that we would find very odd today, with our regimented and bureaucratic world of qualifications, identity passes and health-and-safety strictures. He liked to steer

2. Introducing Whitman as Guru

the vessels of friendly captains in Brooklyn harbor, but gave up eventually when he nearly caused an accident. He was particularly fond of the Broadway stagecoach drivers, as he found them "uncommonly talented" with their horses in the most difficult of roads, and would join them up on the box – he spent the whole of a winter in the 1850s driving a stage for a sick driver, so that the driver "might lie without starving his family."[23] Towards the end of the 1850s he was a frequent visitor to the New York Hospital where he looked after disabled drivers.

Whitman appeals to me here because my own mother brought me up to have the same indifference to social status. I have had refreshments with a peer of the realm in the House of Lords tearoom; I have sat on park benches talking with down-and-outs. I seek out neither one nor the other, but listen equally, or am equally moved to press my ideas on them. However I find myself *far* less generous with my time and resources in the service of others than Whitman and so am baffled that Hourihan criticized Whitman for failing to "amend his ways" after his illumination.

Leaves of Grass brought Whitman notoriety and fame, and through its publication he later met some of the literary notables of his age: Emerson, Thoreau and Oscar Wilde. In 1861, when Whitman was forty-two, the American Civil War broke out and Whitman's brother George joined up; he was injured at the Battle of Fredericksburg, and Walter travelled to be with him. He spent time with the wounded, comforting the injured and dying young soldiers, and also spent much of his spare income (which was small in the first place) on treats for them. At Fredericksburg the field hospitals consisted of shabby tents, where the wounded were lucky if the blankets they lay on had a layer of leaves or grass between them and the hard ground. Whitman not only tended to the wounded but mixed with the soldiers in the camp in his usual informal way and commented that he found himself "always well used." A correspondent of the *New York Herald* wrote this about Whitman's ministrations:

> I first heard of him among the sufferers on the Peninsula after a battle there. Subsequently I saw him, time and again, in the Washington hospitals, or wending his way there, with a basket or haversack on his arm, and the strength of beneficience suffusing his face. His devotion surpassed the devotion of woman. It would take a volume to tell of his kindness, tenderness, and thoughtfulness. [Did Hourian know of these writings?]

> Never shall I forget one night when I accompanied him on his rounds through a hospital filled with those wounded young Americans whose heroisms he has sung in deathless numbers. There were three rows of cots, and each cot bore its man. When he appeared, in passing along, there was a smile of affection and welcome on every face, however wan, and his presence seemed to light up the place as it might be lighted by the presence of the God of Love. From cot to cot they called him, often in tremulous tones or whispers; they embraced him; they touched his hand; they gazed at him. To one he gave a few words of cheer; for another he wrote a letter home; to others he gave an orange, a few comfits, a cigar, a pipe and tobacco, a sheet of paper or a postage-stamp, all of which and many other things were in his capacious haversack. From another he would receive a dying message for mother, wife, or sweetheart; for another he would promise to go an errand; to another, some special friend very low, he would give a manly farewell kiss. He did the things for them no nurse or doctor could do, and he seemed to leave a benediction at every cot as he passed along. The lights had gleamed for hours in the hospital that night before he left it, and, as he took his way toward the door, you could hear the voices of many a stricken hero calling, "Walt, Walt, Walt! Come again! Come again!"[24]

Whitman wrote to his mother:

Mother, I have real pride in telling you that I have the consciousness of saving quite a number of lives by keeping the men from giving up, and being a good deal with them. The men say it is so, and the doctors say it is so; and I will candidly confess I can see it is true, though I say it myself. I know you will like to hear it, mother so I tell you.[25]

In a later letter he says:

Nothing of ordinary misfortune seems as it used to, and death itself has lost all its terrors; I have seen so many cases in which it was so welcome and such a relief.[26]

In 1865 he was appointed as a clerk in the Department of the Interior, only to be dismissed shortly afterwards when it was discovered that he was the author of *Leaves of Grass*. Whitman's friend William Douglas O'Connor published a defense of Whitman in which he attacked the Secretary of the Interior, James Harlan, for dismissing him (the pamphlet may have been the first time that the epithet "The Good Grey Poet" was associated with Whitman). Secretary Harman of the State Department had sacked Whitman for "being the author of an indecent book," and went so far as to say that even if the President had ordered it he would not reinstate him.[27] However Bucke reports this about Abraham Lincoln from an eye-witness:

> ... Walt Whitman went by, on the White House walk in front, quite slow, with his hands in the breast-pockets of his overcoat, and a sizeable felt hat on, and his head pretty well up, just as I have often seen him on Broadway. Mr. Lincoln asked who that was, or something of the kind. I spoke up, mentioning the name, Walt Whitman, and said he was the author of *Leaves of Grass*. Mr. Lincoln didn't say anything, but took a good look, till Whitman was quite gone by. Then he says – (I can't give you his way of saying it, but it was quite emphatic and odd) – "Well," he says, "*he* looks like a *Man*." He said it pretty loud, but in a sort of absent way, and with the emphasis on the words I have underscored.[28]

Whitman in turn had great respect for the President and on his assassination in April 1865 wrote "When Lilacs Last in the Dooryard Bloom'd," a great elegy for the dead man, and included it amongst a series of poems in the section of *Leaves* called "Memories of President Lincoln."

In 1868 an edited version of *Leaves* was published in England by William Michael Rossetti. This was read by Anne Gilchrist, widow of Alexander Gilchrist (the biographer of William Blake), who then received the unexpurgated version and becomes one of its champions, leading her to visit Whitman in 1876. Meanwhile, in 1873, and at the age of only fifty-four Whitman suffered his first paralytic stroke, leaving him lame. His mother died in the same year, and Whitman was now far from the peak of health and good cheer that he described in "Song of Myself." He visited Emerson on his sick-bed in 1881, a year before Emerson's death, and in 1882 met Oscar Wilde. In 1883, Richard Maurice Bucke, by now a close friend of Whitman's, published his biography, which includes many letters and articles from both hostile and friendly press. In 1884 Whitman was finally able to buy his own house from profits made from *Leaves*. He lived there until his death in 1892, known to all as the "Sage of Mickle Street." It was four years before his death that a second stroke rendered him, at the age of seventy-three, almost immobile, though he continued to receive a stream of visitors, many of them writers.

We will uncover more biographical detail about Whitman when looking at his disciples in Chapter 7, but the key portrait of him will be drawn from his writings. Taking both together we can be sure of one thing: Whitman's spirituality was not of the monastic kind but lived out in the ordinary details and encounters of American life of the nineteenth century.

Evidence from Richard Maurice Bucke

From the writings of late twentieth century writers such Cowley, Hutchinson, Kuebrich, Robertson and Hourihan it should be clear that there is a strong case to see Whitman as a religious figure. However these scholars all drew on much earlier writings, and amongst those who lived in the time of Whitman and knew him none is more important to me than Richard Maurice Bucke. Re-reading his *Cosmic Consciousness* makes me realize the extent to which this book shaped my subsequent research and thinking about the spiritual life. For a start it led me to Whitman, but also to a series of figures that showed me how Christianity was not at all the sum total of Western religious thought. At the time of first reading it I had studied many Eastern masters and so was receptive to Bucke's eclectic and wide-ranging choice of figures to write about. However I have always rejected or at the very least doubted one theme of his book, influenced by the evolutionary thinking of his day, which suggests that the human race is collectively becoming more spiritual; that more and more cases of "cosmic consciousness" – to use his phrase – would occur. This is now a common New Age theme for which I can see no evidence.

Bucke listed a set of characteristics of the mystic which became the basis for later lists within the scholarly discipline of studies in mysticism. What was remarkable I think is that he found mystics where others had not, divided into what is effectively an "A" list and a "B" list. I don't at all accept his categorization into A and B here, but his lists set me off exploring the thought of such figures as Socrates, Plotinus, Blake, Spinoza … and of course Whitman. Using his method as a starting point I soon expanded Bucke's list, though I now realize there are some individuals on his list I never got round to looking at. His legacy on my own writing shows in my concept of Neoplatonism – a broad current of non-Christian thought as I define it – as the "counter-religion of the West" and also my concept of the "lost buddhas of the West" as mentioned earlier. Something else I owe to Bucke is the very sense that in reading a spiritual text one can come close to its originator and so become his or her disciple in a meaningful way. Bucke wrote that when he first encountered *Leaves of Grass* only small pockets of it "lit up" for him here and there, but after more extensive acquaintance with it the whole thing was illuminated. This is very much my experience with some of the texts that Bucke led me to. For example I bought the collected works of Blake and the *Ethics* of Spinoza, both on Bucke's list, and found initially that neither spoke to me at all. Now and again I would take them off the shelf, but still nothing. At some point over the years I went to one or other of them – along with many sacred texts in my possession – and for no particular reason found my mood receptive. I was ready you could say. Then, reading a bit each day, the whole thing lit up, as Bucke declares. Only one at a time does so I have found, because one has to tune in to the teacher, "walk" solely with him or her, and only then does the text reveal itself. Over time and with exposure to other teachers this depth of experience with any one text fades, though one does not forget them, or the impact of them.

More important than texts here is the impact of the living teacher on the pupil, and there is no doubt that Bucke's various accounts of his discipleship to Whitman are deeply moving. When I read or re-read the various scholarly accounts of Whitman by recent authors, however open to the religious nature of his teachings, I found them mostly hedged around with criticisms of Whitman, particularly that he cultivated an image of himself to promote his work. With Bucke I find none of that. Instead there is the simplicity of discipleship at its best: a relationship of equals underpinned on both sides by the recognition of some kind of *transmission*. Bucke was worldly enough with a steady career in the mental health system of his day, a competent administrator, and clearly a researcher whose work, though not academic, is rigorous in its own way. The friendship he offered to Whitman was not an ordinary friendship however but based on an appreciation that he had been blessed by the presence and religious thought of Whitman.

We return later to the Whitman-Bucke relationship but first we will make a considerable detour into firstly Whitman's religious system and then into the more general history of gurus in the West and the problematics of hierophancy.

3
WHITMAN'S SYSTEM

When I first encountered Whitman through Bucke and began to read *Leaves of Grass* I was better informed about Eastern spirituality than Western traditions. This made it easy for me to consider Whitman's spiritual worldview or system in the light of the Eastern notion of spiritual enlightenment. Bucke presents Whitman as mystic, a category I accepted, found of great significance to myself, and exemplars of which I was always on the search for. I studied mysticism at Masters level at a British university and recall a moment when our tutor asked each student to give their definition of mysticism. Mine was this: "a permanent orientation to the infinite and the eternal." This can also serve as my definition for enlightenment, though the subtlety of this condition requires many similar complementary definitions and elaborations. I can't remember how my definition of a mystic was received but, on suggesting that Krishnamurti was a mystic on this basis, I was told that Krishnamurti was perhaps better understood as a healer. Healing is certainly part of what all mystics do, but I stand by my definition. With this in mind it is easy to work through Whitman's writings on the lookout for references to the infinite and eternal, of which there are many.

Another characteristic in the literature on enlightenment is that it is, or begins as, an event in a person's life. There is before and after enlightenment. Here we find no difficulty in identifying an event for Whitman as a possible moment in which enlightenment came to him; many commentators have pointed to this passage:

> I believe in you my soul, the other I am must not abase itself to
>   you,
> And you must not be abased to the other.
>
> Loafe with me on the grass, loose the stop from your throat,
> Not words, not music or rhyme I want, not custom or lecture,
>   not even the best,
> Only the lull I like, the hum of your valvèd voice.
>
> I mind how once we lay such a transparent summer morning,
> How you settled you head athwart my hips and gently turn'd
>   over upon me,
> And parted the shirt from my bosom-bone, and plunged your
>   tongue to my bare-stript heart,
> And reach'd till you felt my beard, and reach'd till you held my
>   feet.
>
> Swiftly arose and spread around me the peace and knowledge
>   that pass all the argument of the earth,
> And I know that the hand of God is the promise of my own,
> And I know that the spirit of God is the brother of my own,
> And that all the men ever born are also my brothers, and the
>   women my sisters and lovers,
> And that a kelson of creation is love, ...
>   (Song of Myself, v. 5)

Bucke amongst others suggests this passage as indicating the moment of illumination for Whitman, though my own experience suggests, as I mentioned earlier, that "enlightenment" may be more of a drawn-out process than an event. Nevertheless this line "I mind how once we lay such a transparent summer morning" has suggested to myself and others a key moment in Whitman's spiritual awakening. The imagery is sexual ... yet not of sex. As in my poem "The Petals of Me" I think Whitman is conveying a truth about illumination, which is that a union takes place both intense and the closest to sexual union out of all our known human experience. When he says that he likes the hum of his lover's "valvèd" voice he is talking about nothing physical at all; when he says that the lover plunges his tongue into his "bare-stript heart" he is talking about no possible physical congress. Neither can a tongue reach to one's beard or feet after entering one's body at the chest. No analysis at the level of physical sexuality will reach to the meaning of Whitman's poetry; likewise no analysis of its aesthetics will give any clue. Instead I draw throughout this book on the thought of the mystics East and West – those who have known mystical union – as giving immediate and direct clarity to Whitman's intentions and the spiritual system that lies behind them.

A first look: "Song of Myself"

To gain some insights into Whitman's system I will work through his major poem "Song of Myself." My reading is both personal and informed by the various scholars mentioned earlier and of course the writings of Whitman's disciples including Bucke. Another disciple, the English social reformer and mystic Edward Carpenter, reported this conversation about Whitman's spiritual insights (Whitman is talking first):

> "What lies behind 'Leaves of Grass' is something that few, very few, only one here and there, perhaps oftenest women, are at all in a position to seize. It lies behind almost every line but concealed, studiedly concealed; some passages left purposely obscure. There is something in my nature *furtive*, like an old hen! You see a hen wandering up and down a hedgerow, looking apparently quite unconcerned, but presently she finds a concealed spot, and furtively lays an egg, and comes away as though nothing had happened! That is how I felt in writing 'Leaves of Grass.' Sloane Kennedy calls me 'artful' — which about hits the mark. I think there are truths which it is necessary to envelop or wrap up."
>
> I [Carpenter] replied that all through history the old mysteries, or whatever they may have been called, had been held back; and added that probably we had something yet to learn from India in these matters.
>
> W.: "I do not myself think there is anything more to come from that source; we must rather look to modern science to open the way. Time alone can absolutely test my poems or any one's. Personally, I think that the 'something' is more present in some of my small later poems than in the 'Song of Myself'".[29]

We note in this extract that Carpenter like many others at the time drew parallels between Whitman's work and Indian spirituality, though Whitman – perhaps correctly – is dubious that more is to come from that source, suggesting instead that science may open the way (in turn I am highly skeptical of that). He also thinks that later poems contain more insights perhaps than "Song of Myself," but as so many commentators take it to be a crucial Whitman text we start with that. Here are the first few verses of the first edition:

> I celebrate myself,
> And what I assume you shall assume,
> For every atom belonging to me as good belongs to you.
>
> I loafe and invite my soul,
> I lean and loafe at my ease observing a spear of summer grass.
>
> Houses and rooms are full of perfumes, the shelves are crowded with perfumes,
> I breathe the fragrance myself, and know it and like it,
> The distillation would intoxicate me also, but I shall not let it.
> The atmosphere is not a perfume, it has no taste of the distillation, it is odorless,
> It is for my mouth forever, I am in love with it,
> I will go to the bank by the wood and become undisguised and naked,
> I am mad for it to be in contact with me.[30]

What "eggs" has the furtive Whitman hidden here? For there are many possible readings of these passages, so typical of his style. I suggest the following. First of all he acknowledges each person as inheritor of the earth; second he takes time out to be with his soul or inner being, observing the simplest things. Existence is benign, as suggested by "perfumes," or perhaps endowing us with a myriad good things, the distillation of which could be intoxicating. He will not let himself be intoxicated however by the wonders of the manifest world, bringing his attention instead to the "atmosphere" that which is the source or ground of all things – in the Greek system the quintessence – something that is odorless, i.e. without qualities. He is mad for this, in love with it, so he retreats from the busy world of men to a natural spot to be stripped of all his constructs, ready to engage with the Absolute, or whatever name you may want to give it.

3. Whitman's System

Note that I have presented this almost as a rebuke to Hourihan. Whitman here is certainly in love with creation, but tells us at the very outset that the creator *is* more important, or at least as important, and will devote himself to it, or "Him" in the Christian system. Better than "the creator" of course is "the uncreated" though perhaps the unfamiliarity of this term in a Christian context is why Hourihan misses the rather oblique reference to it. However the perception must stay with us that Whitman celebrates the creation far more than the Christian mystics, for example Teresa of Avila, who said that to know the Creator one must deny the creation. Whitman mentions "The feeling of health, the full-noon trill" a little later. He was writing this in his prime – aged thirty-seven – and the question must always remain in the spiritual life: are you building your castle on sand? If your spirituality depends on your vitality, what happens when you lose it? For Whitman certainly did in later life, laid low by a stroke.

Whitman has a sense of the "eternal present," widely recognized as typical of the mystic, and set out in verse 3:

> There was never any more inception than there is now,
> Nor any more youth or age than there is now;
> And will never be any more perfection than there is now,
> Nor any more heaven or hell than there is now.

I have partly selected this as a contrast to Bucke who saw in Whitman's system, or perhaps just made central to his own, the idea of evolution. Later in the same verse Whitman alludes to God:

> As God comes a loving bedfellow and sleeps at my side all night
>   and close on the peep of the day,
> And leaves for me baskets covered with white towels bulging the
>   house with their plenty,
> Shall I postpone my acceptation and realization and scream at
>   my eyes,
> That they turn from gazing after and down the road,
> And forthwith cipher and show me to a cent,
> Exactly the contents of one, and exactly the contents of two, and
>   which is ahead?

One should be confounded by this, because who sleeps so benignly, with the sense of God close to one all night, and particularly at the peep of day? We are all grumpy in the morning. It is inhuman to wake so bright and have a sense of gifts lavished upon one, scattered metaphorically about the "house." Jumping to a very different context, we may feel equally skeptical when learning that a friend of Socrates once came past his house at daybreak and spotted him dancing.[31] Who dances first thing in the morning? The classic answer is: only the one with a spotless conscience, an untroubled psyche, a subconscious rid of all complexes. In other words an enlightened one. In the second half of this extract Whitman rejects the idea that "realization" is a matter of postponing the here and now and must be a matter of intellectual deciphering, of judging what is ahead or behind.

Whitman is detached from self, just as he adheres to the quintessence rather than the intoxication of the manifest world which he endlessly describes to us. In verse 4 he is conscious of all that is good in the world as a blessing, but also of sickness and ill-fortune: "The sickness of one of my folks—or of myself, or ill-doing, or loss or lack of money, or depressions or exaltations, / They come to me days and nights and go from me again, / But they are not the Me myself." As with many Indian mystics Whitman appears to describe a "Me" that is not the ordinary "me" and which is unaffected by pleasure or pain, success or failure, gain or loss. The verse continues:

> Apart from the pulling and hauling stands what I am,
> Stands amused, complacent, compassionating, idle, unitary,
> Looks down, is erect, bends an arm on an impalpable certain rest,
> Looks with its sidecurved head curious what will come next,
> Both in and out of the game, and watching and wondering at it.

Here Whitman is giving a classic account of detachment as put forward, for example, by both Eckhart and the Buddha. The difference here, particularly with the Buddha, lies in the curiosity: this is a world-curious spiritual path. Whitman's "Me" – the part of him separate from his personality and experiencing – is however characterized in some important ways. His "what I am" is unitary, a perception that is central I think to all religion, mysticism and spirituality. The manifest world is manifold, meaning made up of myriad parts interacting with each other: where is peace to be found in this maelstrom? The common answer is: in the still point of the turning world, in the unitary sense of being the observer, a conclusion drawn to our attention in countless spiritual texts. Whitman further characterizes it as "idle," which gives fuel perhaps to Hourihan's criticism of him but can be interpreted not as lazy but as non-acting, the "non-doing" of Taoism. If we practice detachment in the system of Eckhart or the Buddha then this "Me" that emerges out of it is without body, parts or passions (as in the Westminster Confession of Faith) and therefore does not act. In all the systems I am aware of this "Me" is also compassionating, as Whitman terms it. Compassion for all sentient beings is at the core of the Buddha's teachings for example. But we are perhaps a little surprised at two more qualifiers that Whitman introduces: "amused" and "complacent." As both poet and spiritual teacher Whitman is entitled to employ words in slightly unfamiliar ways, but I think both of these terms at face value are a little hard to reconcile with "compassionating."

Whitman is comfortably dualistic about soul and body. For example in verse 5 he says "I believe in you my soul, the other I am must not abase itself to you, / And you must not be abased to the other." Clearly in whatever sense Whitman is modern here he nevertheless stands in opposition to the entire recent philosophical tradition of the West in its rejection of Cartesian dualism. There *is* a soul as well as the body, declares Whitman, and they are of equal importance. I have thought much about the so-called "Cartesian split" and find myself a good Cartesian, partly because of my perception of him as more than a philosopher. My point is that if body and soul are of equal importance and we live in a culture where soul is denied as separate from body, and that denial is backed up by all our great intellectuals, then the religious or spiritual life has to claw back "soul" from the materialist morass. They are equal, let us go with Whitman on that, but soul now needs the greater advocacy.

In Whitman's days that was not so. The religious heritage was still strong, particularly in America, and this was during the prudish Victorian era which saw strong condemnation of Whitman's earthy and downright sexual material in *Leaves of Grass*. What has happened since that time, as I point out in my book *Secularism: The Hidden Origins of Disbelief*, is the universal reverence for the works of Marx, Darwin and Freud, perhaps the three most important executioners of the "soul." In the early twenty-first century we are only body; a body, that is, which has evolved from monkeys, is primarily sexual, and is organized socially with other bodies along economic and political lines.

Verse 5 brings us to where Whitman describes what many take to be his enlightenment experience or conversion experience, as cited earlier. He completes it by saying: "I know that the hand of God is the promise of my own" though in other versions it is this: "I know that the hand of God is the elderhand of my own." I prefer "elderhand" and am not sure which version came first. Crucially he adds: "And that a kelson of creation is love." A kelson is the inner keel of a ship, so Whitman clearly means that the core of creation is love, an important statement for a mystic. Ultimately I know of only two really significant paths in the spiritual life, that of detachment and that of love. Whichever of these is emphasized – and Eckhart for example is explicit that he places detachment over love – I think one is always the corrective for the other. A detachment run cold may become indifference, while a love run cold often manifests as control. If Whitman stands "amused, complacent, compassionating, idle, unitary" we need to be sure that love is his corrective for amused idle complacency. Love manifests in various ways but for many religious people the emphasis is on good works, and I think there are enough in Whitman's life to answer any charge by Hourihan of laziness.

Whitman's real love, judged from "Song of Myself," is for the stuff of existence as described at the end of verse 5, including leaves of grass, brown ants and "mossy scabs of the wormfence, and heaped stones, and elder and mullen and pokeweed." Many times he tells us that he favors the outdoors, both wilderness and cities, both the products of the natural world and the products of the human world. "What is grass?" he imagines a child asking in verse 6 and has to reply he has no more clue than the child, going on to offer this however:

> Or I guess it is the handkerchief of the Lord,
> A scented gift and remembrancer designedly dropped,

> Bearing the owner's name someway in the corners, that we may
>   see and remark, and say Whose?
> Or I guess the grass is itself a child, the produced babe of the
>   vegetation.

"Song of Myself" has long sections listing things that Whitman observes as compassionater and lover, no two alike and every one good as he says in verse 7. This habit of listing natural and man-made phenomena led to the famous suggestion in Emerson's letter to Carlyle that he might think *Leaves* "only an auctioneer's inventory of a warehouse."[32]

Whitman is not shy of using "Lord" or "God," though in a way more Deist than classically Christian. Grass, or all plants and animals, are a gift from God, a sentiment that is religious and in contradistinction to both the hard materialist who conceives of living things in terms of molecules and DNA, and the aesthete who experiences them only aesthetically. To see the parts of the world and find each them bearing the owner's name – God – and a "remembrancer" – of God – is surely a religious outlook.

Whitman is not in the least perturbed by death, his own or that of any other living thing as is clear from verse 7:

> Has any one supposed it lucky to be born?
> I hasten to inform him or her it is just as lucky to die, and I
>   know it.
>
> I pass death with the dying, and birth with the new-washed
>   babe, and am not contained between my hat and boots,
> And peruse manifold objects, no two alike, and every one good,
> The earth good, and the stars good, and their adjuncts all good.
>
> I am not an earth nor an adjunct of an earth,
> I am the mate and companion of people, all just as immortal and
>   fathomless as myself;
> They do not know how immortal, but I know.

In reverse order we can explore this passage for more clues to Whitman's system. He, as teacher, knows he is immortal and knows that all people are immortal. We have to agree with him that people by and large do not believe they are immortal, but having spoken about death he clearly does not mean immortality of the body as some people might understand it. But what exactly is immortal in a person? This is a question of great spiritual significance and cannot be settled either in Whitman's writings or my own; we have to leave it open. Here is a clue though: Whitman also tells us, that despite finding all earths good and all their adjuncts good, he is neither an earth nor an adjunct. The secular or atheist reader might give up on this all as gobbledygook, but not any serious seeker; such will suspect reference here to the quintessence, or comparable term by which others have hinted at the immortal in us.

Unlike most Christian or Buddhist mystics, Whitman sees Nature as a teacher. The look of an ox that plows or rests in the shade is important to him; the look in its eyes "seems to me more than all the print I have read in my life," as he says in verse 13. Ducks scared by his tread in a day-long ramble rise into the sky: "... I believe in those winged purposes." He finds their feathers and colors intentional and says of the bay mare that it "shames the silliness out of me." A goose leads its flock in the night saying "ya-honk!" Whitman thinks that the pert find it meaningless, "but I listen closer, I find its purpose and place up there toward the November sky." Summing up in verse 14 he declares: "I see in them and myself the same old law."

The Buddha often talks about the ancient "law" (*dharma*) meaning not those created by man but of the cosmos, waiting to be discovered, not, one has to add by the scientific method, but by *insight*, the key term in Buddhism. Whitman returns a number of times to the ancient law, as discoverer anew of it, and as teacher of it. Of course his system diverges radically from the Buddha's because where the Buddha stays with the unitary, the stainless, the spotless, the imperishable – you can choose other terms for the same thing – Whitman moves cyclically from the unitary to the manifold. He says in verse 16 "I resist anything better than my own diversity." I don't quite believe him of course: he does not resist the unitary at all, but the point is that if he is not also the poet and teacher of diversity he is nothing. His departure from the Buddha, and from Christ and the Gnostics too, is the conviction that there is nothing "fallen" about this world. He is clear in verse 20 that he has no patience for such views:

> I do not snivel that snivel the world over,
> That months are vacuums and the ground but wallow and filth,
> That life is a suck and a sell, and nothing remains at the end but threadbare crape and tears.

All very good, but Whitman was young and fit when he wrote that. How does one carry this sentiment with one when coming close to the coffin's shroud and tears of the bereaved? In the modern age we die terribly slowly, far too often in a hospital with its fluorescent lights; its plastics, glass and steel; its antiseptics and interventions; and all far removed from street, meadow or forest. Can Whitman's teachings carry us through that? Did they carry him through his long years of semi-paralysis and general infirmity?

Whitman knows the quintessence, to use the Greek term, or the imperishable, to use the Indian term. That is what remains when we lose vitality and fall out of the sky to our graves. He has many metaphors for it; the next in our progression is this: "Shall I make my list of things in the house and skip the house that supports them?" "House" can only be the unmanifest, the uncreated, the quintessence here. But Whitman's earthiness has to embrace everything. If that is so he has to embrace evil, and many times he confirms this. For example, in verse 22: "I am the poet of commonsense and of the demonstrable and of immortality; / And am not the poet of goodness only, I do not decline to be the poet of wickedness also." He continues:

> What blurt is it about virtue and about vice?
> Evil propels me, and reform of evil propels me, I stand indifferent,
> My gait is no faultfinder's or rejecter's gait,
> I moisten the roots of all that has grown.

When we look at religious groups that are world-engaged we often find a form of activism that sets out to reform evil wherever it finds it, such as injustice or the violation of human rights or to combat global warming or pollution. These groups do not stand indifferent to such reforms and generally are not indifferent at all to evil. Most religions posit a *moral* universe in which transgression is met with suffering. In the West it is God that judges and punishes; in the East it is the less personal workings of karma. Either way much religious thought is devoted to moral questions, so we have to say that Whitman's system here is rather different. Of the religious forms I know I would have to place this *relative* indifference to good and evil along with the animist religions, though Whitman is imbued with none of that sensibility. He has nothing of condemnation in him; neither is he one who pulls away from the mediocre or desperate or those who, by common measure, have fallen to the bottom (verse 24):

> Through me many long dumb voices,
> Voices of the interminable generations of slaves,
> Voices of prostitutes and of deformed persons,
> Voices of the diseased and despairing, and of thieves and dwarfs,
> Voices of cycles of preparation and accretion,
> And of the threads that connect the stars—and of wombs, and
>   of the fatherstuff,
> And of the rights of them the others are down upon,
> Of the trivial and flat and foolish and despised,
> Of fog in the air and beetles rolling balls of dung.

How different to Nietzsche, for instance, who has his religious character Zarathustra declare himself far beyond all those who are the "flies of the marketplace" or the "bungled and the botched" or characterized in other contemptuous phrases. But how does one cope when one has placed no barrier between self and all of manifest creation? A longer passage gives us a clue as to Whitman's perhaps rare moments when he is close to being overwhelmed. I am thinking of when he describes the soprano and orchestra in an opera which raise tumultuous feelings in him (verse 26): "I am exposed, cut by bitter and poisoned hail," he writes, after which he is:

> Let up again to feel the puzzle of puzzles,
> And that we call Being.
>
> To be in any form, what is that?
> (Round and round we go, all of us, and ever come back thither,)
> If nothing lay more developed the quahaug and its callous shell
>   were enough.

> Mine is no callous shell,
> I have instant conductors all over me whether I pass or stop,
> They seize every object and lead it harmlessly through me.

The quahaug is a hard-shelled clam; Whitman has no hard shell but has a sensory system that lets everything through, harmlessly, he claims. But is it so harmless? He goes on to say that to touch his person to another's is about as much as he can stand, and that this sense of touch "immodestly" dominates the other senses to the point of being traitorous. I'm not sure what exactly to make of this passage except that to permit all things to impinge upon him without exclusions has its dangers. Then, in verse 31, one of my favorite passages includes the line "a mouse is miracle enough to stagger sextillions of infidels," and leads to this verse:

> I find I incorporate gneiss and coal and long-threaded moss and
>   fruits and grains and esculent roots,
> And am stucco'd with quadrupeds and birds all over,
> And have distanced what is behind me for good reasons,
> And call any thing close again when I desire it.

Here Whitman is not overwhelmed by all that he finds to himself to be – and the image of being "stucco'd" with animals and birds is verging on the shamanic. But the last two lines give us another clue: the profusion of all that Whitman finds good can be "distanced" behind him. His "good reasons" are not spelled out, but could be read as follows: so as not to be overwhelmed.

The creatures are everywhere in Whitman's thoughts: "I think I could turn and live awhile with the animals," he says in verse 32, "because they do not sweat and whine about their condition; "They do not make me sick discussing their duty to God." He adds: "Not one is respectable or unhappy over the whole earth." More obscurely he says that "They bring me tokens of myself, they evince them plainly in their possession. / I do not know where they got those tokens, / I must have passed that way untold times ago and negligently dropt them." I believe I am not the only one to take this as yet another reference to reincarnation, and certainly I feel the same: each animal I encounter I experience as part of my history. This is the essence of shamanism I believe, but it is important to say that Whitman does not make his home there.

Instead Whitman is here for us humans and feels everything we do. This section of verse 33 is sobering indeed:

> I am the hounded slave, I wince at the bite of the dogs,
> Hell and despair are upon me, crack and again crack the marksmen,
> I clutch the rails of the fence, my gore dribs thinned with the ooze of my skin,
> I fall on the weeds and stones,
> The riders spur their unwilling horses and haul close,
> They taunt my dizzy ears and beat me violently over the head with their whip-stocks.
>
> Agonies are one of my changes of garments;
> I do not ask the wounded person how he feels, I myself become the wounded person,
> My hurt turns livid upon me as I lean on a cane and observe.

We are uncomfortable I think with the dry-eyed tone in the recounting of the murder of a black slave. We are uncomfortable I think that Whitman leans on his cane and observes the wounded person. Why is he not rushing around like a madman crying "doctor!" "nurse!"? But these and similar verses with their measured detailing of our miseries stand with the measured detailing of our joys. If one is to be co-extensive with all that is one cannot exclude anything and Whitman does not hold back: next in verse 34 he recounts in the same studiously neutral fashion the "murder in cold blood of four hundred and twelve young men." I don't know what event in the American Civil War this refers to but these fighting men surrendered to superior forces, were promised safety, but as prisoners of war were not to benefit from the rights later enshrined in the Geneva Convention. Instead the following morning they were brought out in squads and massacred. Whitman fills out some details for us and finishes: "And that is the tale of the murder of the four hundred and twelve young men." In one edition there is a further line: "And that was a jetblack sunrise." Only that last image of the jetblack sunrise conveys even the slightest horror at what took place, and is an unusual image for Whitman, perhaps very unusual, perhaps jarring even. Is it enough though? That depends on one's feelings about detachment perhaps. Interestingly it looks like Whitman was himself dubious about the line, because in one version it as the end of the account, in another at the beginning, and in a third it is absent.

If Whitman is a spiritual teacher, then his teachings at times are hard going, it cannot be denied. He turns to face the manifest; he turns to face the unmanifest. He turns to describe our greatest joys; he turns to describe our greatest horrors. He identifies with the greatest of men; he identifies with the most corrupt. This journey is not for the faint-hearted.

Whitman had in his unstructured way absorbed much about religion and has this to say in verse 41 on the religious teachers of the past and how he will surpass them:

> Magnifying and applying come I,
> Outbidding at the start the old cautious hucksters,
> The most they offer for mankind and eternity less than a spirt of my own seminal wet,
> Taking myself the exact dimensions of Jehovah and laying them away,
> Lithographing Kronos and Zeus his son, and Hercules his grandson,
> Buying drafts of Osiris and Isis and Belus and Brahma and Adonai,
> In my portfolio placing Manito loose, and Allah on a leaf, and the crucifix engraved,
> With Odin, and the hideous-faced Mexitli, and all idols and images,
> Honestly taking them all for what they are worth, and not a cent more,
> Admitting they were alive and did the work of their day,
> Admitting they bore mites as for unfledged birds who have now to rise and fly and sing for themselves,
> Accepting the rough deific sketches to fill out better in myself, bestowing them freely on each man and woman I see.

Commentators have made much of this passage of course. Is it bombast? Is it a poetic flight of fancy? Personally I take it at face value –

Whitman is founding a religion that he hopes will outstrip the others. We have seen that Whitman holds dear all those at the bottom of the supposed human pile, the prostitutes, the criminals, the young men killed in war, the unlucky, the rebel, much as Jesus did when he defended all those spurned by the elites of his day. Jesus called himself the son of God and presented his teachings as superseding what went before, so why cannot Whitman do the same?

I had an argument about the Buddha once, in the London centre for the Friends of the Western Buddhist Order, a spiritual community or *sangha* I spent much time in. The subject of the spiritual teacher Andrew Cohen came up and the swift consensus on him was this: "I don't like people who set themselves up that way." I pointed out that the Buddha had set himself up in exactly the same way, as documented in the Pali Canon. "Ah, but he was *the Buddha*," came the tautological response. I just shook my head but should have responded: "No. He was not *the* Buddha then. It is people like you over thousands of years that have turned him into '*the* Buddha.'" Whitman is not "the" Messiah, Christ, Buddha, Savior or anything like that because his system was never promoted in the way that Constantine made Christianity a religion of state, or the emperor Ashoka made Buddhism a religion of state, and therefore placed Jesus and the Buddha at the centre of mythologizing public opinion. But in his day Whitman's influence was great enough for William James to write this:

> Thus it has come about that many persons today regard Walt Whitman as the restorer of the eternal natural religion. He has infected them with his own love of comrades, with his own gladness that he and they exist. Societies are actually formed for his cult; a periodical organ exists for its propagation, in which the lines of orthodoxy and heterodoxy are already beginning to be drawn; hymns are written by others in his peculiar prosody; and he is even explicitly compared with the founder of the Christian religion, not altogether to the advantage of the latter. [33]

James is expressing a certain discomfort here at the idea of Whitmanism, yet this passage remains a tribute to what was then a significant phenomenon, a new religion. Working through "Song of Myself" we are piecing together the first outlines of that religion through fragmentary hints here and there.

3. Whitman's System

A throwaway comment is important when Whitman says in verse 41: "the supernatural of no account ..." For me it says two things: firstly that Whitman did not necessarily deny the supernatural, but that secondly it had no special place in his system. I understand the Buddha in the same way: he had no difficulty acknowledging all that is regularly called supernatural but was clear that none of it was part of his system or practice.

For the religious left who want Whitman to have a socialist political consciousness there are many disappointments. For example he sees clearly enough what separates those with capital and those without (verse 42): "Many sweating and ploughing and thrashing, and then the chaff for payment receiving, / A few idly owning, and they the wheat continually claiming." But that is it: he passes over the issue neutrally as he does the slaughter of prisoners of war or any other evil he records as part of the fabric of life.

As mentioned, a number of commentators are persuaded that reincarnation is part of Whitman's system; verse 43 contains another passage that supports this interpretation:

> I do not despise you priests;
> My faith is the greatest of faiths and the least of faiths,
> Enclosing all worship ancient and modern, and all between ancient and modern,
> Believing I shall come again upon the earth after five thousand years, ...

We saw that Whitman's positivity irritated William James, and here is a reminder that Whitman feels no grudge against existence for his life to date (verse 44):

> Were mankind murderous or jealous upon you my brother or my sister?
> I am sorry for you, they are not murderous or jealous upon me,
> All has been gentle with me, I keep no account with lamentation,
> (What have I to do with lamentation?)

Whitman may have nothing to do with lamentations, but does that not rather separate him from the rest of us? His life circumstances were largely benign though of course they did not place wealth or privilege at his feet. But what of those pushed down from birth, the ones, as he says, that toil all day in the fields for chaff while making others rich on the wheat? If religion in the modern world has to take Freud in its stride, and if all kinds of religious thinkers, including Richard Maurice Bucke have attempted to incorporate Darwin's discoveries into the religious life, then Marx too must have his place. There is no doubt that when Whitman encountered the working poor he gave them his love, his time and what possessions he had. He was a communitarian. What he did not give the working poor was a socialist doctrine, and when enthusiastic socialists took up the ideas in *Leaves* and came on pilgrimage to him he mostly found them too doctrinaire. We cannot deny then that there is a Marx-shaped gap in Whitman's system, even if it is easy to add such socialist reform to it, as many did.

Let us return to what *is* in Whitman's system. Here is a passage – still in verse 44 – on what one could say is immortality, but couched in terms of the distant past, not future:

> Afar down I see the huge first Nothing, the vapor from the nostrils of death,
> I know I was even there, I waited unseen and always,
> And slept while God carried me through the lethargic mist,
> And took my time, and took no hurt from the foetid carbon.
>
> Long I was hugged close – long and long.
>
> Immense have been the preparations for me,
> Faithful and friendly the arms that have helped me.

I too have this sense of having existed in some form or other for aeons; I recognize too that Thomas Traherne writes in the same way (more of him later). Here is a passage from Whitman towards the end of "Song of Myself" that I read decades ago and which I have made mine and meaningful to me (verse 48-49):

> And I call to mankind, Be not curious about God,
> For I who am curious about each am not curious about God,
> No array of terms can say how much I am at peace about God
>   and about death.
> I hear and behold God in every object, yet I understand God not
>   in the least,
> Nor do I understand who there can be more wonderful than
>   myself.
>
> Why should I wish to see God better than this day?
> I see something of God each hour of the twenty-four, and each
>   moment then,
> In the faces of men and women I see God, and in my own face in
>   the glass;
> I find letters from God dropped in the street, and every one is
>   signed by God's name,
> And I leave them where they are, for
> I know that others will punctually come forever and ever.
>
> And as to you death, and you bitter hug of mortality, it is idle to
>   try to alarm me.
>
> To his work without flinching the accoucheur comes,
> I see the elderhand pressing receiving supporting,
> I recline by the sills of the exquisite flexible doors, and mark the
>   outlet, and mark the relief and escape.
> And as to you corpse I think you are good manure, but that does
>   not offend me,
> I smell the white roses sweet scented and growing,
> I reach to the leafy lips, I reach to the polished breasts of melons.
>
> And as to you life, I reckon you are the leavings of many deaths,
> No doubt I have died myself ten thousand times before.

It is most telling here that while Whitman is not curious abut God, he is curious about each and every one of us. He is at peace with God and with death and thinks he has died ten thousand times before.

These thoughts conclude our whistle-stop tour through "Songs of Myself." Hopefully the few extracts indicate the outlines of Whitman's system, though they cannot of course convey the experience of reading the poem as a whole. We look at more of it in Chapter 7; here my aim was to pull out enough to confirm what other scholars have said, that Whitman's work is religious and his intention is religious.

Whitman's system and the East

Both Western and Eastern scholars wrote widely and approvingly of Whitman in their comparisons with Indian thought. For example Dorothy Mercer submitted a PhD thesis in 1933 entitled "Leaves of Grass and the Bhagavad Gita." This remains unpublished, but there exists a series of articles by her in the journal *Vedanta and the West*, published by the Vedanta Society of Los Angeles. In one of them she observes that a number of passages in *Leaves* suggest that Whitman believes in reincarnation,[34] and comments that though his work bears resemblance to Vedic thought, he does not share some of its attitude to suffering. Mercer's work is illuminative, although, as the Indian scholar V. K. Chari (introduced below) has commented, she probably over-emphasizes the evolutionary aspect of *Leaves*, perhaps influenced in this by Bucke.

Romain Rolland, the French writer and correspondent with Freud, published works in the 1920s that were also sympathetic to Whitman. Rolland charted the role of the great Indian teacher Vivekananda in the establishment of Vedanta in the West, in the USA in particular, and recognized the American Transcendentalists (Emerson and Thoreau) as important figures in the introduction of Hindu thought into the US. For Whitman however Rolland reserves an unconditional salute as the equal of anything Hindu, at the same time lamenting that Vivekananda did not praise him enough (beyond calling him the "American Sannyasin").[35] Rolland calls Whitman the "dead giant," "whose shade was a thousand times warmer than such pale reflections of the Sun of Being seen through their cold Methodist window panes. He stood before Vivekananda and held out his great hand to him. ... How was it that he did not take it?" This was meant metaphorically, as Whitman had died in the year previous to Vivekananda's arrival in the States.

Rolland says of Whitman's religious thought that it "has come least into the limelight – and at the same time is the kernel [of his poetry]." He regretted also that beyond his immediate disciples Whitman was not recognized in the States:

> But this is true of all real Precursors. And it does not make them any the less the true representatives of their people that their people ignore them: in them is liberated out of due time the profound energies hidden and compressed within the human masses: they announce them; sooner or later they come to light. The genius of Whitman was the index of the hidden soul sleeping — (she is not yet wide awake) — in the depth of his people of the United States.[36]

In his preface to *Maha Yogi: Walt Whitman - New Light on Yoga*, published in 1978, O. K. Nambiar comments on Hindu reactions to Whitman:

> It is a curious fact that the Hindu mind has shown an instant capacity for responsive incandescence when brought into contact with Whitman's works. I remember an occasion when I read out passages from *Leaves of Grass* and translated them for the benefit of a Brahmin pundit. The pundit's eyes lighted up with a flash of recognition, and he exclaimed from time to time — "He is a realized soul," "that is the cream of the Vedanta," "those are the signs of Bhava Samadhi" — a joyous recognition of the familiar Upanishadic landmarks all along the route. I know also a few Hindu professors of American Literature who have cheap jibes ready when they talk of Whitman — "homosexual," "egotist," "cataloguer," etc., all of which reveal how little they have tried to know him.[37]

Note that *Bhava Samadhi* is one of many technical Sanskrit terms in the religious life and means approximately a state of ecstasy brought about by devotional practice, as for example common in the life of Ramakrishna. The ecstasy bit may be right, but the devotional is not Whitman's path at all. As another example of the Indian response to Whitman, it is interesting to note that Asit Chandmal ends his introduction to his photo-essay on Jiddu Krishnamurti with passages from "Song of Myself."[38] As a contemporary academic Nambiar is unusually receptive to Whitman, and makes many interesting connections and comparisons between Whitman and other mystics of various tradition, though mainly Indian. He is able to describe various contemporaries of Whitman, such as Bucke and Horace Traubel, as Whitman's disciples, and him their guru, without any of the embarrassment or distaste that a Western academic would show. Here is the passage in which he declares Traubel a disciple:

> An interesting fact about Horace Traubel may be mentioned here. Whitman was Traubel's Guru. Traubel had served him devotedly during the last fifteen years of Whitman's life during his illness. Traubel had his first *samadhi* experience at the age of thirty one, followed by two successive experiences at two year intervals. The last one, a particularly overwhelming experience, happened when he was crossing the ferry, leaning over the railing of the boat. He then "lost this world for another" and saw revealed for a few minutes "things hitherto withheld from him." "The physical body went through the experience of a disappearance in spiritual light."... "I was one with God, Love, the Universe, at face to face with myself." He was sensible of particular mental and moral disturbances and readjustments, ... "an indissoluble unity of the several energies of my being in one force." He stood so profoundly lost in this blissful state that a deckhand who knew him had to tap him on the shoulder to bring him back to normal consciousness. There was such a heavenly look in his face that the deckhand exclaimed: "You look wonderfully well and happy tonight, Mr. Traubel." He continued in a state of ecstasy for full twenty-four hours before he met Walt Whitman. The first words that Walt addressed to him when he sallied into his room reassured him: "Horace," he said, "you have the look of great happiness in your face tonight. Have you had a run of good luck?" Traubel explained in a few words that he had indeed a run of good luck though not perhaps the good luck he had in mind for him at the moment. Walt put his hand on Traubel's shoulder and looked deep into his eyes and said one of the strangest things he ever said, "I knew it would come to you." Traubel said, "I have been wondering all day if I am not crazy." Walt laughed gravely. "No, sane. Now at last you are sane." The Guru knew instinctively that the disciple had made the grade.[39]

We return to this passage later, just noting for now the use of the term *samhadi* again in an Indian assessment of Whitman's hierophancy. Nambiar's analysis is also conscious of the division that Whitman himself makes between his ordinary and cosmic self:

> Whitman speaks to us from two levels. He has got himself misunderstood, sometimes, because he commutes between the two levels without warning us. He shifts his standpoint. There are two Whitmans. One is

3. Whitman's System

the "son of Manhattan." The other is "a Kosmos." The former, somewhat unreasonably calls himself "one of the roughs," just for the sake of being all inclusive. The latter during his cosmic moments believes himself, to be an "incredible God." The two have to be carefully separated lest their voices should mix. The Manhattan voice speaks of the earthly show: it talks about politics, wars, presidents, the Broadway pageant and the human scene. The "incredible God" swiftly leaps over them and speaks of the soul, the cosmic plan, divine purpose and of the "light untellable." Since the son of Manhattan is intermittently aware that he is a Kosmos, there are two voices heard in *Leaves*, and we are apt to treat them alike. However, sensitive readers can note a difference. When he speaks from the "Manhattan level" he appears to be speaking out to us in a "yawp heard over the roofs of the earth." The reader is obliged to shift his viewpoint back and forth between the immanent and the transcendent levels of consciousness to follow the transition of thought. This movement on the part of the reader is necessary.[40]

I am curious that Nambiar thinks Whitman "unreasonable" for calling himself one of the roughs. It is true that by the standards of his day Whitman was a cultured man, a man of letters. He loved opera. But Whitman's claim rings true, I feel, because of his faith in the ordinary man and his acute mistrust of the elevated person, whether through wealth, erudition, political status or anything that makes for conventional success. Whitman always looked beneath that social sheen to find the authentic individual underneath, and for those where no such barriers had to be stripped off – the roughs – he had an immediate affection. Whitman's inclusivity is central, I would say, something that Nambiar does not quite recognize.

On the question of the two selves of Whitman it is true that he does distinguish between his soul and the rest, but he always does so in the context of explaining their equality and inter-manifestatory nature (i.e. that one begets the other). Interestingly a scholar writing on the Theosophical Society website claims: "The concept of the 'self' in 'Song of Myself' can be fully understood only from a Theosophical standpoint. Throughout the poem, every use of the words 'I,' 'Soul,' 'Self,' and 'Body' is consistent with the ideas brought forth in the writings of Helena P. Blavatsky, A. P. Sinnett, and William Q. Judge, three Theosophical contemporaries of Whitman's."[41] This Theosophical interpretation is again broadly Indian, a per-

49

spective not unknown to Whitman when he told his friend Horace Traubel in 1888 that "Even the Theosophists claim me."[42]

V. K. Chari, an Indian scholar mentioned above, first wrote *Whitman in the Light of Vedantic Mysticism* as his PhD thesis, and subsequently published it in 1964. The 1976 edition[43] has an introduction by Gay Wilson Allen – one of Whitman's biographers[44] – who praised Chari's work as a thorough study of Whitman in the context of Indian thought. Allen recounts how Thoreau asked Whitman if "he had read any of the great works of India," to which Whitman is supposed to have replied "No, tell me about them." Whitman claims however to have read "the ancient Hindu poems" before writing *Leaves of Grass*, and Nambiar's *Maha Yogi: Walt Whitman*, shows in the frontispiece a photograph of a page from Whitman's copy of the *Gita* with a handwritten commentary.

Chari gives a good introduction to the literary controversies surrounding *Leaves* though he prefers the Upanishads to the *Gita* for comparison. In *Whitman and Bharati: A Comparative Study* another Indian scholar, V. Sachitanandan, shows how the Tamil poet Bharati was influenced by Whitman in the introduction of free verse into his tradition.[45] Sachitanandan also investigates the affinity of the two poets in terms of Vedantic mysticism, in particular the Advaita (non-dual) school of Vedanta, but on the whole the study is more oriented towards a literary analysis than a mystical one.

This is a good place to introduce a few Indian terms belonging to the spiritual life, beyond the familiar "guru" and the term *samhadi* discussed above. They are needed not just because Indians have claimed Whitman as one of their own and so more is needed to understand why, but because I have adapted a limited number of these terms to help understand the history of Western spirituality. I explain them in detail in my book *Secularism*; here I introduce just a few that are necessary for our discussion. Firstly I have adopted the Hindu term *sangha* to mean spiritual community, generally gathered around a spiritual teacher, as used earlier for the community of the Friends of the Western Buddhist order. If a permanent residence for the guru and their following arise, then that is called an "ashram," a term I have also used a number of times already. It has no direct translation into

English, though an ashram might have some common ground with the seminary, monastery or convent. The small group of people that gathered around Whitman can be called a *sangha* perhaps, though his home was too small and too devoid of devotees to call it an ashram. The second, which has again no Western equivalent, is *darshan*, meaning to sit in the presence of the spiritual teacher (I have also used this term earlier). In the first instance it means to sit in silence, though it may be followed by a talk, or questions and answers or any kind of ritual. In the West it might be considered odd to sit for an hour or two in complete silence with an Anglican priest; we cannot imagine the point of it. We will see that some accounts suggest that merely being in the presence of Whitman, even if there is no conversation, has a spiritual impact on the person; that would be *darshan*. A third, and less-needed term than the previous two, is *siddhi*, meaning occult power. We will see that for some teachers and seekers such occult powers are important; we will find that they are irrelevant to Whitman.

Finally, I have to explain my repurposing of two Sanskrit terms, *bhakti* and *jnani*, meaning respectively the devotional and non-devotional spiritual paths. A great deal of my book *Secularism* is taken up with explaining my usage of these two terms and why I regard them as virtually a Rosetta Stone for the deciphering of Western religious history. Here I'll just revisit a few of the issues as they help locate Whitman's system.

Don Cupitt, a writer on religion whose book *The Sea of Faith* started a movement of the same name, is aware of *bhakti* devotional religious traditions, but as an obviously *jnani* thinker is puzzled by them, saying:

> It is not necessary here to dwell at length upon the familiar eroticism of wounds, of thraldom, bondage, and ravishment, for everyone knows that both in India and in the West spiritual writing makes extensive use of erotic imagery. What has not hitherto been sufficiently noticed or explained is the extent to which celibate male, as well as celibate female, writers unhesitatingly adopt the point of view and metaphoric of specifically female sexuality for devotional writings.[46]

I think this most interesting. My poem "The Petals of Me" that I included earlier is clearly an example of what Cupitt is talking about (Whitman's passages about the lover's tongue that penetrates his breast is another example). My poem could be interpreted however as merely about sexual longing but the fact is that I wrote it out of the depth of my religious feeling and the difficulties I was going through at the time. We turn to sexual metaphors because they are so cathected with energy, this remaining, I think, a problem in the interpretation of Whitman. However, his system is as far removed from any *bhakti* kind of devotion as is the Buddha's; indeed the only time I know of that the Buddha used the word "love" is when he comments that his monks love him, but it is not as devotion towards the guru that would be found in a *bhakti* system.[47] Indeed he comments on it rather clinically. Whitman on the other hand has love most central to his system, but it is not of the religiously devotional type at all, as in the case of Ramakrishna. Nevertheless the imagery and metaphors he uses to convey this non-sexual love are often sexual, for reasons I have suggested.

A little more of my terminology has to be introduced here, this time of Western origin: the juxtaposition of *via positiva* against *via negativa*. They are theological terms which I have adapted to indicate, respectively, a world-curious spiritual path or a world-denying spiritual path. Whitman, it hardly needs saying, belongs to the former.

Having introduced these terms we can now characterize the Indian tradition known as the Advaita which is relevant to our Whitman exploration. One of its defining texts is Shankara's *The Crest-Jewel of Discrimination* introduced earlier. I think of the Advaita as generally *jnani, via negativa*, meaning that it is a non-devotional, world-denying spiritual path; at the same time we can characterize in advance Whitman's system as *jnani, via positiva*, meaning a non-devotional, world curious spiritual path.

The unchristian Whitman

Being so shaped in my thirties by Eastern systems of thought it has taken many years to realize just how alien Whitman's thinking is to the Christian world he was located in. However it is the comment on Jesus by Rajneesh – being a Jain by birth and therefore also far removed from Christian thought – that has helped me pinpoint where Whitman diverges so much from his religious heritage: there is nothing of *atonement* in his system. Rajneesh thought that this was the great original contribution of Jesus, that by sincere faith in Christ as Redeemer our sins are forgiven. The whole system of confession, repentance, purgatory and salvation is absent in Whitman and I am sure there are many who would say, good riddance. However, at the age of sixty-five and a Quaker, I am not so sure. While the Quaker tradition has perhaps the least of this emphasis on sin than any other branch of Christianity, atonement does remain for me an issue in the spiritual life that cannot be overlooked.

Christianity was Whitman's context however, in days long before comparative religion was taught in schools and long before priests, rabbis and imams gathered for interfaith conferences. Vivekananda introduced Hinduism to America at the Parliament of the World's Religions in 1893, a year after Whitman died. This marked perhaps the beginning of American interest in Indian religions, but it took a century for anything resembling religious pluralism to become widely accepted and even then some would claim that this is only the domain of the liberal educated elite. In Whitman's prime Christianity was however not just the sole religion but in itself a spectrum of faiths, including the Quakerism of Whitman's mother, the Deism of America's founding fathers and the more mainstream Baptist and Methodist traditions.

Whitman's contemporaries found it hard to recognize his faith as Christian; indeed much of what he wrote seemed to undermine it. The most challenging of Whitman's writings on faith must lie in his poem "To Him That Was Crucified:"

> My spirit to yours dear brother,
> Do not mind because many sounding your name do not understand you,
> I do not sound your name, but I understand you,
> I specify you with joy O my comrade to salute you, and to salute those who are with you, before and since, and those to come also,
> That we labor together transmitting the same charge and succession,
> We few equals indifferent of lands, indifferent of times,
> We, enclosers of all continents, all castes, allowers of all theologies,
> Compassionaters, perceivers, rapport of men,

> We walk silent among disputes and assertions, but reject not the
>   disputers nor any thing that is asserted,
> We hear the bawling and din, we are reach'd at by divisions, jeal-
>   ousies, recriminations on every side,
> They close peremptorily upon us to surround us, my comrade,
> Yet we walk unheld, free, the whole earth over, journeying up
>   and down till we make our ineffaceable mark upon time and
>   the diverse eras,
> Till we saturate time and eras, that the men and women of races,
>   ages to come, may prove brethren and lovers as we are.

This passage alone tells us that Whitman counts Jesus as an equal and that while many claim to speak in his name they do not understand him where Whitman does. What would the average Christian preacher of his day make of his remark "we few equals"? Outrage. This was certainly the reaction of Secretary James Harlan in the Department of the Interior – an ordained Methodist minister – who sacked Whitman when he discovered that he was the author of *Leaves*, though that may also have been over its alleged indecency. The English publication *The Critic* sums up the more general Victorian distaste for Whitman:

> Is it possible that the most prudish nation in the world will adopt a poet whose indecencies stink in the nostrils? We hope not; and yet there is a probability, and we will show you why, that this Walt Whitman will not meet with the stern rebuke which he so richly deserves. ... Walt Whitman is as unacquainted with art, as a hog with mathematics. ... The very nature of this man's compositions excludes us from proving by extracts the truth of our remarks; but we, who are not prudish, emphatically declare that the man who wrote page 79 of *The Leaves of Grass* deserves nothing so richly as the public executioner's whip.[48]

Whitman collected all such negative criticism but remained firm in the face of it. His approach to Jesus is further spelled out here:

> I think too much is made of the execution of Jesus Christ. I know Jesus Christ would not have approved of this himself: he knew that his life was only another life, any other life, told big; he never wished to shine, especially to shine at the general expense. ... The masters in history have had lots of chance: they have been glorified beyond recognition: now give the

other fellows a chance: glorify the average man a bit: put in a word for his sorrows, his tragedies, just for once, just for once.[49]

Whitman was not alone however in this period of religious innovation. As Michael Robertson points out, the *Book of Mormon* had emerged in 1830 as a new scripture, and before that, as part of the Enlightenment revolution against the constraints within Christian thought, Blake, as poet, had worked to provide new religious narratives and myths.[50] As Whitman himself wrote in his prose piece *Democratic Vistas*: "The priest departs, the divine literatus comes." According to Robertson, Whitman was not exceptional in this but "responding to a widespread demand among progressive intellectuals and artists." The close relationship between the Transcendentalist writers of Whitman's day and the Unitarian religion was an example of the "literatus" both arising out of a religious movement and influencing it. However all this was a movement with no lasting legacy. The poet in the twenty-first century has not replaced the priest but displaced him, meaning that rather than artists becoming the servants of religion, religion has become the poor relation of art, not to mention science. In my experience those in the arts today are more inclined to atheism even than the general population.

The American Transcendentalists

Contemporary Christianity may have had little influence on Whitman but he can easily be placed in the Transcendentalist movement of the time. This religious movement had roots in the Unitarian and German Romantic traditions and counted Ralph Waldo Emerson as perhaps its most famous adherent. It was an individualist spiritual philosophy with strong interests in Nature and Eastern philosophies. Henry David Thoreau, part of this movement, wrote:

> In the morning I bathe my intellect in the stupendous and cosmogonal philosophy of the *Bhagavat Geeta*, since whose composition years of the gods have elapsed, and in comparison with which our modern world and its literature seem puny and trivial; and I doubt if that philosophy is not to be referred to a previous state of existence, so remote is its sublimity from our conceptions. I lay down the book and go to my well for water, and lo! there I meet the servant of the Brahmin, priest of Brahma, and

Vishnu and Indra, who still sits in his temple on the Ganges reading the Vedas, or dwells at the root of a tree with his crust and water-jug. I meet his servant come to draw water for his master, and our buckets as it were grate together in the same well. The pure Walden water is mingled with the sacred water of the Ganges.[51]

Thoreau's outlook is similar to Whitman's when we consider the aim that Thoreau had set himself in his quest to live simply by Walden Pond: "I went to the woods because I wished to live deliberately, to front only the essential facts of life, and see if I could not learn what it had to teach, and not, when I came to die, discover that I had not lived."[52] Whitman met Thoreau in 1856, the latter knowing and liking Whitman's work. A third party recorded that, "Each seemed planted fast in reserve, surveying the other curiously, like two beasts, each wondering what the other would do, whether to snap or run." Despite all they had in common they landed up having an argument about ordinary people in which Whitman detected in Thoreau a "disdain for men," a complaint he held against Thoreau despite their long-term friendship.

Whitman sent *Leaves of Grass* to Ralph Waldo Emerson, who was even more enthusiastic about it than Thoreau, writing to Whitman that "I am not blind to the worth of the wonderful gift of 'Leaves of Grass.' I find it the most extraordinary piece of wit and wisdom that America has yet contributed."[53] Without asking Emerson, Whitman had the letter published in the New York *Tribune* in 1855, and it was this and Emerson's word-of-mouth enthusiasm that may well have enabled *Leaves* to survive its early years. The two men met, but Whitman and Emerson were poles apart in their temperament, Emerson being a refined establishment intellectual, graduating in divinity, and pastor for a time at the prestigious Second Unitarian Church in Boston, while Whitman was a carpenter's son and a man of the rough outdoors. Whitman took Emerson for a beer in a rowdy pub, but despite this indelicate introduction, and Emerson's public annoyance that Whitman should publish his letter without permission, they saw each other, albeit infrequently, until Emerson's death. Emerson became ambivalent in his attitude to *Leaves*, as the following letter to Carlyle in 1856 shows. It includes the remark about "an auctioneer's inventory of a warehouse" cited earlier:

3. Whitman's System

One book, last summer, came out in New York, a nondescript monster, which yet had terrible eyes and buffalo strength, and was indisputably American — which I thought to send you; but the book throve so badly with the few to whom I showed it, and wanted good morals so much, that I never did. Yet I believe now again, I shall. It is called *Leaves of Grass* — was written and printed by a journeyman printer in Brooklyn, New York, named Walter Whitman; and after you have looked into it, if you think, as you may, that it is only an auctioneer's inventory of a warehouse, you can light your pipe with it.[54]

Emerson also referred to *Leaves* as a singular blend of the *Bhagavad Gita* and the New York *Tribune*. Whether Carlyle lit his pipe on *Leaves*, I do not know, though Whitman was an admirer of his, excepting the gloominess of his later work. Whitman gives us this interesting insight into his relationship with Emerson (and at the same time a foretaste of how he relates to Nature, in this case trees) in the following prose passage:

10 - 13 *October [1881]*: I spend a good deal of time on the Common, these delicious days and nights — every mid-day from 11.30 to about 1 — and almost every sunset another hour. I know all the big trees, especially the old elms along Tremont and Beacon streets, and have come to a sociable-silent understanding with most of them, in the sunlit air, (yet crispy-cool enough), as I saunter along the wide unpaved walks. Up and down this breadth by Beacon street, between these same old elms, I walk'd for two hours, of a bright sharp February mid-day twenty-one years ago, with Emerson, then in his prime, keen, physically and morally magnetic, arm'd at every point, and when he chose, wielding the emotional just as well as the intellectual. During those two hours he was the talker and I the listener. It was an argument-statement, reconnoitring, review, attack, and pressing home, (like an army corps in order, artillery, cavalry, infantry,) of all that could be said against that part (and a main part) in the construction of my poems, "Children of Adam." More precious than gold to me that dissertation — it afforded me, ever after, this strange and paradoxical lesson; each part of E's statement was unanswerable, no judge's charge ever more complete or convincing, I could never hear the points better put — and then I felt down in my soul the clear and unmistakable conviction to disobey all, and pursue my own way. "What have you to say then to such things" said E., pausing in conclusion. "Only that while I can't answer them at all, I feel more settled than ever to adhere to my own theory, and exemplify it," was my candid response. Whereupon we went and had

a good dinner at the American House. And thenceforward I never waver'd or was touch'd with qualms, (as I confess I had been two or three times before.)[55]

I think that Whitman's response here is both that of the true artist and the true religionist. Whenever a creative person ushers the new into the world there follows a reaction just like Emerson's, and the tougher the arguments go against this new thing, the more the creator of it – if it is truly genuine – is persuaded of its truth, even if they cannot answer the arguments at their own level. One has indeed to adhere to one's own theory and exemplify it. The question in a hierophantic setting is: what is valuable in the guru's theory – or system – and in exemplifying it does she or he set me an existential challenge? When I ask myself that of Whitman my answers are respectively everything, and yes.

Whitman and Nature Mysticism

In the above passage, taken from some of Whitman's prose writings, we see Whitman talk about his "silent sociable" relationship with the trees. From this and many other comments of his we can relate Whitman's system to that of the Nature mystics, a category largely associated with the Romantics. Personally I like to divide Nature mystics between a Romantic and a non-Romantic branch, the latter having less of a purely aesthetic relationship with Nature and certainly less problem with predation and death. Three important contemporaries of Whitman might be counted as non-Romantic Nature mystics, these being John Muir (1838-1914), Richard Jefferies (1848-1887) and John Burroughs (1837-1921), though only the latter was known to Whitman – indeed he was an important disciple as we shall see.

However in *Leaves*, Whitman's celebration is so comprehensive, and so inclusive of man's arts and industries, that Nature, in the modern sense of being in opposition to industrial and urban life, does not stand out. He is not therefore a "Nature writer" as Muir, Jefferies and Burroughs are. A comment of his to Bucke gives us an interesting insight into his attitude to writing on Nature:

> All such things need to be at least the third or fourth remove; in itself it would be too much for nine out of ten readers. Very few care for natural

3. Whitman's System

objects themselves, rocks, rain, hail, wild animals, tangled forests, weeds, mud, common Nature. They want her in a shape fit for reading about in a rocking-chair, or as ornaments in china, marble or bronze. The real things are, far more than they would own, disgusting, revolting to them. This may be a reason of the dislike of *Leaves of Grass* by the majority.[56]

In *Leaves* the descriptions of Nature are often in the form of lists, but effective in spite of that. There is also a description in *Specimen Days* – a collection of prose from later in Whitman's life – that perhaps comes closest to telling us how he really sees Nature:

> 1 *September*: I should not take either the biggest or the most picturesque tree to illustrate it. Here is one of my favorites now before me, a fine yellow poplar, quite straight, perhaps ninety feet high, and four feet thick at the butt. How strong, vital, enduring! how dumbly eloquent! What suggestions of imperturbability and *being*, as against the human trait of mere *seeming*. Then the qualities, almost emotional, palpably artistic, heroic, of a tree; so innocent and harmless, yet so savage. It *is*, yet says nothing. How it rebukes by its tough and equable serenity in all weathers, this gusty-tempered little whiffet, man, that runs indoors at a mite of rain or snow. Science (or rather half-way science) scoffs at reminiscence of dryad and hamadryad, and of trees speaking. But, if they don't, they do as well as most speaking, writing, poetry, sermons — or rather they do a great deal better. I should say indeed that those old dryad-reminiscences are quite as true as any, and profounder than most reminiscences we get. ("Cut this out," as the quack mediciners say, and keep by you.) Go and sit in a grove or woods, with one or more of these voiceless companions and read the foregoing, and think.
>
> One lesson from affiliating a tree — perhaps the greatest moral lesson anyhow from earth, rocks, animals, is that same lesson of inherency, of *what is*, without the least regard to what the looker on (the critic) supposes or says, or whether he likes or dislikes. What worse — what more general malady pervades each and all of us, our literature, education, attitude towards each other, (even towards ourselves,) than morbid trouble about *seems*, (generally temporarily seems too,) and no trouble at all, or hardly any, about the sane slow-growing, perennial, real parts of character, books, friendship, marriage — humanity's invisible foundations and hold-together? (As the all-basis, the nerve, the great sympathetic, the plenum within humanity, giving stamp to everything, is necessarily invisible.)[57]

Clearly it was an endless pleasure for Whitman to simply be in Nature, spending time in the countryside, enjoying the ordinary as much as any spectacular scenes like canyons or great waterfalls or brilliant sunsets. Having said that, Whitman's ultimate preference is for the scene to include people, perhaps ideally by rivers or the sea, but never rejecting the busiest streets of the inner city either. Bucke saw that natural things gave Whitman a pleasure that ordinary people never experience, and credited him with above-average hearing and sense of smell (I think this unlikely: Whitman may have just been more alert to his sensations). Whitman's opinion of Thoreau is interesting: he suspected that the romantic view of Nature expressed in Thoreau's *Walden* and in his life was not so much from "a love of woods, streams, and hills, ... as from a morbid dislike of humanity. I remember Thoreau saying once, when walking with him in my favorite Brooklyn — 'What is there in the people? What do you (a man who sees as well as anybody) see in all this cheating political corruption?'"[58] This is echoed in a passage from Thoreau himself:

> I walk towards one of our ponds, but what signifies the beauty of Nature when men are base? We walk to lakes to see our serenity reflected in them; when we are not serene, we go not to them.[59]

Neither I nor Whitman believe that "men are base;" mostly people miss out on Nature not by choice but because of the hardships of wresting a living. Whitman does not of course turn to Nature out of a "disdain for men." On the contrary "The Lesson of a Tree" is telling us how to let Nature instruct us in our human sphere, and in the foundations of our being; it is teaching us sobriety, a willingness to allow the important things to mature at their own mysterious pace, and not to apply the modern haste to our foundations. Beyond this lesson, and it is fundamental to Whitman's teachings I think, there is also the sheer exuberant delight in Nature, and also an almost painful wonder at it:

> As I have walk'd in Alabama my morning walk,
> I have seen where the she-bird the mocking-bird sat on her nest
>   in the briers hatching her brood.
>
> I have seen the he-bird also,

3. Whitman's System

> I have paus'd to hear him at hand inflating his throat and joy-
> fully singing.
>
> And while I paus'd it came to me that what he really sang for was
> not there only,
> Not for his mate nor himself only, nor all sent back by the ech-
> oes,
> But subtle, clandestine, away beyond,
> A charge transmitted and gift occult for those being born.
> (Starting from Paumanok v. 11)

I too experience birdsong as a "gift occult" – in certain moods the call of a thrush for example gives me the feeling of primal newness, charged as Whitman says with something unnamable, wild, and healing of human hurt and history.

Turning now to Richard Jefferies, this English contemporary of Whitman was a journalist and writer by profession. That he is considered as a mystic is due to his book *The Story of My Heart* which was published in 1883.[60] At times there is an extraordinary parallel with Whitman, and at other times Jefferies seems to say the opposite; certainly he shares Thoreau's "disdain for men" or perhaps just a despair of them. Jefferies' love of Nature runs along the same stream as Whitman's thoughts in "The Lesson of a Tree," only he describes his raptures at greater length, and in terms of the empowering of his "soul life." Again and again he describes how he seeks solitary moments away from his family and work, and climbs a local hill, or seeks the sea, and strides across the human-remote countryside or beach in order to wrest the nourishment for his soul-life from Nature; or he lies under a tree or by a brook and stares up at the sky and lets it fill him. His book is a careful prose, and in great contrast to Whitman's free verse, but he sings of Nature, and, oddly for a Victorian Englishman, the body too:

> There came to me a delicate, but at the same time a deep, strong and sen-
> suous enjoyment of the beautiful green earth, the beautiful sky and sun; I
> felt them, they gave me inexpressible delight, as if they embraced and
> poured out their love upon me. It was I who loved them, for my heart was
> broader than the earth; it is broader now than even then, more thirsty and
> desirous. After the sensuous enjoyment always come the thought, the de-

sire: That I might be like this; that I might have the inner meaning of the sun, the light, the earth, the trees and grass, translated into some growth of excellence in myself, both of the body and of mind; greater perfection of physique, greater perfection of mind and soul; that I might be higher in myself.[61]

For Jefferies his mysticism is one of longing, a desire that he calls his "single thought" or prayer, and the beauty of Nature raises it to the highest degree. Unlike those that run away from the human to Nature, Jefferies finds the human body to be the sum of all beauty in Nature:

Not only in grass fields with green leaf and running brook did this constant desire find renewal. More deeply still with living human beauty; the perfection of form, the simple fact of forms, ravished and always will ravish me away. In this lies the outcome and end of all the loveliness of sunshine and green leaf, of flowers, pure water and sweet air. This is embodiment and highest expression; the scattered, uncertain, and designless loveliness of tree and sunshine brought to shape. Through this beauty I prayed deepest and longest, and down to this hour. The shape — the divine idea of that shape — the swelling muscle or the dreamy limb, strong sinew or curve of bust, Aphrodite or Hercules, it is the same. That I may have the soul-life, the soul-nature, let the divine beauty bring to me divine soul. Swart Nubian, white Greek, delicate Italian, massive Scandinavian, in all the exquisite pleasure the form gave, and gives, to me immediately becomes intense prayer.[62]

If Whitman can bring one to walk down the street looking at people that pass one in a new way — a kind of curious touch to each person — then Jefferies can cause one to see in them the distillation of sun, rain, and air on trees; a new gift to us.

Where Whitman is at pains to praise the body and the soul equally, letting neither "abase" itself before the other, Jefferies is quite sure that the soul is higher, more important, and that the soul or the spirit is *entirely lacking* in Nature, in the rocks, trees and sky, where Whitman sees "God's handkerchief" dropped at every corner. Jefferies goes further: he comments on the immense inhospitability of Nature, the very sun that sends him into raptures burns and kills, the very sea is an undrinkable poison. It is a baffling contrast to Whitman at first, and is not easily resolvable; however we can leave it for now as a mark of the genuine expression of a mystic: that it is unique, and will not agree with another's tale of the ultimate. We can also find references in his book to having lived a hard life; one has the impression that he was as poor as Whitman, and as unpracticed in economics, but his situation was worse, for he had a wife and children to support. The sheer hardness of extracting a living in Victorian England for a man so averse to the material spirit of that age may have found expression in his views on the in-humanness of Nature.

The second of our Nature mystics, John Muir, was not only a naturalist, writer and Nature mystic, but also the founding father of ecology as a discipline and political force, instigating the American National Parks system. I'll provide just one extract from his writings to demonstrate his Nature mysticism. He is pursuing his scientific research in the Sierra and writes the following in his diary in a little log cabin far from "civilization:"

> These earthquakes have made me immensely rich. I had long been aware of the life and gentle tenderness of the rocks, and, instead of walking upon them as unfeeling surfaces, began to regard them as a transparent sky. ...
>
> We had several shocks last night. I would like to go somewhere on the west South American coast to study earthquakes. I think I could invent some experimental apparatus whereby their complicated phenomena could be separated and read, but I have some years of ice on hand. 'Tis most ennobling to find and feel that we are constructed with reference to these noble storms, so as to draw unspeakable enjoyment from them. Are we not rich when our six-foot column of substance sponges up heaven above and earth beneath into its pores? Aye, we have chambers in us the right shape for earthquakes.[63]

To assert, in the face of the very real terrors of possible crushing rock-fall, that we have "chambers in us the right shape for earthquakes" is remarkable and the mark of a mystic. Muir exemplifies for me the non-Romantic Nature mystic; one with more of a scientific than a poetic eye; one for whom the very real beauty of Nature is not compromised by recoil from its dangers. In contrast we can look at a Romantic like Tennyson who introduced the phrase "Nature red in tooth and claw" into the English language in his poem "In Memoriam A. H. H." The poem also says that that Nature's ravines "shriek" against the creed of man, his faith in

God. Muir sees no such betrayal in Nature; neither does Whitman. Both see more of God in Nature than in the world of the priest; indeed, although Muir's father was a Christian fundamentalist, Muir rejected the entire Christian church. Where Whitman goes far beyond Muir however is that he sees no such betrayal in the world of men either, their faults observed keenly enough but overwhelmingly countered by their divinity.

Traherne and Blake: "Poets of the *via positiva*"

In some of my books I refer to William Blake, Thomas Traherne and Walt Whitman as the "three poets of the *via positiva*." What they have in common is a world-celebrating or world-curious outlook or what I term the *via positiva*, as explained earlier. Whitman would have had no knowledge of Traherne but was quite aware of Blake, even basing a sketch for his proposed tomb on a Blake engraving.[64] Although Blake was born before Traherne I will look at Blake second because where he and Whitman part company in their systems is highly instructive and therefore useful in the following evaluation of what is missing in Whitman's system.

The works of Thomas Traherne were not discovered until long after his death in 1674. The earliest publication of the "Dobell" poems was in 1903 and followed by a prose collection in 1908 known as the *Centuries*. Further poems were discovered at the British Museum shortly after, and more works found in 1964 and 1967. Traherne's work contains a seemingly endless recitation of the joyfulness of his soul's simplicity and abundance, as reflected in and engendered by the abundance of creation. One has to search quite hard for the negative in it, where Whitman is at pains to speak of depression for example or any of the low states of human emotion as a necessary correlate to the higher more positive moods. Traherne emphasizes the innocence of childhood and speaks of his emergence from "unbeing" to life and the delight in the treasures of the senses (in particular sight) and the sense that all *belongs* to him (and at the same time to all other men and women: in turn they are also his treasures). We are presented with a conundrum: how is that a grown man can speak so clearly of a childhood innocence and bliss, one that we all recognize, however dimly, yet earnestly maintain it to be his present, adult, reality? One possibility is that he was gifted with a quite extraordinary memory for the childhood state, and furthermore that he was quite precociously gifted with wisdom at that age. More likely, in the context of mysticism, is that he travelled the same road as all of us: the gradual loss of innocence into a worldly-wise adult, then followed by a "rebirth" of some kind into spiritual awareness. Let us look at some typical Traherne passages. Here are the first four verses of "The Salutation," the opening poem of the Dobell collection (all selections from the Penguin edition[65]):

1
These little limbs,
These eyes and hands which here I find,
These rosy cheeks wherewith my life begins,
Where have ye been? Behind
What curtain were ye from me hid so long!
Where was, in what abyss, my speaking tongue?

2
When silent I,
So many thousand years,
Beneath the dust did in a chaos lie,
How could I smiles or tears,
Or lips or hands or eyes or ears perceive?
Welcome, ye treasures which I now receive.

3
I that so long
Was nothing from eternity,
Did little think such joys as ear or tongue,
To celebrate or see:
Such sounds to hear, such hands to feel, such feet,
Beneath the skies, on such a ground to meet.

4
New burnish'd joys!
Which yellow gold and pearl excel!
Such sacred treasures are the limbs in boys,
In which a soul doth dwell;
Their organized joints, and azure veins
More wealth include, than all the world contains.

These verses introduce many of Traherne's themes: that it is blessed to be born (quite at odds with mainstream Christianity's concept of original sin), that the sense organs themselves are treasures (reminiscent of some Upanishadic and Tantric themes and practices); and that the objects of those senses are also treasures. All this is perfectly Whitmanesque, and reminds us of a verse we looked at earlier: "I waited unseen and always, / And slept while God carried me through the lethargic mist." Both have a sense of existing before physical birth and both carry into physical life a blissfulness from the pre-physical. Traherne concludes his poem with this verse:

> A stranger here
> Strange things doth meet, strange glories see;
> Strange treasures lodg'd in this fair world appear;
> Strange all, and new to me.
> But that they mine should be, who nothing was,
> That strangest is of all, yet brought to pass.

This verse repeats the idea that all *belongs* to him. For a mystic on the path of the *via positiva* no other conclusion is possible of course: one sees directly that one is coterminous with all that is; "belong" simply expresses a form of ownership far more profound than the legal equivalent. Leaving this point for a moment let us compare the above extract to verse 5 of Wordsworth's "Intimations of Immortality:"

> Our birth is but a sleep and a forgetting:
> The Soul that rises with us, our life's Star,
> Hath had elsewhere its setting,
> And cometh from afar:
> Not in entire forgetfulness,
> And not in utter nakedness,
> But trailing clouds of glory do we come
> From God, who is our home:
> Heaven lies about us in our infancy!
> Shades of the prison-house begin to close
> Upon the growing Boy

> But He beholds the light, and whence it flows
> He sees it in his joy;
> The Youth who daily travels farther from the east
> Must travel, still is Nature's Priest,
> And by the vision splendid
> Is on his way attended;
> At length the Man perceives it die away,
> And fade into the light of common day.[66]

There are some similarities (though we can be confident that Wordsworth would not have read Traherne): Wordsworth recognizes the "heaven that lies about us in our infancy" and the "vision splendid." But he is less optimistic: birth is a "sleep and a forgetting;" the "clouds of glory" that we trail have another origin than the wondrous world of the senses; and of course the "shades of the prison-house" close in until the grown man sees his vision die away into "the light of common day." What is absent in Wordsworth perhaps is the "rebirth" that spiritual awakening brings and in which the "shades of the prison house" not so much evaporate as prove to be illusory. Wordsworth, I would suggest, is a typical Romantic. Whitman's system goes far beyond the Romantic because, like Traherne, he is convinced that to be born is no "fall" into the valley of the shadow of death – death being the great indigestible in the Romantic tradition – but an extraordinary privilege or at least adventure.

As with Whitman there is no elevation of Nature over the human world; stars and clouds feature, but streets, cities, and above all people count as much amongst Traherne's treasures. His love of creation rests on what is beyond creation, which is what we would expect to find in a mystic, but it is a Christian God and a Christian message that restores him to the innocence-in-adulthood that is the mark of the mystic. It is also worth mentioning that his *Centuries of Meditations* may have been written as spiritual instruction for a friend who had supplied the notebook they are written in, which would make Traherne a hierophant in relation to a particular disciple.[67]

Perhaps Traherne's best prose on the subject of bodily life is in the *Meditations*:

By the very right of your senses you enjoy the world. Is it not the beauty of the hemisphere present to your sight? Is not the vision of the world an amiable thing? Do not the stars shed influences to perfect the air? Is not that a marvelous body to breathe in? To visit the lungs: repair the spirits: revive the senses: cool the blood: fill the empty spaces between the earth and heavens; and yet give liberty to all objects? Prize these first: and you shall enjoy the residue.[68]

Prize these first: and you shall enjoy the residue. This is a remarkable statement in the spiritual life and one entirely consonant with Whitman's system. Traherne goes on to recommend a most un-Christian insatiableness for life: "It is the nobility of man's soul that he is insatiable." One suspects that Whitman, had he been in possession of this text would have agreed with that.

William Blake was born not long before Traherne, though they would have most likely been unknown to each other. Blake is an extraordinary spiritual thinker, and as mentioned above I am grateful to Bucke for introducing him to me. Blake shares the world-celebratory stance of Whitman and Traherne but there is a significant difference to his system: he is also what many call a "sensitive," meaning that he claims access to the spirit world. This is a world of spirit beings, "disembodied" in the usual sense but embodied in another way perhaps. Blake was also a visual artist. As an artist, musician and novelist myself I relate more directly to the impulses that drove Blake than those that drove Traherne or Whitman, and in addition as slightly "sensitive" I find Blake's system more complete than those of the other two. However, although Blake's engravings and writings have an obviously didactic purpose in the spiritual life, I am not aware of him operating as a spiritual teacher with disciples. He certainly had a following in the group known as The Ancients, but these were in the first instance artists of a Romantic inclination and followers of Blake's visual style. I have been unable to find any suggestion that their aims were also spiritual or religious in the way that for example the Transcendentalists married literature and religion.

A single Blake aphorism is for me telling of his whole system: "eternity is in love with the productions of time." If Whitman stands for anything it is for being in love with the productions of time, but for both men the other half of the story is eternity, or to put it another way, the infinite, the imperishable, the stainless, or the "unmoved mover" or the "still point of a turning world" to use phrases from widely different sources. Blake's opening quatrain of his poem "Auguries of Innocence" are well known and acknowledge both the infinite and the eternal:

> To see a World in a Grain of Sand
> And a Heaven in a Wild Flower
> Hold Infinity in the palm of your hand
> And Eternity in an hour.

The atheist Richard Dawkins once wrote: "word for word, I wish I had written the following famous quatrain ..." and goes on to claim that the lines just quoted are all about science.[69] Leaving aside that claim, the presence of the terms infinity and eternity as non-scientific terms is, I would claim, often the mark of a mystic's writings.

We are interested here in the spiritual teacher and their relationship with their pupils, but it is worth emphasizing that the projects of Blake and Whitman seem to have many common features, as remarked upon for example in Algernon Charles Swinburne's book on Blake:

> I can remember one poet only whose work seems to me the same or similar in kind; a poet as vast in aim, as daring in detail, as unlike others, as coherent to himself, as strange without and as sane within. The points of contact and sides of likeness between William Blake and Walt Whitman are so many and so grave, as to afford some ground of reason to those who preach the transition of souls or transfusion of spirits.[70]

Whitman himself would not have agreed with Swinburne. Here are some of his thoughts, extracted from a piece he wrote in the guise of independent reviewer:

> Of William Blake & Walt Whitman. Both are mystics, extatics but the difference between them is this—and a vast difference it is: Blake's visions grow to be the rule, displace the normal condition, fill the field, spurn the visible, objective life, & seat the subjective spirit on an absolute throne, willful & uncontrolled. ... To the pe[rfect] sense, it is evident that [Whitman] goes off because he permits himself to do so, while ever the director, or direct'd principle sits coolly at hand, able to stop the wild teetotum & reduce it to order, at any a moment. In Walt Whitman, esca-

pades of this sort are the exceptions. The main character of his poetry is the normal, the universal, the simple, the eternal platform of the best manly & womanly qualities. [71]

Though I think Whitman's analysis is insightful – and useful to see that he is comfortable to describe himself as an ecstatic and mystic – I do not reject Blake's system at all. Crucially, Whitman is the teacher of the "normal, the universal, the simple, the eternal platform of the best manly and womanly qualities," as he puts it; Blake the teacher of what lies beyond that. What both have is a world-curiosity, whether of the material one or of the spirit world. It is important however to acknowledge that their systems are profoundly different and therefore that is unlikely that Whitman is the reincarnation of Blake as Swinburne appears to suggest. Blake's occultism better places him in the company of hierophants like Emmanuel Swedenborg, Rudolf Steiner and Paramahansa Yogananda. Indeed the comparison between Blake and Swedenborg has been well argued, particularly by Blake's first biographer Alexander Gilchrist, impressed it seems by the possibility that the boy Blake might have passed the eighty-year old Swedenborg in the streets of London just prior to his death.[72] Blake in fact studied and then criticized Swedenborg's system. Of systems Blake writes:

I MUST Create a System, or be enslav'd by another Man's;
I will not Reason and Compare: my business is to Create.

(*Jerusalem*, f. 10, ll. 20–1.)

One could take Blake's dictum here, that he must create his own system or be enslaved by another's, as emblematic for modern individualism. At the same time Blake, like Whitman, is skeptical of the purely rational, but is more emphatic than Whitman: Blake's purpose is to create. His creativity spanned the fields of fine art, poetry, prose and even, according to one witness, music. Equally important was his creativity in religion. I relate to all of this, but not to Blake's use of the Bible as a foundational document. The point of course is that as unique modern individuals with a Western heritage we create our own systems. What the hierophant makes available to us are their own or prior systems, elements of which we can adopt, adapt or discard at will, as Whitman says:

3. Whitman's System

> You shall no longer take things at second or third hand, nor look through the eyes of the dead, nor feed on the spectres in books,
> You shall not look through my eyes either, nor take things from me,
> You shall listen to all sides and filter them from yourself.
>
> (Song of Myself, v. 2)

Whitman says that one should examine many sources of truth and filter them from oneself. I take it to mean that one's own system may well be built from listening to what others have to say, but whatever is not true to oneself has to be filtered out. This is pretty much how I would describe my approach, for example, in all the live discourses of Rajneesh that I sat through.

We can note in passing that Whitman read Alexander Gilchrist's *Life of William Blake* in 1881, a few years after Gilchrist's widow, Anne, moved to be near Whitman, having read his *Leaves of Grass* and written an essay "A Woman's Estimate of Walt Whitman."[73] A writer herself, she had become a disciple of the poet, as we explore later on.

Gaps in Whitman's system

In my book *Secularism* I develop a comprehensive taxonomy of spiritual impulse or orientation, drawing on various existing schemes. Without going into detail here it is enough to say that once one sets out such a comprehensive scheme no existing single system of spiritual or religious insight will turn out to be complete. There have been systematizers in the past who have listed the spiritual paths of their day; for example both the *Bhagavad Gita* and the *Yoga Sutras* of Patanjali cover a wide spectrum. Iran has historically produced not one but two syncretic religions, these being Manichaeism in the third century and the Baha'i in the nineteenth century. Both attempted to bring together the known religions of their period. However I don't think it possible for any system to be entirely comprehensive and perhaps not desirable anyway. It is enough to be able to locate and characterize a spiritual system and simply note what it cannot include and how it speaks to one.

With that in mind we can now sum up Whitman's system as a transcendent, world-celebrating spirituality of body and soul, located firstly within the American Transcendentalist movement and more broadly as resonating with the systems of Blake and Traherne. It has some Romantic and Neoplatonist elements and so is better located in the history of Hellenic rather than Hebraic religion. Many parallels are also usefully found in Upanishadic thought or other Indian traditions. However a short consideration of the work of Blake shows that by comparison Whitman's system is devoid of interest in the spirit world. A longer consideration of the Christian tradition shows that by comparison Whitman's system is devoid of devotionality of the more pious Catholic type and entirely missing of the concept of spiritual atonement. Any moralizing element is nowhere to be found. Neither does it include socialism or the solutions for the predicament of working people found in the Marxist tradition where it mingles with religion, as is the case for example in Liberation Theology.

Because the outdoors, or Nature, is important to Whitman it is useful to triangulate how he relates to it against those of the indigenous Americans. I often quote Jung's dictum that a colonizing people inherit the racial memory of the natives they displace.[74] Robert Pirsig, author of *Zen and the Art of Motorcycle Maintenance*, maintained that the laconic speech and manly silence in the personality of actors such as Robert Redford derives from the white man's contact with the Plains Indians.[75] So did Whitman "inherit" some elements of the Native American psyche? John Burroughs, an important disciple of Whitman's, tells of a trip in 1879 or 1880 where Whitman visited Red Indian prisoners in the company of well-known politicians and government officials. The sheriff explained to the Indians who the distinguished men were, but they paid little attention as they filed past until Whitman brought up the rear. The old chief looked at him steadily, then extended his hand and said "How." All the other Indians followed suit.[76] In fact Whitman had a fairly extensive interaction with Native Americans through his life and worked in 1865 in the Indian Bureau of the Department of the Interior where he met a number of impressive Indian delegates. His writings make many references to them, and he insists on calling many places by their Indian names, saying at one point that "all aboriginal names sound good."[77]

Despite all this I detect little of the Native American in Whitman in the sense that Jung or Pirsig suggest. That is because, as pointed out above, Whitman's interests do not lie in the spirit world, or putting it another way, there is little of the animist or shamanic in his worldview or instincts. True, in his essay on the tree he made reference to dryad and hamadryad, and wrote of trees "speaking," so we cannot be dogmatic about this. All we can say is that if his system is placed alongside that of key Native American medicine men such as Crow Dog, Yellow Tail or Black Elk, it is palpably modern, and silent on the animism that pervades the thought of the Native Americans. What Whitman's system has great resonance with are the "poets of the *via positiva*," that is Blake and Traherne, perhaps more so with the latter, whose focus on felicity – happiness – has all the positivity of Whitman. It also has great resonance with the non-Romantic Nature mysticism of his approximate contemporaries, Jefferies and Muir.

4

GURUS IN THE WEST

Before looking at Whitman as hierophant we turn in this chapter to the more general picture of spiritual teachers in the West. We look at this under three categories: Western teachers through history, including spiritual advisors; those arriving from the East; and some modern teachers who draw on the world's great spiritual traditions whether of East or West. Clearly it is spiritual teachers from the East who have not only introduced the term guru to the West but also perhaps the very category of spiritual teacher.

First we return to the rise of individuality and what this means for religion and spirituality. The elevation of personal goals over collective ones in the spiritual life is part of the general revolt against religion that began in the Enlightenment period of the seventeenth and eighteenth centuries. The majority of Westerners today are more likely humanists than religionists and for the humanists at least the term "atheism" holds no fears. Some are indifferent to atheism; some revel in it; some tentatively reject it in favor of agnosticism, a simple not-knowing. But atheism in Whitman's time was a term of high condemnation, as it had been through the history of Christianity. Whitman was not much different to his contemporaries in regarding atheism as at least an affliction of the soul, as in this passage in verse 43 of "Song of Myself" where he claims comradeship with all those in the grip of negative emotions: "Down-hearted doubters, dull and excluded, / Frivolous sullen moping angry affected disheartened atheistical, / I know every one of you, and know the unspoken interrogatories, / By experience I know them." In verse 7 of the poem "Starting From Paumanok" Whitman uses an interesting term: "I am the credulous man of qualities, ages, races, / I advance from the people in their own spirit, Here is what sings unrestricted faith." I think "credulous" is a good alternative to more ostensibly religious terms and a good opposition to "atheist." If Whitman means anything to the twenty-first century it is a gentle encouragement to move from an unthinking collective atheism to a position of informed individualistic credulity.

Michael Robertson's analysis of Whitman as religious thinker acknowledges the individualism of his approach:

> He was never a systematic theological thinker, but in "Democratic Vistas" he sketched out a religion appropriate for American democracy, one freed from all links to Old World feudalism. *Individuality was at the core of the new American religion.* "Bibles may convey, and priests expound," he wrote, "but it is exclusively for the noiseless operation of one's isolated Self, to enter the pure ether of veneration, reach the divine levels, and commune with the unutterable."[78] [My italics.]

Writing in the aftermath of the American Civil War, Whitman used his essay "Democratic Vistas" to argue that the Union best served individualism, and vice versa:

> This idea of perfect individualism it is indeed that deepest tinges and gives character to the idea of the aggregate. For it is mainly or altogether to serve independent separatism that we favor a strong generalization, consolidation. As it is to give the best vitality and freedom to the rights of the States, (every bit as important as the right of nationality, the union,) that we insist on the identity of the Union at all hazards.

Whitman is both honest about the moral failings of ordinary people and the American institutions and businesses of his time; his remedy is the new religion of which he is one prophet. While Robertson and Whitman use the word "religion" to describe Whitman's ambition for his writings, I would suggest that spirituality better describes it, simply because we use that term more often for the "isolated Self," as Whitman puts it, in search of the sacred. When Whitman writes "it is exclusively for the noiseless operation of one's isolated Self, to enter the pure ether of veneration, reach the divine levels, and commune with the unutterable", it could, with a little adoption of close synonyms, have as easily been spoken by Plotinus, who summed up spirituality as the "flight from the alone to the Alone."

If the conventionally Christian world of Whitman's day cold-shouldered him, then the conventionally humanist world of today is equally indifferent, beyond the aesthetic and cultural appreciation of him as literary figure. In the two-hundredth anniversary year of his birth no doubt Whitman's literary achievements will be lauded and perhaps a whole new generation will read him with enthusiasm. But his religious or spiritual intent will be easily overlooked, just as Whitman hinted at that he intended. It is only the determinedly *credulous* individual that will seek out his spiritual meaning.

There is however a sense in which Whitman's spiritual teachings are possibly more relevant to us now than in the middle of the nineteenth century. As mentioned earlier I think this is down to the leisure made possible since the industrial revolution and which has been spread – albeit unequally – throughout society. Relative greater wealth brings relatively greater economic independence and leisure time and through all of that – alongside humanistic philosophies and psychologies – we have become enormously greater individualists. Old religion emphasized the eradication of self-will in favor of God's will; a philosophy not much popular today. Despite the condemnation implied in the term "self-spirituality" it is a significant phenomenon most amongst those turning away from raw materialism and yet not willing to adopt old religion. Whitman's system and his method of guruship may be eminently suitable to that constituency.

If we are more individualist now than in Whitman's time then it is also due to the recent shapers of modern thought, not just those of the Enlightenment. None is more important here than Freud as I have suggested, though as I show in my book *Secularism*, Marx and Darwin are at least as significant. Rajneesh said this:

> After Freud the world of religion is not going to be the same as before him. Freud stands as a watershed between the religions of the past and the religions of the future. ... A new peak of consciousness has been touched and a new understanding, an altogether new perspective, a new vision of life has come into being. ... The old religions taught suppression as the way to God. Man was asked to suppress everything – his sex, his anger, his

greed, his attachments – and then alone would he find his soul, would he attain to God.[79]

I think Rajneesh is half-correct here. Certainly at the heart of modern individualism and personal identity is sex, and Freud's liberation of us from Victorian sexual repression was a watershed. And we can agree that religion and spirituality have to take this into account because our individualism is deeply entwined with our sexuality. The very title of Whitman's poem "Song of Myself" and the often rather explicit sexual descriptions in it therefore make it a candidate source for contemporary spirituality. But Rajneesh is wrong I would suggest to say that Freud represents a new peak of consciousness. At best it recovers for us something that the highly mannered Victorian society had delegitimized, but at worst the work of Freud leaves only sex standing while utterly denying the validity of religion or any of the nobler ambitions of mankind. The title of Freud's influential book "The Future of an Illusion" points to its thesis, that religion is no more than a crutch, a relic of the past and an illusion. No, if we are looking for a modern seer who is able to both welcome the return of our natural sexuality and point to a new peak of consciousness I would nominate Whitman as candidate, not Freud. The individualism of Whitman, as William James regretfully points out, is that of the "healthy-minded," whereas that of Freud I would suggest confines itself to the small spectrum that ranges from the completely pathological to the resignedly adjusted to society.

If everybody is unique, as the individualism doctrine asserts, then everybody's spirituality is unique. John Locke recognized this in the late seventeenth century when he suggested in his famous "A Letter Concerning Toleration" that "everyone is orthodox to himself."[80] A hierophant operating in the modern world has to negotiate this as much perhaps as the aspirant has to negotiate the natural tendency of the hierophant to construct their system exclusively out of their own experience. This is important to recognize, the Buddha being a good example. Based on his own experience he came to believe that the onset of enlightenment is inevitably heralded by complete recall of previous lives, and in *The Elders' Verses* his pupils dutifully declare the same thing; something I find implausible. A brief survey of the many accounts of enlightenment does not support the Buddha's assumption. One thing is sure however: in the history of spiritual teachers most of them have taught an entirely prescriptive system and their followers have appeared to excel by repeating its major and minor features without question. Our individualism now makes that suspect.

Romanticism, Neoplatonism and the New Age

Romantic thinkers and writers of the eighteenth century were anticlerical, meaning against the priesthood but not necessarily against religion. They were also individualistic, and spiritually they had more in common with the Renaissance and Ficino than with the emerging materialist science of their time. J. A. Stewart sums up what he terms the "Platonism" that infused the Romantic poets:

> Platonism I would describe, in the most general terms, as the mood of one who has a curious eye for the endless variety of this visible and temporal world and a fine sense of its beauties, yet is haunted by the presence of an invisible and eternal world behind, or, when the mood is most pressing, within the visible and temporal world, and sustaining both it and himself – a world not perceived as external to himself, but inwardly lived by him, as that which, at moments of ecstasy, or even habitually, he is become one.[81]

The individualism of the Romantics was a natural expression of a period during which the dominant role of the Church waned (and was fragmented in fringe movements and schism) and the fascination with science grew, not to mention the equally growing disquiet with industrialization. It was its *aesthetic* impulse which drew Romanticism close to the spiritual, quite unlike the rational impulse that drove Descartes, Spinoza and Leibniz. Romanticism also turned to Nature as the source of its aesthetics, its values and its spiritualities. We could say that Romanticism as a spiritual movement rather than as an aesthetic movement was part of the "counter-religion" of the West. In turn what we now term the New Age spiritual movement extended the popular interest in such things down the social pyramid as an increasingly important phenomenon through the twentieth century, though we note that most Romantics were drawn from the upper, leisured echelons of that pyramid. In the twenty-first century social media is creating virtual spiritual communities or what are known as "hyper-religions" with a markedly populist or New Age basis.

4. Gurus in the West

Roughly speaking the New Age movement began with a British literary magazine of that name edited by A. R. Orage, an important disciple of G. I. Gurdjieff (a hierophant we look at in Chapter 6). It was hardly a populist venture and it was not until the 1970s that the major movements and beliefs we now term New Age came into being. However from the time of Gurdjieff to the present day, spiritual teachers in the West operate in a milieu increasingly shaped by New Age prophets such as Deepak Chopra, Elizabeth Clare Prophet, Neale Donald Walsch and Sir George Trevelyan. I have picked these at random; lists can run into the hundreds and include many who might not care for the label. My own experience of New Age ideas is that there is much in them that is genuine and also much that is shallow and fantastical. For me the crucial cut-off lies in the issue of self-aggrandizement, often framed in the sentiment that through some meditation or mind-control technique one can change reality, a proposition backed up by a New Age reading of quantum theory. For individuals with low self-esteem, unhappy lives or struggling with a pervasive sense of meaninglessness, such New Age doctrines come as a balm which may alleviate symptoms but address nothing of root causes. It hardly needs to be said that New Age gurus emerge to serve this market, armed with an extensive pre-existing mystical literature of which a deep understanding is not always present. Negotiating all this is a matter of considerable discernment and at the same time forms part of the larger context for the potential reception of Whitman as guru.

Non-Christian Western Spiritual Teachers

If we make a rapid trawl through Western spiritual teachers of the pre-Freudian eras we find of course a bewildering variety of systems and teaching methods. More bewildering still for many will be the proposition that Pythagoras and Socrates were spiritual teacher. Surely they were philosophers? And Plotinus; was he not also a philosopher? And Descartes, Spinoza and Leibniz? Why on earth should we see them as spiritual teachers? The answer to this question lies in my concept of the "counter-religion of the West," a broad current of spiritual thinking that ran underground to the mainstream of Christianity though often influencing it, as in for example the Cambridge Platonists of the seventeenth century. In many periods Christianity fiercely suppressed it. The term "the counter-religion of the West" is my coinage but I intend it to have roughly the same meaning as Platonism, or Neoplatonism or another common term: "the Western esoteric tradition." However, "counter-religion" conveys two ideas not so easily read into those other terms, firstly that these traditions operate as a religion no different to Christianity, and secondly that they both counter Christianity in their spiritual systems and were deeply opposed by it. Crucially, they derive more from the Hellenic mind than the Hebraic.

By labeling such luminaries as Pythagoras, Socrates and Plotinus as philosophers we have lost their spiritual-religious dimension. But Pythagoras and Plotinus were gurus who founded spiritual communities and Socrates had a following whose religious intent is not hard to identify. While Plato gives his name to "Neoplatonism" – or just "Platonism" – I argued in my Master's thesis and elsewhere that Pythagoras is properly the founder of this tradition, Socrates a prime example, Plotinus its key early proponent and Plato a mere hanger-on, or worse, one who attributed words and beliefs of his own to his master, Socrates. Much later it is clear that Descartes was a deeply religious thinker with a following including his last employer the Queen of Denmark; Spinoza taught a spiritual system to those that had been influenced by Descartes; and Leibniz was in turn a teacher of his own system with pupils that included royalty.

Out of these six teachers only Plotinus was able to teach in relative safety, and it is clear that in the time of Descartes, Spinoza and Leibniz their writings had to remain unpublished or hedged around with circumlocutions and metaphor to avoid being labeled heretics or atheists. Descartes fled France to avoid the authorities, and then again fled the relatively tolerant Holland for Denmark. Worse fates befell others who were more obviously Neoplatonist in their thinking; the year 1600 marking the burning of Giordano Bruno for his heresies. Sir Isaac Newton had also to be careful to hide his interests in alchemy, astrology and numerology as all associations with such traditions – key currents in Neoplatonism – were inimical to public life.

What is of interest here is how many of these various figures operated as gurus or hierophants, especially as they mostly had to be careful of the authorities of their day or mobs that took a dislike to them. In the case of Socrates we see most clearly perhaps where the confusion over religion and philosophy emerges for the West. My Master's thesis explored the question of him as a mystic of a certain type operating as a religious or spiritual teacher, the issue lying in how *speculative* his system was intended or received, and how his pupils regarded him. I say "speculative" because I see Western philosophy as largely a series of speculative propositions, mostly of a rarified nature that neither relate to the outer mechanics of physical nature nor the inner mechanics of the soul. In Chapter 6 we look at Socrates as hierophant in relation to Alcibiades and others.

Rabbis, priests and imams as Western spiritual teachers

If the spiritual teachers just discussed have often been wrongly categorized as philosophers then we can say that many who have officiated within mainstream religion – that is rabbis, priests and imams – have been wrongly categorized as *not* being spiritual teachers. Moses, Jesus and Mohammed have been promoted beyond anything as prosaic as teachers, while their priests have been demoted to mere functionaries. Many priests may be simple office-holders but to some degree all are spiritual teachers, and in exceptional cases are hierophants in their own right with systems only nominally conforming to their tradition. Meister Eckhart would be a prime example of this, where his popularity as a teacher was matched only by the radical nature of his teachings, which brought charges of heresy evaded only by dying before trial. To fully examine how exceptional rabbis, priests and imams become hierophants in their own right and to fully examine their relationship with their disciples would take another book. To some extent at least the relationship is governed by the religious mainstream they operate in, whereas we are mostly interested here in the hierophant operating outside of the mainstream with no traditional checks and balances on their power.

Having said that, the "spiritual advisor" in the Catholic tradition is worth commenting on precisely because of the conventional structures surrounding it. Known also as "spiritual director," one Catholic has this to say about it in the modern context:

> Many religious traditions encourage the use of a spiritual guide to facilitate and assist believers on the path of spiritual growth. What makes a Catholic spiritual director different is that he or she is not a guru whose

81

words are to be obeyed blindly, but rather a companion and resource on your own personal journey of faith.

The goal of a spiritual director is to help you recognize how the Holy Spirit is working in your life. The emphasis is deepening one's relationship, not with the spiritual director but with God, by developing an active, vital prayer life. While a spiritual director can and should offer advice, you are always free to make your own decisions and choices.[82]

Note two caveats in this explanation: firstly that the spiritual director is not a guru to be blindly obeyed; secondly that the relationship to be deepened is not with the spiritual director but with God. The statement is clearly responding to modern realities, including both the emergence of the guru in the West and the fear present in all situations of religious and spiritual instruction that one might not be free to make one's own decisions and choices. The tradition of spiritual advisor or director goes back centuries however and I have always like the example of Jean Pierre de Caussade in the seventeenth-eighteenth century, or at least the man revealed in a famous work attributed to him, *Abandonment to Divine Providence*. De Caussade was spiritual director to the Nuns of the Visitation at Nancy, France from 1733 to 1740 and wrote letters of instruction to the nuns. Such letters of instruction are a form of hierophancy; the great medieval work *The Cloud of Unknowing* is one example, and Traherne's *Meditations* is possibly another, as we saw. De Caussade's *Abandonment to Divine Providence* is a beautiful book of exhortations to love God, but we learn nothing from it of the day-to-day hierophancy that the man's direct exchanges with the nuns would have involved. Instead I want to dwell for a moment on an equivalent spiritual instructor engaged to assist the nuns in a UK convent as followed by TV cameras for a period, which I was fortunate enough to watch. I was greatly taken by the role of this male instructor with his female clients who were grateful to talk over with him the problems they faced in the spiritual life. The greatest of these, it struck me, were those of all aspirants when the initial enthusiasm gives way to perhaps rather arid periods. For the nuns this would mean that prayer was not perhaps as rewarding as it had been, but there could be many other reasons why they were glad to receive encouragement from the priest. Amusingly, as they were in a silent order he ate separately from them during his stay in order to listen to the radio. Whether his inability to cope with silence made him quite the right advisor I cannot tell.

Just because an imam, priest or rabbi is a religious functionary does not prevent them being a gifted spiritual teacher in their own right, though the deeper the gift the more likely it is that traditionalists within their religion will resist them, just as the rabbi Jesus was resisted by his tradition. However there is humorous saying that the job of a Church of England vicar is to inoculate their congregation against religion. Too many functionaries do that so successfully – meaning that they dull all sense of enquiry – that serious spiritual seeking normally has to be done in the marginal worlds of maverick hierophants – hence the risks involved.

Eastern Gurus in the West

The Catholic spiritual director is not a guru, we are told, but to even make that distinction is to recognize that both the term and the system it stands for have made a mark on the West. From the late nineteenth century, when Vivekananda burst upon the Western religious stage, Eastern spiritual teachers have had a great impact on many Westerners. While Vivekananda merely visited America, many stayed and built up substantial followings; in Europe too. Societies and institutions formed for the propagation of their teachings including the Vedanta Society which published various positive essays on Whitman. There are excellent studies of the many, many Eastern teachers who came to the West; here we introduce just five of them: George Ivanovich Gurdjieff (1866-1949) from Armenia, Jiddu Krishnamurti (1895-1986) from India, Bhagwan Shree Rajneesh (1931-1990) from India, Chögyam Trungpa (1939-1987) from Tibet and Mother Meera (born in 1960) from India. Gurdjieff mostly taught in France and Mother Meera in Germany, the others mostly in America as well as India. As mentioned, I took discipleship with Rajneesh, attended talks by Krishnamurti and have had *darshan* with Mother Meera a number of times. I have read the writings or transcripts of the talks of all five, and each have been important to me in different ways. All of them brought traditions very foreign to the Christian heritage of the countries they taught in, and all of them counted public figures in the arts and sciences amongst their pupils.

Gurdjieff

After returning from India in the 1980s I "took sannyas" with Rajneesh, though the initiation was through one of his Indian disciples, subsequently excommunicated. I went through a long period of spiritual turmoil (as perhaps my poem "The Petals of Me" might indicate) the most important element of which was past-life recall. Events were bleeding through, as it were, that were highly charged but not obviously related to this life. For example, I recall standing in the Oxford town library at a shelf of Gurdjieff-related books, having been aware of him for a while. I had first seen a poster of him in a toilet in a hippy squat and at that time, from what little I had heard, I regarded him as a charlatan. However Rajneesh praised him highly and so I entirely reversed my opinion, especially intrigued that Rajneesh insisted that many former Gurdieff pupils had been drawn to him because of the resonance between their systems. It took down a volume – I think it was by Gurdieff's pupil Orage – and began to read. The hairs on the back of my neck stood on end. This began a period of intense reading of the Gurdjieff literature, and I still have a considerable shelf of such books. I became convinced that I had been with Gurdjieff in Paris between the wars and that he had been an important spiritual teacher for me. I also thought that perhaps he had pushed me too hard and contributed to a nervous breakdown, though that may also have been the experience of being caught up in both world wars (as fictionalized in my reincarnation novel *Enigma's Coda*[83]). Note that the dangers of nervous breakdown are one of the very real issues to be addressed in negotiating the hierophant.

It is hard to asses the impact of Gurdjieff on me now, nearly forty years after that moment in the library. I tangled a little with the organization left behind him to carry on his "work" – some odd encounters in London – but otherwise I have kept away from his legacy. But I learned two important things from him I think, firstly the nature of sacred dance, and secondly the idea of humans as having three metaphysical centers: head, heart and *hara*; or mind, emotion and movement. If I have two regrets at sixty-five, having lived a very full life, it is that I have not travelled enough or danced enough.

Gurdjieff was a tough hierophant. I find it hard to write about him, so first two seemingly unconnected anecdotes.

4. Gurus in the West

W. G. Gabb was an eccentric Englishman, an accountant by trade, who wrote such convincing Zen stories– under the pseudonym Tokuzan – that they circulated in the Far East as genuine writings a millennium old. It appears that he became enlightened, and what did he do with his enlightenment? He emigrated to South Africa and was never heard of again. Actually, that is not *exactly* the story of Gabb, but never mind. Crucially in his writings he says this in regards to the classic four-line form of the Zen haiku:

> If only I might be allowed full freedom of expression before a completely understanding audience, I should say all I need to say not in four lines, but in two words: the words, "Ah this!"[84]

"Ah, this!" is perhaps one too many words, and the exclamation mark a poor translation of the symbol used in Chinese, or so I learned from T. D. Suzuki. But "this" or "suchness" or similar terms is indeed the essence of it all, as Whitman would recognize in an instant I suspect. The point of Gabb and Zen is the playfulness of it. A huge furor is made about the Zen master, the Zen pupil, the "way" and so on, but after enlightenment, then what? This. You take your family to South Africa and take up farming or whatever.

In the Taoist text, the *Chuang Tzu*, a pupil of Master Hu Zu called Lieh Tzu brought a shaman that he had been greatly impressed with to the master. Hu Zu promptly made a fool of the shaman. As a result of this:

> ... Lieh Tzu realized that he had so far learnt nothing real, so he returned home. For three years he did not go out. He cooked for his wife and tended the pigs as if they were humans. He showed no interest in his studies. He cast aside his desires and sought the truth. In his body he became like the ground itself. In the midst of everything he remained with the One and that is how he remained until the end.[85]

I had to look up this quote, but the funny thing is that I remembered it a little different, that it was the master who gave up and returned to tend his pigs. Either way, the point of both stories is that the everyday is both the destination of enlightenment and where it is tested at every turn. Lieh

Tzu had his pigs; I have a vegetable patch – and cook for my wife as often as she cooks for me.

Life with Gurdjieff was not "everyday" for the seekers with him however but more like some kind of drug they could not get enough of. When you are a seeker, pigs and vegetables don't do it for you. Such everyday things are not yet lit up, as is all of "this" when seen with the light of suchness, and which radiates from the hierophant because of their charisma. The religious scholar Georg Feuerstein records that amongst those influenced by Gurdjieff were Frank Lloyd Wright, Georgia O'Keefe, J. B. Priestly, Moshe Feldenkreis, Aldous Huxley, Arthur Koestler and Katherine Mansfield.[86] The celebrity seekers – an important category in terms of the hierophant's reputation – wanted something exceptional, and they found it with Gurdjieff. Mansfield also met her death in his community, probably a quite innocent and random event, but others were scarred by the experience. In a comprehensively critical survey of gurus by the psychiatrist Anthony Storr there is a satisfyingly thorough twenty-page demolition of Gurdjieff,[87] satisfying, that is, unless you are serious about enlightenment. For me, what Gurdjieff has to say has to be negotiated with even now, and my renewed contact with his thought is the renewed contact with a deep life-spring.

For those prepared to give Gurdjieff the benefit of the doubt, I reproduce a passage that I spotted in Andrew Rawlinson's book of enlightened masters, for which I am most grateful. It is an account by another of Gurdjieff's key disciples, John Bennett, in the aftermath of a car crash that left Gurdjieff severely injured:

> For four or five days after the accident, it seemed he either could not or did not feel the need to play a role, to hide himself behind a mask. We then felt his extraordinary goodness and love for humanity. Despite his disfigured face and arms – he was literally black and blue from head to foot – and his terrifying weakness of body, he was so beautiful that we felt that we were looking at a being from another and better world. ... I believe that, for a few days, we caught a glimpse of the real Gurdjieff, and that all his strange and often repellent behavior was a screen to hide him from people who would otherwise have idolized his person instead of working for themselves.[88]

4. Gurus in the West

For some reason the car crash of Gurdjieff preoccupied me twenty-five years ago to the point that I made a digital artwork about it. The piece was exhibited at my university, and as digital art was at that time rather new and daring the show was covered by the arts correspondent of the *Daily Telegraph*, so my picture was reproduced in the paper's culture section. It prompted one of Gurdjieff's biographers, James Moore, to contact me, on the one hand complaining that I had used a copyright photo without permission, and on other suggesting I join a London Gurdjieff group. I never joined but I did once receive an invitation to the private screening of a film about Gurdjieff's sacred dances. I turned up at a cinema booked for the occasion in Leicester Square, London, watched the film quite transported, spoke to nobody and went home again.

We look again at Gurdjieff in Chapter 6.

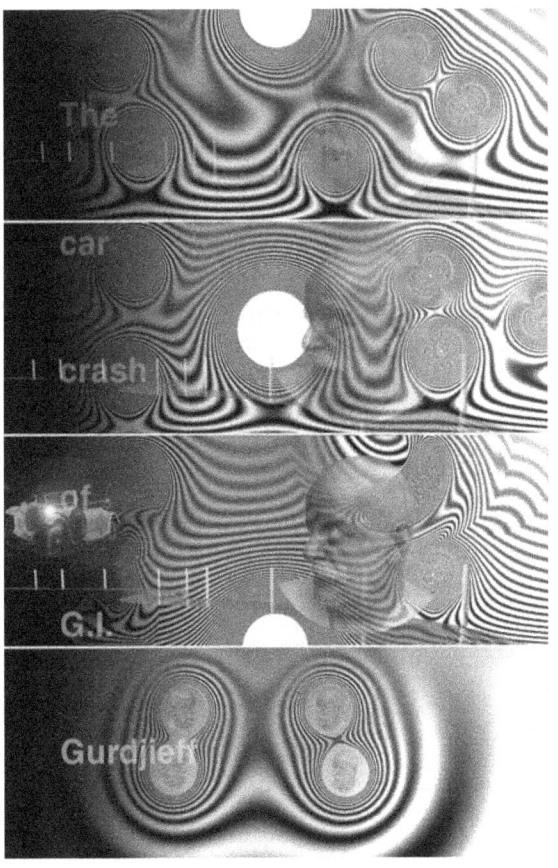

Krishnamurti

Jiddu Krishnamurti was an Indian spiritual teacher with a considerable following in the West. Christ-comparisons were also made throughout his life – here are some comments from contemporary figures:

> George Bernard Shaw called Krishnamurti "a religious figure of the greatest distinction," and added, "He is the most beautiful human being I have ever seen."
>
> Henry Miller wrote, "There is no man I would consider it a greater privilege to meet ..."
>
> Aldous Huxley, after attending one of Krishnamurti's lectures, confided in a letter, "... the most impressive thing I have listened to. It was like listening to the discourse of the Buddha — such power, such intrinsic authority ..."
>
> Kahlil Gibran wrote, "When he entered my room I said to myself, 'Surely the Lord of Love has come.'"[89]

Krishnamurti held dialogues with famous figures of his day, including the Dalai Lama, and scientists such as David Bohm, Fritjof Capra and Rupert Sheldrake. He is also said to have been an influence on the martial arts legend Bruce Lee. Krishnamurti was born in humble circumstances in India, where his mother chose, against the explicit religious and caste instructions regarding birth, to deliver her son in the puja room (shrine room) of her small house. As a child Krishnamurti was not considered unusual in any way, but was discovered in 1909 by Charles Leadbeater, a leading member of the Theosophical Society. His secretary had pointed him out, but was astonished at Leadbeater's prediction that Krishnamurti would one day be a great spiritual teacher, as he found the boy particularly stupid. Krishnamurti was in fact practically educationally subnormal, and even after his private education and strict training repeatedly failed to get into Cambridge University. This would come as a shock to anyone who read his later works, or perused the conversations between Krishnamurti and the eminent physicist David Bohm; perhaps this is a good example of how the conventional assessment of intelligence is often inadequate. The Theosophical Society had as its stated goal the preparation for a new World Leader, and before long it declared that it had found it in the person of Jiddu Krishnamurti. He was prepared for his role through occult initiations at the hands of Leadbeater and Annie Besant, a process that involved communications with so-called disembodied "masters," and ultimately the excruciatingly painful preparation of his body to become the vessel for the (Buddha) Maitreya. In later life Krishnamurti denied recollection of most of these experiences and denied that they contributed to his illumination. He gradually shook off the ministrations of the Theosophical Society, and in a dramatic gesture dissolved the Order of the Star, which was the organization founded to support his work. He could not shake off his destiny however and entered a life of teaching that lasted fifty years. The teachings were his, however, and could be summed up in a single phrase: *choiceless awareness*.

While the totality of Krishnamurti's thought had a great impact on me, one of his specific gifts was to wake me up to Nature through his extraordinary writings on fields, forests and rivers and the simple world of Indian village life. His was also a momentous struggle against the hierarchy implicit in the role of hierophant. Ironically his efforts to not be a guru are only outshone by the "anti-guru guru" bearing the same family name: U. G. Krishnamurti (1918-2007).[90] The two men knew each other and later in life U. G. had his own enlightenment experience, as we explore later.

One can speculate that Jiddu Krishnamurti plotted his course as a spiritual teacher rather out of reaction to the Theosophical society's occultist and hierarchical leanings – including racial stereotyping – and all the complexity that entails. I attended his talks at Brockwood Park, a mansion in Hampshire, England, bought by his followers and now a retreat center and school. At the time I was a follower of Rajneesh, dressed in orange. Although Rajneesh liked the idea of his followers sitting in a row in front of Krishnamurti as something of a provocation I honored instead Rajneesh's acknowledgement of him as equally enlightened. I had no direct contact with Krishnamurti, but his books remain filled with grace for me. Also part of his legacy for me lies in his conversations with the physicist David Bohm. Having a degree in physics myself I find them intriguing from this perspective: Krishnamurti was attempting to place Bohm at his own level of spiritual development by making the conversation one between equals. So Bohm, a confident public speaker in his own discipline, repeats enlightenment wisdom he has heard back at Krishnamurti, who attempts to teach Bohm while not teaching him. It is a painful dialog, recorded in published collections. We return to how Bohm negotiated his encounters with Krishnamurti as reluctant hierophant in Chapter 6.

Rajneesh

I introduced Rajneesh earlier and will dwell on his failings in the next chapter. Here I briefly reflect on his example as an Eastern guru in a Western setting. Rajneesh, born as Chandra Mohan Jain, grew up in a Jain family as a rebel against puritanical Indian tradition – perhaps a little like my other guru Douglas Harding who grew up as a rebel against the strict practices of the Plymouth Brethren of his family. Rajneesh's antinomianism led him to become a controversial lecturer in philosophy and public speaker denouncing various systems such as socialism, organized religion and even the legacy of Gandhi. Just about every position he held on any subject was a reaction to Indian conservatism, drawing instead on Western ideas of sexual liberation, personal freedom and pro-market economics. His central objection was to the life-denying puritanism of Indian religious culture, which elevated asceticism and saintly exemplars that withdrew from the "world." Rajneesh thought there was nothing "spiritual" in what he perceived of as the resulting deadening of the senses and the acceptance of material poverty. Although his initial audience was drawn from Indians including wealthy businessmen, he soon attracted Westerners drawn to India for spiritual enlightenment and attracted by the link Rajneesh made between spiritual growth and sexual exploration as sanctioned through the venerable tradition of Eastern Tantric masters.

One could say therefore that Rajneesh was a Tantric Eastern guru teaching in the West long before he moved to America, though it is also true that he retained a loyal following amongst Indians as well. In the next chapter we will explore how the project of Rajneesh failed in spectacular fashion when transplanted from Pune in India to Oregon in the United States.

Chögyam Trungpa

The parallels between Chögyam Trungpa and Rajneesh are instructive, though Trungpa left for the West at a much earlier age than Rajneesh and prior to that had almost no contact with Westerners. Trungpa, along with Gurdjieff and Rajneesh, are prime examples of the so-called "crazy wis-

4. Gurus in the West

dom" teachers detailed in Feuerstein's book on the subject, more on this idea shortly. Trungpa was a *tulku*, meaning a Tibetan lama or priest confirmed as the reincarnation of a previous lama, just as the Dalai Lama is. Indeed the two mainstream films about the Dalai Lama, *Seven Years in Tibet* and *Kundun*, give some good insights into the tradition that Trungpa emerged from, including the sometimes harsh nature of the *tulku* system against which Trungpa rebelled, though poignantly using the tools of that tradition against itself. Like the Dalai Lama, Trungpa had to escape Tibet when the Chinese took control. Trungpa was, at the age of twenty, already the head of a group of monasteries, his own having been occupied and then destroyed by the Chinese People's Liberation Army. Once in India he became the spiritual head of the Young Lamas Home School with the endorsement of the Dalai Lama. Invited to study in Britain, Trungpa then took over a meditation center in Scotland and had amongst his pupils the pop singer David Bowie. Not long afterward Trungpa moved to the States.

It was in America that Trungpa turned to the so-called "crazy wisdom" teaching methods and published a key work called "Cutting Through Spiritual Materialism." I love this book and what it shows specifically about Tibetan Buddhism and also the universal lesson that tradition in itself is nothing if not fructified by the independent thinker, the radical iconoclast, who understands the tradition, not through its outer rote symbols but directly from within. The thesis of Trungpa's book has guided me much I think, this being that both trying to become a better person and especially holding to any such claim – a form of spiritual materialism – is entirely antithetical to what the spiritual life really means, which is a search for truth. To demolish such preconceptions about the supposed holiness of the exotic Tibetan guru in the eyes of Westerners Trungpa took to drink, smoking, sex and who knows what other pursuits conventionally held as counter to the precepts of classical Buddhism, and like Rajneesh he drew on Tantric ideas. Feuerstein writes of Trungpa:

> In 1973, Chögyam Trungpa finally began to initiate disciples into the esoteric practices of Vajrayana (Tantric) Buddhism. He warned his disciples that "working with the energy of Vajrayana is like dealing with live electric wire." He might have added, and probably did, that working with a Tantric adept is actually touching that live wire with one's bare hands.

The predicable result is a terrific jolt that can wreck a person for life, or at the very least cause emotional trauma.[91]

I quite agree with Feuerstein that working with a Tantric adept like Trungpa or Rajneesh can result in a terrible jolt. I would go further however in saying that the master does not have to operate in a Tantric system. The jolt can be the same, just the methods differ as in my case with Krishnamurti or Douglas Harding. My point, using Feuerstein's metaphor of high-voltage electricity, is that all real hierophants are high voltage and to negotiate them you have to understand the risks. How much sex you participate in along the way makes no difference, though I suppose the average Freudianized Westerner might say in that case the more the better.

I have to add here, and I have not explored this part of my being for a long time, that I feel that have a Tantric past as a *dakini*, a female initiate and helper of others on the way. In the period of intense exploration of my previous lives I became aware that my hands would spontaneously form *mudras* from that tradition. Whenever *mitras* (order members) of the Friends of the Western Buddhist Order spoke about Tantra and in particular its female adepts I got something of an inner shock of recognition. It is the dance forms of this tradition that I miss when I say that I regret not having danced more in my life; Gurdjieff's dances have a family resemblance. The *dakini* period was also a period of rebirths when I regularly took female form – as far as I can make out – and in which I learned how males would take advantage of the Tantric women in that tradition if they could. This is, I think, why I am no fan of sex as a way to enlightenment, despite having been drawn to Rajneesh as my first significant guru. (Bear in mind that his first, and very influential, book was titled "From Sex to Superconsciousness.") However I do not believe that Trungpa was any the less of a great teacher for the fact that he slept with his pupils and even entertained the offer of gay sex – if Feuerstein is correct in reporting this – from the poet Allen Ginsberg.[92] On this subject it is amusing to note that Ginsberg claimed a "gay lineage" back to Walt Whitman: he allegedly slept with someone who had slept with someone who had slept with Whitman.[93]

Trungpa's reputation, along with that of Sogyal Rinpoche and other Tibetan teachers in the West, is dogged by accusations of guru malpractice that for some cannot be justified on the grounds of crazy wisdom. Trungpa was often drunk, apparently, and slept with some of his female students. Feuerstein also criticizes Trungpa in his choice of successor, Thomas Rich, whose promiscuous bisexuality apparently led to Aids.[94] Sogyal Rinpoche, author of the best-selling *The Tibetan Book of Living and Dying*, was the subject of a $10 million civil lawsuit for having sex with a female student.[95] My considered view is that this is simply part of the territory and cannot be avoided but negotiated with, armed with as much background information as possible.

Mother Meera

If Gurdjieff, Rajneesh and Trungpa are crazy wisdom teachers of varying temperament, and Krishnamurti is rather the opposite – meaning sober to the point of earnestness – then it is true to say that Mother Meera is also the polar opposite of a crazy wisdom teacher. I love her equally, and am conscious again that she has taught me something different and precious: the pure presence of the teacher in the total absence of words and in the near-total absence of action or ritual. I can't remember how I first heard of her, but I read the book by her disciple Andrew Harvey with great interest and have been to see her four times, three of them in Germany.

Mother Meera, born Kamala Reddy, says she had her first enlightenment experience at the age of six, following which her uncle promoted her as an incarnation of the Divine Mother. Only in India, one might say (and thank goodness for India). Her life of spiritual insight and teaching included a short period at the Sri Aurobindo Ashram where she met Westerners. Chance brought her to Germany where the first village that hosted her was not so keen on the influx of international visitors who flocked their, but the second one took her to their hearts – I know this from having visited both. While her spiritual system is known through the writings of Harvey and her own short statements, she engages with her followers through silence, avoiding public lectures. Visitors come for *darshan* – sitting with the teacher – an ancient Indian practice that she has adapted. More than a hundred people arrive in a hall, are seated, and after a while Mother Meera makes her entrance: diminutive, fragile-seeming and without looking at anything beyond what is needed to navigate her way to a seat on the stage. Then, over a period of an hour or so, people come up one by one and kneel in front of her. She briefly holds one's head; then she briefly raises the head to look into one's eyes. That's it.

While the impact, as Feuerstein says, of the crazy wisdom teacher may be profound emotional upset, the silence of Mother Meera can be just the same, and I have witnessed it both with friends and with strangers in the conversations that take place afterwards: wracking sobs, profound self-questioning. For myself I find each time that the reverential atmosphere is calming, that I am keenly present to everything that takes place and interested in the proceedings. When I go up to Meera I like to have my head held; I like the brief moment of looking into her eyes. On returning to my seat I find myself in an utterly different space, knocked back as it were into my interiority, filled with peace, with my eyes closed and taking no further interest in the external proceedings.

I made several trips to Germany as part of my work as a digital artist, including those where I also visited Mother Meera, and was conscious that the subject of WW2 had not so far been raised. On the last trip to Meera in Germany I happened to join two other visitors – a woman in her eighties and her young travelling companion – for an evening meal in the valley below her residence. The old woman suddenly asked me if I was English. I said yes, upon which she told me that she wanted to confess something she had never told anyone in her entire life. As a young village girl she had heard on the radio that a British Air Force plane had been shot down not far away and it was the duty of locals to ensure that the pilots did not escape with their lives. She saw villagers gather outside her window, armed with axes and pitchforks, and then leave in the direction of the crashed aircraft. She had lived all her life with the guilt of not doing anything to stop them, she said. Of course I responded by saying something to the effect that there was nothing she could have done, but I remain deeply moved by this encounter. It may be a coincidence of course, but I put the opening up of this old woman's heart to a foreigner at that particular moment down to the impact of Mother Meera. It was also said by sympathetic locals that she had come to heal the psychological wounds still open from the last war.

One would think that negotiating this particular hierophant would present no problems, or even that the term "hierophant" is least suited to her compared to the other spiritual teachers we are considering here.

However, I will show in Chapter 6 that the relationship between Mother Meera and her key early disciple, Andrew Harvey, was as fraught as any, and that it was partly due to the fact that she brought with her a culture alien to Western modernity. The infinite, it seems, is always channeled through a human mind as prone to parochialism as any other. Recognition of that is crucial to negotiating the foreign spiritual teacher.

Modern Western teachers

The five gurus discussed in the last section brought Eastern cultures with them to the West which framed their spiritual systems and shaped the relationship with their pupils to some degree. Western-born spiritual teachers are bound to understand their Western pupils a little better, even if their teachings have Eastern influence. Andrew Rawlinson – mentioned earlier – has made a comprehensive survey of Westerners teaching in Eastern traditions, which covers over a hundred and fifty teachers;[96] clearly this on a significant scale. Here I will mention just four Westerners, all considered enlightened, whose teachings owe much to the East but were made profoundly their own: Douglas Harding (1909-2007), Wayne Liquorman (born in 1951), Tony Parsons (born in 1953) and Andrew Cohen (born in 1955). I like the teachings of all four men, have met three of them, and made one, Douglas Harding, my guru for a while. Of these it is Cohen who is most controversial, but I regard none of them as crazy wisdom teachers and none have significantly broken laws or taboos, not, that is, unless one considers enlightenment itself a taboo subject, which it might as well be.

What Cohen and Liquorman have in common is that they stand third in line to two famous Indian teachers: Cohen being the pupil of H. W. L. Poonjaji, who was the pupil of Ramana Maharshi, while Liquorman is the pupil of Ramesh Balsekar who was the pupil of Nisargaddata Maharaj. I rate all four of those Indian teachers most highly and like it that their teachings are ramified through Americans. Harding was deeply affected by India, as he records in his autobiographical works, but Parsons perhaps the least out of the four. None of them need anything Indian however to convey their teachings, but perhaps they and all similar teachers owe a simple debt to that nation: a certain language to get at what they already know of enlightenment from the *inside*.

The spiritual systems of the four men have much in common, but also enough to set them apart to make all of them worthy of study – not excluding of course countless other Western teachers. Their systems aside, we are interested in how their pupils negotiate these particular hierophants; does it make it easier that they are Western-born? I suspect so, though this is only a matter of degree. If the master is to be taken seriously there will be nothing "easy" in what the pupil goes through.

This is a good point to return briefly to Whitman. The scholar of mysticism Agehananda Bharati once wrote that one of the characteristics of a mystic is no small-talk.[97] The mystic is only interested in conversation that is part of teaching, and this is what I observe in Harding and Cohen. I only met Tony Parsons once at one of his talks and so it is no surprise that we only talked about enlightenment – touching on Douglas Harding – while I have not met Wayne Liquorman. However I *suspect* Bharati's dictum is true of all of them, or that at the very least their role as spiritual teachers leaves little room for anything else. Whitman could be as forbidding as any Zen master, as I gather through testimony of those around him, but his life was not lived as Harding's was, or as Liquorman, Parsons and Cohen continue to do. Neither does Whitman's life look like that of Gurdjieff, Krishnamurti, Rajneesh, Trungpa or Mother Meera. Of course all have "down time" and we know from Harvey that Mother Meera enjoys putting up shelves, and we know from Krishnamurti's writings that he enjoyed watching Clint Eastwood movies, driving a sports car, walking his dogs and reading detective novels. But all of them pursued the vocation of teacher which dominated their lives. One cannot say this of Whitman. I am not even sure that being a poet dominated his life; rather that he fitted it round the much more general vocation of simply being alive. This means that his role as hierophant was perhaps more occasional and so negotiating it may well have followed different contours. We explore that later.

5
CULT CATASTROPHES

What could possibly go wrong in the relationship between a spiritual teacher and pupil?

Everything, seems to be the answer. But why? The spiritual teacher has been through the excruciating stages of seeking answers to life's most profound questions and has emerged the other side fully liberated from personal goals and in possession of simplicity, tranquility and wisdom. Or so the aspirant assumes. It is natural to be in awe of such a person, particularly when they already have a large following. It is natural not to question the radical wisdom and apparent ability to turn every question upon the questioner; not to query why an organization appears around the teacher to help disseminate that wisdom; and not to challenge the inner circle of disciples placed in charge. So why not hand over large amounts of cash when your fully paid-up discipleship might one day transform you into an enlightened one or even a hierophant in your own right? Why not, for now, surrender to the hierarchy of the hierophant all those life-choices you would normally make?

These questions are answered in an instructive if cynical piece of film-making on the subject, *Holy Smoke* (Jane Campion, 1999). The female protagonist becomes the classic seeker of truth in India, finds a guru and rejects her family. They kidnap her, take her home, and make a bargain with her that if she submits to "exit counseling" and still wants to continue her discipleship they'll pay for a flight back to India. So enter exit counselor P. J. Waters (played by Harvey Keitel) who tells her:

> We're talking about your soul here. Have you ever thought about the damage that could be done to your soul, to your very center ... if you hand it over to someone else? To the wrong someone else?

I don't think I could have scripted this better in terms of raising the most fundamental fears we have of the guru. It does appear as if the guru demands of us we hand over our very soul. Waters continues by reminding her of cult leaders including Rajneesh, Moon, Koresh, Manson, Jones (of Jonestown mass suicide) and Applewhite (of Heaven's Gate) using video clips. However in the end Waters appears as manipulative as the gurus he derides, certainly in terms of his sexual appetites. All those who set themselves up as instructors of the soul, it seems, have evil designs on you. We have seen, for example, that Tibetan teachers in the West succumbed to excesses of behavior that for many quite undermined the value of their teachings and the dignity of their tradition. So, here is the key question of this book: is the guru system as adopted by Westerners set up to fail? If so what are the dynamics of its failure?

I am going to suggest that the problem has three dimensions. Firstly there are clearly terrible hierophants. There are plenty of studies of those. Secondly there are clearly pupils whose inner lives are deeply unstable and who place far too much hope in the hierophant. They need support, and ultimately may benefit from some kind of "exit counseling." Thirdly the West has a religious history making it difficult ground for the guru system, an essentially Eastern idea, to operate properly. In this chapter we explore some examples of spiritual teachings gone horribly wrong, on a spectrum ranging from the outright terrible to the debacle to the embarrassing to the merely resented. This clears the ground, as it were, to then examine accounts of more constructive hierophancy.

The terrible: Waco, Heaven's Gate, Jonestown

The film *Holy Smoke* references the Heaven's Gate, Jonestown and Branch Davidians cults all of which met horrible ends. The leaders of these three cults, Marshall Applewhite, Jim Jones and David Koresh, respectively, were Christian preachers however, with no reference to Eastern systems. Cult members of Heaven's Gate and Jonestown died in mass suicides, while the Branch Davidians of David Koresh died in a conflagration that they could have escaped, had they surrendered to the federal agencies besieging their ranch house at Waco. What the three have in common are Christian apocalyptical teachings, though the Heaven's Gate theology owed as much to science fiction.

These examples are very much in the public mind when it comes to charismatic spiritual teachers. How do the parents of young people drawn to such cults know that they will not be "brainwashed" to the point that they eventually follow their leaders to the death, by means possibly including suicide? Nuns and monks in the Catholic tradition take vows of poverty, chastity and obedience. Poverty and chastity are not life-threatening, even if unwelcome to parents, but obedience can be. To look at another example, the word "Islam" means submission to God. In practice it might mean submission to a mullah or religious teacher who preaches jihad – holy war – and sends a son or daughter to fight in foreign conflicts, or worse, to commit acts of terrorism in states not at war. Abandoning one's will to another may mean the abandoning of what, to a parent at least, is the most important instinct of a human being, self-preservation.

It is no surprise then that exit counseling exists in real life, and many organizations exist to extract cult members from the clutches of their guru. I regard all this as an extreme however and from which we do not learn that much. The trajectory of Bhagwan Shree Rajneesh and his followers is more instructive, for example, and I present it here because he was one of my key spiritual teachers.

The debacle: Rajneesh in America

At some point in early 1990s I found myself on my high-powered BMW motorcycle waiting at traffic lights in the East End of London. My head was enclosed in a full-face helmet and tears were coursing down my cheeks. I had just heard that Bhagwan Shree Rajneesh – later just known as Osho – had died and was on my way to the Rajneesh center in North London to participate in one of the first commemorations of his death. I had not been that active a "sanyassin" – as his followers were called – for a while and had no idea that his dying would take me so hard. What little connection I had with the Rajneesh organization faded out completely after that, but I was left in no doubt that he had been an enormously important figure in my life. As mentioned earlier the other two important gurus for me were

Krishnamurti and Douglas Harding, but I was not so affected by their deaths, even despite attending Harding's funeral in Suffolk, England.

I still have two dozen of Rajneesh's books, almost all of which are transcripts of his lectures. I knew from the moment of his death that I would have to re-assess his work at some point later in his life and so do that briefly here. There is no doubt of course that the Rajneesh experiment in its American incarnation culminated in debacle. I don't wish to go into details here, but here are the basic facts as stated in Wikipedia:

> The alleged crimes, which he [Rajneesh] stated had been committed without his knowledge or consent, included the attempted murder of his personal physician, poisonings of public officials, wiretapping and bugging within the commune and within his own home, and a bioterror attack on the citizens of The Dalles, Oregon, using Salmonella to impact the county elections. While his allegations were initially greeted with skepticism by outside observers, the subsequent investigation by the US authorities confirmed these accusations and resulted in the conviction of Sheela [lead disciple] and several of her lieutenants.

This is not how one wants a spiritual community to end. The question is, regardless of whether Rajneesh was unaware of the plans to carry out the crimes for which Sheela was convicted, did he prepare the ground for them? Were his teachings open to such interpretation as would permit or encourage criminal behavior to advance the material cause of his spiritual community? And why did he purchase ninety-two Rolls Royces?

I hesitate here. A huge part of my life is at stake. In my twenties I took up Hatha Yoga and had my first mystical experience while practicing some postures on the carpet in my mother's living room (she was away at the time). The experience was a sense of mild possession, in that my body wanted to make its own movements, to which I abandoned myself. Looking back on that now, I would call the experience the first inklings of mystical union, though only very partial. It was sufficient to set me searching for more, and I took the opportunity to go to India to take a yoga intensive course with B. K. S. Iyengar. The course was grueling, and I found him a man of limited spiritual insight, but chance would have it that in the same town (Poona or Pune) was the ashram of Bhagwan Shree Rajneesh, where I subsequently stayed for five weeks. The ashram, with its luxurious vegetation, fountains, and well-appointed buildings seemed a little unreal, and struck me at the time as a kind of human hot-house.

Rajneesh offered a mixture of meditation and psychotherapy courses which I plunged into, to overwhelming effect (the intensive yoga course and the culture-shock generally contributed to my vulnerability). I fell ill at one point with dengue fever and was confined to bed nearby the ashram in Koregaon Park for nearly a week, during which time I practiced a range of meditations from Rajneesh's *The Book of the* Secrets,[98] a commentary on the "Vigyana Bhairava Tantra" – Shiva's listing of meditation techniques to his consort. At the end of this period, at sunset, I experienced my first *samadhi*, or temporary state of union. It was indescribably blissful, a state in which the mind had slowed down to the merest trickle, and from which I slowly returned to "normality" through an anxiety that I had lost my mind. It was probably the first time that I became aware of thoughts as independent entities, and of an identity beyond them and not constructed through them. I was aware that this is what Rajneesh had been talking about in lectures and in his books, but oddly, I felt that I owed the state more to the scruffy dog that hung around the halls of residence than to Rajneesh. I had been sitting outside still feeling weak from the illness, enjoying the sunset, and observing the dog, rib-thin, but alert and contented on a mound of dirt a little way away. The mind had receded as if a horrible noise – that one had grown so accustomed to that one was no longer aware of its presence – had suddenly stopped; though in fact it had merely slowed down to a rate that made it observable. I was naively hoping that I could share this with someone, but the preoccupied faces of other seekers returning from the ashram stopped me confiding my state to them. Instead I wandered out of the compound in this blissful condition, and gradually became concerned that I would not regain my normal state. In the restaurant of the Blue Diamond hotel I was still hoping for an acknowledgement of my condition, this time from Rajneesh as he often dined there, but he did not show up, and gradually the state wore off.

Always disinclined to rush into things I did not seek initiation until I returned to England. After that I wore orange clothes – including an orange Saville Row suit made to order – a set of beads or "mala" with a picture of Rajneesh, and attended the meditations and workshops on offer at the London centre at the time, having moved into a council flat next to it in Camden. Also, as indicated earlier I read even more widely than before, following many of Rajneesh's eclectic interests. But I kept my day job. This I think was crucial in negotiating this particular hierophant. So how do I assess him today? I made a point recently of re-reading his lectures on Krishna, in which, as mentioned earlier, he explains why he thinks Freud is so important.

Here then is my verdict. He was no fraud. But the debacle at Rajneeshpuram in Oregon was, in hindsight, perfectly predictable from his teachings and from the way he ran his ashram. He boasted, *boasted*, that he set out to take the most power-hungry of his pupils and elevate them in his hierarchy to positions of power over the rest as a way of provoking the other pupils into accelerated spiritual development. It was, in effect, a gigantic encounter group engendered through the reckless actions of the ashram elite, with Rajneesh orchestrating the chaos. I have no reason to make excuses for Rajneesh, even if he was unaware of the crimes carried out in the last stages. What he did ensured the collapse of what could have been a spiritual community of great longevity and worldwide significance.

I do not excuse Rajneesh. I am however not in the slightest bitter or resentful or regretful. I had other teachers and a huge range of other teachings to triangulate against and made my own system, as Blake insists we must. But I enormously value what I gained from Rajneesh and place him in the crazy wisdom context as in Feuerstein's book, the subtitle of which elaborates: "The shock tactics and radical teachings of crazy-wise adepts, holy fools, and rascal gurus." Surely, are not rascal gurus to be avoided? Feuerstein suggests that Rajneesh keeps company with Tibetan and Zen teachers, Gurdjieff, Aleister Crowley and Chögyam Trungpa amongst others. Has not Rajneesh proved they do more harm than good? I can only answer for myself: I agree with Shankara. I was lucky to find Rajneesh, though many would say that even better luck was to have the instincts to safely negotiate that particular hierophant. With hindsight of course I can see precisely where Rajneesh's spiritual system was incomplete, fatally incomplete, and so doomed his legacy. Feuerstein says it better than I can in completing his list of Rajneesh's transgressions: "Then there is Rajneesh's avowed antinomian philosophy and moral anarchism, based on Tantrism and epitomized in the following quotes from his works ..."[99]

I won't list all the quotes provided by Feuerstein but his first is a typical Rajneesh utterance: "Morality is a false coin, it deceives people, it is not religion at all." Unlike Feuerstein I will contextualize this. Having listened to or read so many of Rajneesh's lectures I think this bald statement on morality is not exactly representative of him. It was *prescriptive* morality that he railed against, the dead moralizing code of puritan Hinduism, the sort that forbids married men and women from holding hands when walking down the street. Indian social restrictions had become so stifling that Rajneesh's reaction was both inevitable and necessary. What Rajneesh had no interest in – and the lack of which is the characteristic of Feuerstein's "crazy wisdom" – is moderation, balance and harmony, which for example lies at the core of Taoist religious thought. Rajneesh went from one excess to another, inspiring many people to begin with and taking them down with him in the ignominious end to his project. But I still read the transcripts of his talks and find huge insights there, many of which I first discovered in his work and which have stayed with me.

The embarrassing: Scientology

We turn now to Scientology. There is this guy with an interest in science and religion. He has a keen photographic eye, writes science fiction, and believes in reincarnation, not just on earth but across parallel universes, some populated by advanced technological races thousands of years ago. That's me. It is also L. Ron Hubbard (1911-1986), founder of Scientology, another cult with almost Rajneesh-like debacles to its name, including the making of Hubbard a wanted man in America, dying in hiding from the police. Where Hubbard and I part company is firstly that he made millions and attracted celebrities like Tom Cruise and John Travolta to his cult and secondly that he made science deeply part of his religion. I don't. I keep them quite separate on the basis that the former has utility of decreasing value as one gets older, while religion has truth, the importance of which accelerates asymptotically towards the moment of dying. Put another way, science covers everything you leave behind while religion covers everything you take with you. That instinct, I guess, lay behind the nonchalance with which I used to stroll past Hubbard's London center, chat with the sirens hoping to draw you in for a free "engram" testing, and walk on. I never had to negotiate that particular hierophant, though I read his books as I did those of all other teachers I could potentially learn from.

Scientology has fared better than Rajneeshism however, though the latter may have had a greater following at one point than the former. So why should I suggest that Scientology is an embarrassment? Simple: it's the science / science-fiction thing. I'm trained in the hard sciences and have a keen eye for when claims about science become mere science fiction. Hubbard blurred those boundaries, as have what are now termed a whole range of "hyper-religions" based on science fiction ideas of UFOs (Raelianism) or populist cinema such as Star Trek (Jediism).[100] The venerable tradition of the Church of Christ, Scientist, founded by Mary Baker Eddy in 1879, was not based on science as we understand it today, but on the kind of healing that involves the placing of hands on the sick. Eddy's unconventional use of the term "science" is possibly more forgivable than Hubbard's, I would suggest, because in her day the term "science" was more negotiable.

So what went wrong with Hubbard's spiritual enterprise? Like Rajneesh he appears to have had a strong antinomian streak in his character, but his system owed less to the guru tradition in India than what is termed the "prosperity gospel" or "prosperity wing" of the New Age.[101] The accusations of criminality are more severe however, his "Operation Snow White" being counted as "one of the largest infiltrations of the United States government in history"[102] in contrast to the merely local shenanigans of Rajneeshpuram in Oregon. For a period in the 1960s and 1970s Hubbard was at sea in a luxury yacht in command of a fleet of ships crewed by his followers, but his criminal indictments meant that many nations closed their ports to him as *persona non grata*.

Hubbard's spirituality is eclectic, as is Rajneesh's, and rests considerably on the doctrine of reincarnation. As I recall, the most amusing anecdote I came across in respect to this is when Hubbard handed the captaincy of one of his vessels to a young woman with no naval experience. When she protested he told her that she had been a spaceship commander three thousand years previous for an advanced race elsewhere in the galaxy, and so she should soon get the hang of it. More seriously he claimed in one of his works to be the Buddha Maitreya, the future Buddha, a claim made, as we saw, for the young Jiddu Krishnamurti by the Theosophists.

What I turned down as I passed the Scientology center in London was the offer of a free spiritual auditing conducted through the use of an e-meter, a device that measures galvanic skin response. The idea was that past life traumas known as *engrams* are residual in the psyche and can be detected by the device. Through a process of "clearing" one can be freed of their unconscious restricting of human potential and then make progress up a number of spiritual attainment levels. I am actually perfectly sympathetic to this idea, being an extension of Freud's psychoanalytical techniques of catharsis into previous lives. I explore it in a satirical vein in my novel *Enigma's Coda* about a mathematician who believes he was Alan Turing reborn, but behind the satire lies a confidence in the process as *potentially* genuine and useful. It all depends on the context. With Hubbard, as far as I can see, progress with the e-meter allowed for increased seniority and privilege in the organization's hierarchy. If you couple Hubbard's willingness to break the law with his authoritarian control over his organization with a hierarchy based on what can easily descend into mumbo-jumbo it is no surprise that the venture was as doomed as Rajneesh's.

Having said that, the death of Hubbard left behind a significant organization called The Church of Scientology, led by chief disciple David Miscavige and based around a three-fold creed composed by Hubbard:

1. Freedom to enjoy religious expression
2. Mental healing is inherently religious
3. Healing of the physical body is in the spiritual domain.

I have sympathy with all three of these credal positions and am aware that the church appears to have a successful program of drug rehabilitation with a religious basis perhaps similar to Alcoholics Anonymous.

How does one negotiate the hierophant here? As with Rajneesh after he had amassed a large following one is in fact no longer negotiating with the founder of the spiritual movement but with its hierarchy. One is also faced with a mapped-out path of spiritual progression assessed by the officers of the faith. Given the enormous temptations open to those a little higher up in the hierarchy to abuse those one rung down, I would say that quick wits and a profound sense of self-preservation are required to come out as a net beneficiary from membership of anything like Scientology.

The resented: Cohen

While I count Rajneesh, Krishnamurti and Douglas Harding as my three principal gurus it is fair to say that I learned a great deal from Andrew Cohen. He came into my orbit while I was studying for my Master's at Canterbury as a mature student (this was my fourth degree). Six of us classmates attended the first of two day's talks by Cohen in London in the 1990s and at the end of the first day we hummed and hawed. "It was okay," we conceded and left it open as to whether any of us would bother to turn up on the second day. All of us did. He was that good.

As mentioned earlier, Cohen is third in a lineage going back to Ramana Maharshi, through a teacher called Poonjaji, who once said of Cohen that he had seen pure emptiness in the eyes of only three people: his master Maharshi, himself in the mirror and Andrew. As far as I am concerned Hubbard lives the wrong side of that cusp between genuine teacher and charlatan, while both Rajneesh and Cohen are on the right side even though both are at some level showmen.

I think I once upset friends of mine who had not long gone through the trauma of parting from their hierophant, Andrew Cohen. Although they did not detail their perceived losses in having devoted themselves to running his London center only to find it abandoned by its teacher, I understood that they were upset if not angry. "But surely," I suggested breezily, "it was all worth it to have been so close to a great spiritual teacher?" It was only afterwards that I realized how their polite response hid real hurt. I made my apologies later on as I reflected how they were probably "in recovery" – as the phrase goes – from what they saw as an abusive relationship. From the clues I have picked up from them and other ex-Cohen disciples, alongside a book-length exposé by disgruntled former disciple William Yenner, I have an estimation of the resentment built up against him. For some at least their involvement with their hierophant was indeed a catastrophe.

In 2009 I published two reviews of books centered on Andrew Cohen, the first a positive account by Michael Wombacher of an eleven-day retreat with Cohen and the second the negative account by William Yenner and other former disciples who are fiercely critical of Cohen. Yenner knew of my interest in Cohen and sent me his book for review. On the first page of Yenner's introduction he writes:

> When I left Andrew's community, and for many years after, anger and blame dominated my emotions. I was nearly consumed by a paralyzing resentment. The notion that I might ever be able to forgive Andrew was inconceivable to me.[103]

I wonder how many gurus have over the millennia left behind angry and disgruntled students? Is it the case that genuine gurus do not create this kind of resentment and fake gurus inevitably do? Or is it more that a certain type of seeker – who fails to gain what they are looking for – lands up blaming even the perfectly genuine guru? Certainly the accounts in Yenner's book are damning, and suggest that the fault lies entirely with Cohen.

"No one knowingly joins a cult," Yenner begins, explaining how what had been his choice at the outset "gradually came to feel less like a life freely chosen than forced enlistment in the service of an individual bent on total control." First of all, I disagree about "cult" because who is to decide? A small religious group with absolutely no history of abuse and only positive feedback is just a small religious group. Religions on the other hand which are shown to be extremely abusive, are they not cults then? So no, for me a cult is a small religion; a religion is a large cult, and I have knowingly joined some of both. Secondly, what does Yenner mean by "forced enlistment?" Of his own choice he abandoned his career, wife and family to join Cohen's inner community. The Buddha also abandoned his career (as prince), wife and family. Once Yenner had decided that he was in an abusive relationship, what stopped him walking? Of course we ask that of all partners who stay in abusive relationships, the answer for the bulk of them through history, being women, is that men had the economic upper hand. But the key of course is what attracted Yenner in the first place. What did he want so badly as to put up with the abuse? When I was introduced to Cohen at his London center there was nothing I wanted from him and so no question of abuse. Indeed his first question to me was why I disagreed with his evolutionary enlightenment; I answered that in my view humans today are structurally the same as when they first emerged on the planet; how could enlightenment change? The context changes that's all. We formed something of a friendship and at one point Cohen invited me as one of two guest speakers for a day seminar, the first being, amusingly, the occultist Gary Lachman who had formerly been the bass player for the pop group Blondie.

But what does any aspirant want? The master has described a state of perfection, of complete unassailable happiness – or so the aspirant thinks – and they want the same. As Yenner says: "Initially, Andrew Cohen seemed to many of us to embody perfection." That is the problem, and I think Cohen contributed to it with many assertions or hints about the possibility of such perfection. Yenner must have felt deeply imperfect and deeply unhappy with his work and marriage to throw those things away in favor of discipleship. His book is however a significant exploration of the master-disciple relationship in the West and where it can go horribly wrong – at least from the perspective of the student. I once asked Andrew if any of his students had *really* understood what he was teaching. He was a little guarded. "Perhaps a few of my senior students," was the gist of his reply. I have no doubt that the curse of the spiritual teacher is that very few pupils ever understand them, and this can drive them to more and more unusual if not extreme teaching methods. What Yenner does, which initially surprised me, is suggest that Cohen is a "crazy-wisdom" teacher. I never got that from him or his organization in the sense that I got it from Rajneesh, and know of it in the life of Gurdjieff. But it seems that Cohen himself described his teachings as an updated version of this tradition "designed to cut through a student's ego and resistance to facilitate awakening."[104]

I don't want to detail the indignities and cruelties that Yenner and other students claim that Cohen inflicted upon them as reported in Yenner's book. I don't know if they are true or false. But Cohen's apology to his students issued in 2015, two years after the collapse of his spiritual community, appears to acknowledge the general drift of these accusations.[105] In my own many years of searching and in my own encounter with many teachers the worst I can say that happened to me was being slapped in a Rajneesh encounter group – it was actually a badge of honor amongst those attending these things to emerge with a broken arm – and receiving a hurtful remark from Douglas Harding. I simply never placed myself in a position where a guru could demand of me any kind of self-humiliation, let alone verbal or physical abuse. But then I never gave up my career and family to join a community cut off from the mainstream and in which the guru and the spiritual hierarchy had control over every minute of my day. Such communes belong to the larger picture of so-called "elective communities" which may purchase land or housing collectively and live away from the mainstream in the pursuit of an ideology, religious or otherwise. For example the first five years of my life were spent in an elective community of artists in North London centered around a visionary art collector and gallery owner. Poignantly he had bought the grand house and outbuildings – including the shack in which we lived – from a religious group. I should add that I probably acquired my deep instincts for shamanism from the collection of ethnic art housed in what had served as the central chapel for the former religious community.[106]

But what made Cohen drive his students so hard that it became abuse leading to "paralyzing resentment?" We note that unlike Rajneesh, Cohen was never charged with anything criminal, even though it took lawyers to force Cohen to return some of the cash donated to the community. What drove and probably still drives Cohen is his belief in the *evolutionary* side of enlightenment, as this passage from his apology spells out:

> As the years went by I gradually began to define the meaning of the spiritual life lived in earnest in our post modern era as the willingness to be someone who would care so passionately about what appeared to be humanity's next step at the leading edge, that they would be willing to make any sacrifice and take any risk, so that that future could emerge here and now in the present between us, as our very own selves. (Cohen's italics.)

I see two things wrong with this. Firstly it is fine for a person to make any sacrifice and take any risk in some venture so long as all the negative consequences fall only on themselves – and even then the law prohibits many such behaviors because the community has to pick up the pieces. To believe that one's insight as a spiritual teacher is so profound as to take the risk with *other* people's lives is more problematic however, though again, did not Cohen's pupils knowingly take on that risk? Did they not want something so badly that they placed themselves in harm's way to obtain it? The second problem with Cohen's statement here is what strikes me as a lack of faith. If humanity is indeed evolving and the next stage in nearly upon us – statements I anyway would only accept if enormously hedged about with qualifications – then why is there so little trust in the universe that one should assume that this evolutionary leap will not happen anyway? Why would the universe need Andrew Cohen to push it along if it is clearly a collective phenomenon? The boss of any organization might well see a once-in-a-lifetime opportunity for huge beneficial change and give everything to usher it in. But humanity has no boss and why on earth imagine that this *is* a once-in-a-lifetime opportunity that can somehow be missed? Clearly the human world changes over time; I see each phase as significant; but what is coming is firstly only dimly comprehensible and secondly I for one am in no hurry to usher it in, given that however good the new, it will no doubt displace much that is good in the old.

Cohen's students, as believers in evolutionary enlightenment, signed up to this however. They were also not blind to the possibilities that Cohen was out of control as he says in his apology:

> My closest and most devoted senior students were beginning to see through my façade, could see that I was out of control, and see that I didn't even know it. What made matters much worse is that I ignored the evidence; I ignored their respectful pleas for me to slow down and listen to them. For over six months during this period I literally couldn't sleep, and night after night I convinced myself that I had no idea why this was the case. My self became more and more divided. I was still an inspired teacher and speaker, but I adamantly remained steadfastly and obstinately oblivious to the growing storm I was creating.[107]

We note that the attempts by pupils to negotiate this particular hierophant's behavior fell on deaf ears – I imagine it mostly does. Significantly, Cohen goes on to suggest that his treatment of his pupils was similar to the famously harsh treatment meted out by Tibetan master Marpa to Milarepa, two gurus allegedly in a direct line of teaching back to the Buddha and discussed further in Chapter 6. Cohen has said sorry, and that the only way to make amends is become a better teacher. Love is needed in his system, he says. He has realized that he has something called a "shadow side" – a Jungian idea that I am inclined to see as largely psychobabble – and that he had not properly dealt with it, "despite being lucky enough to have access to Enlightened awareness." He goes on to make the point central to this book:

> I know this is hard to fathom, but it certainly has been true in my case, and has been true in many other cases where powerfully awakened Teach-

ers have acted out in either destructive or self-destructive ways ... or both. It's been a significant part of the rocky legacy of eastern Enlightenment coming to the psychologically informed west. Ironically, I spent much of my early career speaking and writing about this very issue.

It is certainly true that Cohen spent much time criticizing other spiritual teachers for their shortcomings, including Rajneesh. I wrote many years ago that this might backfire on him. It did.

I was on the podium with Andrew Cohen and Gary Lachman at Cohen's London center when the topic came up of the then recent mass murders by the Norwegian Anders Behring Breivik. Cohen asked me for my response and this is roughly what I said:

> There are three stages to this. Ordinary people, when confronted with something so horrible, simply call the perpetrator evil and that is that. The more sophisticated say "there but for the grace of God go I." The response of an enlightened person is different however. He or she says "There go I."

Cohen's response to this was most instructive. He denied his identity with Breivik, drawing on a saying by Shankara, which I did not fully follow. What I take from it is that Cohen has retained a separate sense of identity from which it is possible to hold the moral high ground over others, possibly including his pupils. From there it is not just possible to judge others, but, if they have placed themselves at your feet as master, also possible to sentence them to various forms of atonement or "improving" discipline. That's quite a trap.

Cohen's spiritual system is inherited from the Advaita tradition in which his master Poonjaji was located, but was much adapted and developed by Cohen. In particular Cohen's system rejects what perhaps many Westerners perceive as the passive nature of the Advaita, as we shall see. Although the failure of Cohen's hierophancy can be mostly put down to his personality we can also ask whether the system as he developed it did not also contribute to the problem. One must also add that the story of Cohen's hierophancy is not over and that in his efforts to learn and renew his calling there may well emerge a more positive outcome.

6

INSTRUCTIVE NEGOTIATIONS

I am conscious of examples of benign hierophancy through history and in my own life and will look at some here as a contrast to the list of terrible, catastrophic, embarrassing or merely resented cases of hierophancy we have just examined. We are not interested here in teachers who are obvious fakes, though a case can be make that even then an aspirant can, in the right cultural context, gain something from the relationship. Again it is from Rajneesh that I gained this insight, that if the devotion of the pupil is deep enough it does not matter if the guru turns out to have feet of clay – their office is in effect still efficacious. In any case unless you jettison the guru in the end you live only in his or her shadow.

It is clear that for one pupil the relationship can be experienced as benign and for another abusive, even though the hierophancy is with the same guru. As with all relationships, then, it is greatly a matter of chemistry. I include cases here that are perhaps marginal in terms of how benign the pupil viewed the experience, but are still instructive. Because of the sheer intensity of the experience the pupil can live almost perpetually on the cusp of giving up, despair, hatred of the teacher, or just plain bewilderment. What is never plain is the sailing, as my poem about masters included earlier certainly shows; my resentment at the time, even if short-lived, was very real.

Socrates / Alcibiades

It is a radical proposition that Socrates was a teacher of enlightenment, that Plato was his pupil, and that the pupil betrayed his master by putting

6. Instructive Negotiations

words into his mouth. That roughly was my Master's thesis.[108] What I engaged in was a kind of spiritual archaeology, digging Socrates out from under Plato, partly by triangulating Socrates against known mystics and partly by drawing on sources normally ignored such as Xenophon. As mentioned before the whole exercise meant immersing myself in the Socratic texts from various sources and by the end of it I felt that I walked with this man through ancient Athens and saw the world through his eyes. Rajneesh used to say that each enlightened one colors eternity in a unique way, or words to that effect, and I think the power that a figure like Socrates has over me is down to this lingering presence or energetic thread that runs through history and which one can tune into with sufficient effort. I "twang" as it were to the vibrations set off through history by all of these teachers, from before Socrates to after Whitman.

I'll start with some passages regarding the relationship between Alcibiades – destined to become a tyrant – and Socrates, his teacher for a period. In the manner common to the Greek men of the period Alcibiades sought Socrates' physical love, and received at one point only a lecture in philosophy. Alcibiades records ruefully:

> I swear by all the gods in heaven that for anything that had happened between us when I got up after sleeping with Socrates, I might have been sleeping with my father or elder brother. ... On the one hand I realized that I had been slighted, but on the other I felt a reverence for Socrates' character, his self-control and courage; I had met a man whose like for wisdom and fortitude I could never have expected to encounter."[109]

Alcibiades also tells us: "Whenever I listen to him my heart beats faster than if I were in a religious frenzy, and tears run down my face, and I observe that numbers of other people have the same experience."[110]

Socrates has a shaming effect on him:

> He is the only person in whose presence I experienced a sensation of which I might be thought incapable, a sensation of shame; he, and he alone, positively makes me ashamed of myself. ... The Socrates whom you see has a tendency to fall in love with good-looking young men, and is always in their society and in an ecstasy about them. ... , but once you see beneath the surface you will discover a degree of self-control of which you can hardly form a notion, gentlemen. Believe me, it makes no difference to him whether a person is good-looking — he despises good looks to an

> almost inconceivable extent — nor whether he is rich nor whether he possesses any of the other advantages that rank high in popular esteem; to him all these things are worthless, and we ourselves of no account, be sure of that. He spends his whole life pretending and playing with people, and I doubt whether anyone has ever seen the treasures which are revealed when he grows serious and exposes what he keeps inside. However, I once saw them, and found them so divine and precious and beautiful and marvelous that, to put the matter briefly, I had no choice but to do whatever Socrates bade me.[111]

The religious scholar Jacob Needleman comments in connection with this passage that "the impact of Socrates is to produce upon man a specific sort of suffering that involves seeing oneself against a very high criterion of what man should be."[112] Needleman is influenced in this comment by the teachings of Gurdjieff, who often said that the purpose of a master was to induce this specific form of suffering in the disciple (he referred to the process of creating it as "friction"). The following passage reinforces this impression of Socrates as spiritual master (Alcibiades is speaking again):

> But our friend here is so extraordinary, both in his person and in his conversation, that you will never be able to find anyone remotely resembling him either in antiquity or in the present generation, unless you go beyond humanity altogether, and have recourse to the images of Silenus and satyr which I am using myself in this speech. ... Anyone who sets out to listen to Socrates talking will probably find his conversation utterly ridiculous at first, it is clothed in such curious words and phrases, the hide, so to speak of a hectoring satyr. He will talk of pack-asses and blacksmiths, cobblers and tanners, and appear to express the same ideas in the same language over and over again, so that any inexperienced or foolish person is bound to laugh at his way of speaking. But if a man penetrates within and sees the content of Socrates' talk exposed, he will find that there is nothing but sound sense inside, and that this talk is almost the talk of a god, and enshrines countless representations of ideal excellence, and is of the widest possible application; in fact that it extends over all the subjects with which a man who means to turn out a gentleman needs to concern himself.[113]

Alcibiades concludes his speech with another useful clue to Socrates' behavior: "I may add that I am not the only sufferer in this way; Char-

6. Instructive Negotiations

mides the son of Glaucon and Euthydemus the son of Diocles and many others have had the same treatment; he has pretended to be in love with them, when in fact he is himself the beloved rather than the lover."[114] *He himself is the beloved* — an indication that Socrates as spiritual master is loved, though as a *device* he pretends the opposite (not that the master's love is not genuine, but it is not of the familiar sort). We also saw that John Bennett thought that Gurdjieff's persona was a mask designed almost to repel, or at the least to hide his saintly character. I think that an enlightened person does have to hide their true nature in various ways, or at the least hide their insights, because they are so counter-conventional.

A longer immersion in the Socratic literature gives many more clues as to Socrates' possible role as hierophant. What we know nothing of however is how Plato negotiated that relationship because Plato absents himself from the dialogues. We can assume that Plato was profoundly influenced by Socrates and that his eventual distaste for democracy was because he saw it as mob rule which sentenced his master to death; beyond that we cannot say. I do find however that the passages concerning Alcibiades speak volumes. Amongst other things it is clear that Socrates delivers a moral shock to this young man, an element in the hierophant-aspirant relationship that appears absent or reversed in crazy wisdom teachers. On the other hand Plato has Socrates say this about craziness:

> If it were true without qualification that madness is an evil, that would be all very well, but in fact madness, provided it comes as the gift of heaven, is the channel by which we receive the greatest blessings. Take the prophetess at Delphi and the priestesses at Dodona, for example, and consider all the benefits which individuals and states in Greece have received from them when they were in a state of frenzy, though their usefulness in their sober senses amounts to little or nothing.[115]

We may also be intrigued by the comparison made by Meno of Socrates to a stingray:

> Socrates, even before I met you, I heard others talk about how you are always completely perplexed about everything, and how you drag everyone else down into the same pit of perplexity. Now I think you have been bewitching and bewildering me. You've cast some spell over me, so now I'm completely at a loss. In fact, if you don't mind me turning the whole business into a bit of a joke, on the inside you're like one of those stingrays

115

that paralyzes everything it touches; you look a bit like one, too – broad and flat. Anyway, now you've done it to me; both my mind and my tongue are completely numb. I've got no answer to give you. And yet I must have made a thousand speeches about virtue before now – in front of large audiences, too; but now I cannot even say what it is. I think you are wise not to sail away from Athens to live in some foreign city. Because if you behaved like this, as a stranger in a strange land, you would be driven out of town as an evil enchanter.[116]

What is crucial for me in contemplating Socrates as hierophant is that he stands close to the dawn of Western philosophy, a tradition that now excludes the language of the spiritual, of the spiritual teacher, of the hierophant, of the one who "shows us the holy." Instead figures like Socrates are more likely to be cast as philosophers in a technical sense, intellectuals who attempt to build speculative systems of rational thought the merits of which are judged on various criteria all far removed from the master-pupil relationship in the spiritual life. Meno's recourse to the metaphor of stingray is interpreted in the philosophical tradition as merely the state one enters into on defeat in rational argument. Instead, I suggest, there are enough examples in the spiritual literature to make the better analogy with the hierophant who brings about an end to thought altogether and engenders the accompanying encounter with the ultimately real. In any case Socrates' behavior is so *bizarre*, as I have shown in these few extracts, as to make his labeling as philosopher appear to me absurd. In my opinion it is mostly the dead hand of Plato that has engendered this category mistake.

If we grant that evidence points to Socrates as hierophant, not philosopher, then his example raises another frequent misunderstanding in the spiritual life: homosexuality. Should we take the term "satyr," as Alcibiades says, to mean that Socrates was neither philosopher nor hierophant but best understood as an ageing queen with an endless appetite for pretty young men? The testimony of Alcibiades refutes that of course, but throughout the spiritual life the fact that our recorded interactions are mostly between a male master and a male pupil, and that love is clearly part of this relationship, has suggested to the modern mind at least that we are dealing with a phenomenon that can adequately be described as homosexual and nothing more. This issue comes up with Whitman of course and also with Jalāl ad-Dīn Muhammad Rūmī and Ramakrishna Paramahansa, Robertson referring to it as the "erotics of discipleship."[117] We examine this in Chapter 7.

Marpa / Milarepa

The story of the discipleship of Jetsun Milarepa to the Tibetan Buddhist teacher Marpa Lotsawa is retold by Chögyam Trungpa as a case study in the dangers of spiritual materialism. Its original and best-known telling is in the book *The Life of Milarepa*, a classic of Tibetan Buddhism much loved in the West, for example by the sculptor Constantan Brancusi. I don't think I have touched my own copy for twenty years, but find the notes I made in it then of interest and a reminder that, like all such sacred texts, they have become part of my inner firmament: I remain tinged with its color even if I forget the detail. The story is set in the eleventh-twelfth century at a time when Buddhism had long displaced the indigenous shamanic religion of Tibet known as the Bon. Milarepa is supposed to have studied "sorcery" which would no doubt have been practiced and taught by surviving adepts of Bon techniques, and used it to murder his aunt and uncle and their family who had forced his own family into cruel servitude. He then underwent dreadful remorse.

I didn't originally intend to include the Marpa-Milarepa hierophancy in this book, it being presented to us in exotic and rather fabulous terms. But I realized I needed something like this to represent the whole issue of atonement in the master-disciple relationship. My major work on religion and film has a chapter titled "Violence, Compassion, Forgiveness and Atonement," where the section on atonement and redemption quite naturally deals with the film *Atonement*, an adaptation of the novel by the eminent British author Ian McEwan.[118] As a determined atheist it is not surprising that McEwan set out to show how atonement is a mere fiction. In real life, he seems to be saying, the opportunity to make amends for actions or words that have hurt others are rarely presented or taken up. In the world of the spiritual seeker it is however a major issue.

Milarepa begins his discipleship to Marpa quite explicitly as a murderer seeking atonement for his crime. Yes, he his seeking enlightenment by studying with a recognized enlightened master of his day, what is more a master in a lineage purporting to go back to the Buddha himself. But Milarepa brings with him this complication of guilt, for which Marpa prescribes the harshest penances; until these were completed he would not accept the young man as a pupil. He forced Milarepa to build a stone house for him by cutting the rocks, hauling them into position and completing the structure completely by himself, a physically grueling task. He would then tell Milarepa to demolish it and return the stones to their quarries, an emotionally devastating punishment. Marpa made him do this a number of times but Milarepa did not give up and in the end Marpa accepted the final nine-story structure. This was not to be demolished – and allegedly still stands in the Lhodrak district of Southern Tibet – but Marpa declared it insufficient. He wanted payment, knowing full well that Milarepa was destitute. Marpa's wife, Damema, took pity on Milarepa and secretly provided him with suitable goods as payment, but Marpa recognized them as his own property and was furious.[119] He kicked Milarepa out, who became suicidal. It was only then, when the young man was completely broken down, that Marpa finally accepted him as pupil. Many more penances were still required but Milarepa's long discipleship brought him enlightenment in the end.

Looking at photographs of Milarepa's Tower it is hard to believe a single man could build it, and scholars dispute other elements of the story; Tibetan Buddhism is anyway always interlaced with the supernatural. All this means that this particular hierophancy has less believable grit and detail than most in this chapter, but it helps us consider the case where a spiritual teacher appears to behave with utmost cruelty to a pupil. In the Eastern system Milarepa had to suffer intensely to purify himself of the bad karma of his murders, and Marpa, understanding this, enforced both physical hardship and mental humiliation on him. But what right does any spiritual teacher have to do that? My own theory on this, for what it is worth, is that reincarnation is true; the workings of karma are true; all crimes are paid for ultimately, with or without the intervention of the human justice system; and that there are as many people seeking punishment and humiliation from others as there are those willing to dish it out. The context does not have to be spiritual at all; consider these lines from a popular song by Annie Lenox:

Sweet dreams are made of this
Who am I to disagree?
I travel the world
And the seven seas,
Everybody's looking for something.

Some of them want to use you
Some of them want to get used by you
Some of them want to abuse you
Some of them want to be abused.

Of course, that does not answer the question, what *right* has a spiritual teacher to abuse the pupil? The answer to the modern mind of course is none.

Shams-e Tabrizi / Rumi

One might guess that Jalāl ad-Dīn Muhammad Rūmī – known simply as Rumi in the West – was America's favorite dead spiritual teacher, loved by such celebrities as Madonna, Goldie Hawn and Deepak Chopra. At one point he seemed at least to be America's favorite *poet*, as the BBC commented upon in 2014,[120] and nobody can approach his work unaware that his poems are in the Sufi spiritual tradition. He was a thirteenth-century Persian who moved westwards into what is now Turkey, with spiritual influences working on him that span both Islam and Buddhism. But the most powerful spiritual influence on him came from one man, Shams-e Tabrizi, and it is their relationship that is one of the most striking in the history of hierophancy.

Rumi is of interest in the context of Whitman because he is also a poet and because a life-changing event turned him into a spiritual teacher. Rumi was however much better understood in his cultural context than Whitman in his. Rumi has been described as:

> A figure of almost prophetic dimensions, he became for some Muslims almost a second Muhammed, for Christians a second Christ, and for Jews a second Moses. Among those present at his funeral procession were people of different religious traditions each of whom claimed that Jalāluddin had brought him to a deeper understanding of his own faith.[121]

Although commented upon less often, I also detect a great deal of Buddhist thought in Rumi's works. He grew up in what is now Afghanistan, an area with a Buddhist legacy that only slowly faded under Muslim onslaught, and was born a Persian, a race that seems to have an instinct for religious syncretism. However, we are more interested here in his relationship with Shams-e Tabrizi, whose name is given to one of Rumi's major works: *Dīwān-e Shams-e Tabrīzī*, also know simply as the "Great Work" or alternatively "diwan" or "divan" meaning collection of poems. This alone runs to 40,000 verses, though when pressed to write more Rumi referred to his poems as "tripe." Here is the opinion of scholar and translator A. J. Arberry:

> Rumi affected an astonishing contempt for his own poetry. On one occasion he remarked, "I am affectionate to such a degree that when these friends come to me, for fear that they may be wearied I speak poetry so that they may be occupied with that. Otherwise, what have I to do with poetry? By Allah, I care nothing for poetry, and there is nothing worse in my eyes than that. It has become incumbent upon me, as when a man plunges his hands into tripe and washes it out for the sake of a guest's appetite, because the guest's appetite is for tripe."[122]

Arberry refuses to be influenced by Rumi's own assessment, but I do not share his opinion that this was an affectation. I have nothing against art; I come from artistic families on both sides and practice various branches of the arts. None the less I think that however far art can go in revealing to us the deeper nature of things it always stops short – mostly well short – of the ultimate. So one who knows the infinite may also be artistic – as Blake and Whitman were – but will not make the mistake of making their home there. "Tripe" is of course a little harsh, and we are lucky of course that Rumi wrote beautiful poetry because we discover his spirituality that way and also his relationship with Shams. Inelegant prose would have served just as well though.

Rumi was in effect a hierophant before he met Shams, being a Sunni religious scholar and jurist. This combination of theologian and magistrate appears bizarre perhaps to Westerners, but is the norm in Muslim countries where the idea of separation of church and state is unthinkable. The encounter with Shams transformed Rumi, but here is not a classic master-

6. Instructive Negotiations

disciple relationship because it seems that Rumi more or less instantly learned what Shams had to teach, and their subsequent relationship appears to be one of equals. I cannot unpick the rather mythologized nature of the various accounts of their meeting and would probably need to study Rumi's vast outpourings at length to give a better-informed opinion. As it is I have only dipped into his verse, which is of course tremendously beautiful and a prime example of the love-oriented mystic's outpourings, or *bhakti*. It is also exemplary of the Sufi tradition.

Shams was seeking a pupil it seems and some divine intuition led him to Rumi. In most of the hierophants I have examined it is quite clear that their need for pupils matches the pupils' need for a master. However most pupils seem obdurate and slow to learn, to say the least, where here the transformation of Rumi was instantaneous. What is unusual, I think, in the history of hierophancy is that these two hierophants then spent an intense period together, traditionally held to be forty days. What do two enlightened masters do in the same room together? Mostly those who think about this question are clear: it is somehow wrong. The universe throws up so few of these individuals that they should be out there teaching, not enjoying each other's company. This was the view of Rajneesh who commented on a famous meeting between Kabir and Nanak, Indian spiritual teachers either in the Sufi tradition or close to it. Actually he may have made it up, or I remembered it wrong, but he suggested that their respective disciples insisted on the meeting against the instincts of the teachers, and were then disappointed when the two sat in silence for the duration. Rajneesh suggested that when pressed on it the response was something like this: "We had a choice, either to argue about absolutely everything in the spiritual life or sit there and enjoy silence together." I also recall Tony Parsons saying in the middle of a talk that enlightenment was so rare that if there was another enlightened person in the room they should leave immediately as they should be spending their time teaching lost souls elsewhere, or words to that effect. (Whether I failed to leave because I think myself unenlightened or because I didn't agree with him I shall keep secret.)

Rumi's spirituality is of a kind with all the love-mystics in Christianity, Islam and Hinduism. You don't find it in Judaism, Buddhism, or Taoism, and it is alien to Whitman. Just two examples from Rumi's poetry give the temper of it:

> If once in my life I pass a moment without You,
> I repent my life from that moment on.
> If once in this world
> I should win a moment with You,
> I will put both worlds below my feet
> and dance forever in joy.
> Oh Shams of Tabriz, I am so drunk in the world
> that except for revelry and intoxication
> I have no tale to tell.[123]

The unprepared secular reader would assume that "You" mentioned in the first line is a lover, and that intoxication meant the kind induced by alcohol. Any longer exposure to the culture and history of Rumi's time, his own life, and that of other devotional mystics instantly recognize that "You" is God and that the "intoxication" is the love of God which, once experienced, is longed for in its absence and reveled in during its presence.

Here is another extract:

> The soul, by reason of the mingled fires, was wailing "Where shall I flee?"
> In the world of Divine Unity is no room for Number,
> But Number necessarily exists in the world of Five and Four.
> You may count a hundred thousand sweet apples in your hand:
> If you wish to make One, crush them all together.
> Behold, without regarding the letters, what is this language in the heart.
> Pureness of color is a quality derived from the Source of Action.
> Shamsi Tabriz is seated in royal state, and before him
> My rhymes are ranked like willing servants.[124]

These stanzas dwells less on love and more on the unitive, but still, the "language of the heart" is what Rumi speaks with and of. Note I have chosen two extracts that reference Shams. His name crops up again and again as the source of love, or the "sun" blazing with divine love. Perhaps

Rumi regarded himself as less than his master, or simply felt undying gratitude for the transformation wreaked upon him by Shams.

The love-mysticism context of the Shams-Rumi relationship makes this example less relevant to our discussion of hierophancy for the modern age than other types of spiritual context. I mourn that. I am no enemy of modernity, for reasons I explore in my novel *Mountain Calls*, but I can be clear-eyed about what the trade-offs entail and why I find myself lucky to be an anachronism, i.e. capable of living in the mindset of any era from the far future to pre-history. The loss of the devotional as a legitimate cultural expression is a Western modernist phenomenon and my personal leanings towards it is one reason I am sympathetic to Islam as a cultural location where it will possibly survive.

We should note in passing that the secular mind – even including some Iranian thinkers of today – assume that the relationship between Rumi and Shams is homosexual. I don't need to reprise the many thoughtful refutations of that hypothesis in the public domain other than to say I agree with them.

Gurdjieff / Ouspensky

It is hard for me to write briefly about Gurdjieff and the crucial relationship between him and his chief disciple P. D. Ouspensky. I have to enter a universe the major and minor landmarks of which I spent a decade exploring through its extensive literature, and dogged all the time with the vague feeling that I had *been there*, at the center Gurdjieff ran near Paris in the 1920s. If I have mixed feelings about the whole venture of hierophancy, then these must centre on this extraordinary man. While the re-reading of many landmark writings in my lifelong spiritual journey have left me mostly feeling inspired, elevated, and warmed of heart, the Gurdjieff literature, while doing those things, has also left me battered. A longer explanation of that and also a longer evaluation of Gurdjieff's system would have to be presented elsewhere. All I will do here is present the bones of the system and elaborate a little on the relationship between Gurdjieff and Ouspensky as an example of a promising pupil who was subjected to the harshest of treatment by a guru and who quit in despair and in order to become a hierophant in his own right.

First a few words about Gurdjieff's system. At first glance, and indeed even after considerable exposure to it, one is impressed at its breadth. It looks comprehensive indeed with its equal acknowledgement of three major paths in the spiritual life. Ouspensky learned them from Gurdjieff in this form:

1. The way of the fakir: physical discipline, power over the body.
2. The way of the monk: faith, religious feeling, religious sacrifice.
3. The way of the yogi: knowledge, development of mind.[125]

In his explanation of these three paths and how he envisaged the harmonious integration of them Gurdjieff shows himself to be deeply acquainted with spiritual traditions of both East and West and the different ways in which spiritual development takes place. I greatly sympathize with Gurdjieff when he speaks of European knowledge as having gained the ascendency over the development of the *being* of a person; he is bringing a largely Eastern perspective to the Western condition. He explains it in this passage:

> Take for instance the being of a mineral and of a plant. It is a different being. The being of a plant and of an animal is again a different being. The being of an animal and of a man is a different being. But the being of two people can differ from one another more than the being of a mineral and of an animal. This is exactly what people do not understand. And they do not understand that *knowledge* depends on *being*. Not only do they not understand this latter but they definitely do not wish to understand it. And especially in Western culture it is considered that a man may possess great knowledge, for example he may be an able scientist, make discoveries, advance science, and at the same time he may be, and has the right to be, a petty, egoistic, caviling, mean, envious, vain, naive, and absent-minded man. It seems to be considered here that a professor must always forget his umbrella everywhere.[126]

Like Socrates and Whitman, Gurdjieff has more respect for the practical disciplines than for the work of the philosophers. I have always felt the same: you cannot bullshit in wood, stone and metal. Like Gurdjieff I have always admired the crafts and have made many attempts to master the basics of them, conscious that the more I learn the more I have to respect the professionals in the field. When it comes to philosophers I am not so impressed I am afraid. Having read some of the works of Louis Pierre Althusser for example I am not surprised that his life was a complete mess and that his mental condition was so deranged in the end that he murdered his wife. The British philosopher Bertrand Russell was once described as a "brain on a stick," an unkind jibe that nonetheless usefully indicates an overdeveloped intellect. Gurdjieff had little time for Western philosophy or science and dismissed Darwin's evolutionary ideas in their totality. For him the term "evolution" was reserved exclusively for spiritual development of the *individual*; humanity as a whole was incapable of it.

So, I find a great deal to admire in Gurdjieff's system, but am wary of where it strays into the occult. He had learned his system in secret schools in the Middle East but the system it ultimately most reminds me of is that contained in the *Yoga Sutras* of Patanjali, a system of transcendence coupled with detailed occult practices. That system involves the refinement of the will. For Gurdjieff too, the spiritual development of man, or "evolution" as he calls it "is the evolution of his will, and 'will' cannot evolve spontaneously."[127] In other words the whole task of the aspirant is the development of the will, and the master is there to push the aspirant. That to me makes the apparent breadth of his system much narrower – it removes for example the possibility of grace or that the "way of the monk" – through devotion and sacrifice – may be adequate.

The emphasis on will made Gurdjieff a hard task-master, as the relationships between him and each of his pupils testify. We are lucky to have many accounts of this particular hierophancy, but here I focus on Ouspensky, a philosopher whose own work I place as only marginally more interesting than Althusser's. What initially drew him to Gurdjieff is clear in this passage:

> In the course of one of our talks I asked G.:
> "What, in your opinion, is the best preparation for the study of your method? For instance, is it useful to study what is called 'occult' or 'mystical' literature?"
> In saying this I had in mind more particularly the "Tarot" and the literature on the "Tarot."
> "Yes," said G. "A great deal can be found by reading. For instance, take yourself: you might already know a great deal if you *knew how to read*. I

mean that, if you *understood* everything you have read in your life, you would already know what you are looking for now. If you understood everything you have written in your own book, what is it called?"— he made something altogether impossible out of the words "Tertium Organum"— "I should come and bow down to you and beg you to teach me. But you *do not understand* either what you read or what you write. You do not even understand what the word 'understand' means. Yet understanding is essential, and reading can be useful only if you understand what you read. But, of course, no book can give real preparation. So it is impossible to say which is better. What a man knows *well*" (he emphasized the word "well")—"that is his preparation. If a man knows how to make coffee well or how to make boots well, then it is already possible to talk to him. The trouble is that nobody knows anything well. Everything is known just anyhow, superficially."[128]

This rather lengthy extract contains many interesting points. For a start it is clear that Ouspensky is interested in the occult, including Theosophy, and in particular the Tarot. I have to confess I have been allergic to the Tarot all my life and find it amusing that I should use the Tarot card known as "The Hierophant" as the basis for the cover illustration for this book. However I did have a friend who once insisted on reading the Tarot for me and deciphering the "life lines" on the palm of my hand. He was nonplussed: everything indicated I had no future. I have always agreed with that and perhaps that is why no form of divination or prophecy of the future, either for myself or for others, holds any interest for me. Gurdjieff makes a different response however: he says that reading even the occult can be useful if you know how to read but that the preparation for this is to know something – anything – well. He gives the example of making coffee or boots, and perhaps he would also include those that understand and use the Tarot well. I agree here, and think that Socrates was saying the same thing about "blacksmiths, cobblers and tanners," as recounted by Alcibiades. To take a *profound* interest in anything in the universe is to humble oneself in front of the entire universe. In that frame of mind one can learn anything. But Gurdjieff is hard on poor old Ouspensky. Gurdjieff tells him that not only has he not understood anything he has read, neither has he understood anything he *wrote* in his great book *Tertium Organum*. What's more he mocks him over the title, which one has to admit is grandiose. Ouspensky explains the title in a passage in his book on "The Higher Logic," which he claims to find in its most precise and complete formulation in Plotinus. He goes on to say: "I have called this system of higher logic *Tertium Organum* because for us it is the third canon—third instrument—of thought after those of Aristotle and Bacon. The first was *Organon*, the second, *Novum Organum*. But the third existed earlier than the first."[129]

When I look at photographs of the two men I see in Gurdjieff's eyes the deepest knowledge a human can have and in Ouspensky's eyes only the knowledge of an academic. Gurdjieff only has to look into Ouspensky's eyes to know that his book is gobbledygook. I love them both and the drama that played out between them as master and disciple is honestly and endearingly recounted by Ouspensky.

In another encounter we see again how little Gurdjieff thinks of Ouspensky's work and preoccupations. Ouspensky is in a bad mood and Gurdjieff decides to humor him on the issue of eternal recurrence, an idea mooted in ancient Greece, resurrected by Nietzsche and one of Ouspensky's major obsessions (the other being the fourth dimension). Having given the philosopher some crumbs of encouragement over this, Gurdjieff comments, smiling:

> You see how easy it is to *turn* you; but perhaps I was merely *romancing* to you, perhaps there is no recurrence at all. What pleasure is it when a sulky Ouspensky sits there, does not eat, does not drink. "Let us try to cheer him up," I think to myself. And how is one to cheer a person up? One likes funny stories. For another you must find his hobby. And I know that Ouspensky has this hobby—"eternal recurrence." So I offered to answer any question of his. I knew what he would ask.[130]

Is this not deeply insulting to the philosopher? Yet Ouspensky records that his mood was indeed lifted and that he took no offence. One also sees much of Gurdjieff's humor here and perhaps also the love he feels for his pupil, or otherwise why bother to cheer him up? Ouspensky could not take this kind of treatment for long however, as he was an accomplished author and public speaker with a large following, and whatever Gurdjieff said about *Tertium Organum*, it remained a best-seller.

The relationship eventually broke down as it did for many other pupils bewildered by Gurdjieff's bizarre behavior and baffling system. To give just two examples, Ouspensky was summoned from far away, arriving through enormous personal sacrifice, only to be told to go away again, while another pupil, A. R. Orage, was told to dig a trench only to be made to fill it in again.[131] As mentioned earlier Orage was the editor of the prestigious literary journal *The New Age*; in the same vein Rajneesh would boast that he had PhDs cleaning the toilets in his ashram. Gurdjieff was continuously testing his pupils while at the same time providing a spiritual environment that meant everything to them. Towards the end of Gurdjieff's experiment in religious community at Le Prieuré, known as the Institute for the Harmonious Development of Man, scandals emerged of suicides, not to mention the death of the writer Katherine Mansfield.

The contradictions surrounding Gurdjieff are perhaps those of all hierophants but presented in the starkest contrast. For every catastrophically disillusioned pupil of his you can find one whose loyalty was lifelong. For every negative aspect of one's love for this man one can find a positive. Ultimately however unless one can look into those eyes and say as Whitman does of the great spiritual teachers of this world "we few equals" Gurdjieff remains one of the most disturbing challenges to one's worldview. Personally I don't believe in evading that challenge.

Ramana Maharshi / Paul Brunton

Paul Brunton was the pen name of Raphael Hurst (1898-1981), an early British enthusiast for Indian spirituality and co-founder of the Atlantis Bookshop in Bloomsbury. Like Ouspensky, Brunton was originally a Theosophist but an encounter with an Indian guru in the 1930s rather changed his outlook. That guru was Ramana Maharshi (1879-1950) who is important to our exploration of hierophancy in various ways; as mentioned earlier he is the teacher of the teacher of Andrew Cohen.

Brunton introduced Maharshi to the West in his best-selling book *A Search in Secret India*. Just as Ouspensky set out to find certain "mysteries" in the subcontinent with little success, Brunton hunted down reports of miracles performed by fakirs, encountering plenty of fraud along the way. In one example a yogi called Vishudhananda is able to conjure the scent of specific flowers onto Brunton's silk handkerchief and bring a dead bird to life, both feats inexplicable to the scientifically-minded Brunton.[132] Having encountered such things without understanding them or being much edified Brunton was left with enduring respect for only two of the gurus he encountered, Ramana Maharshi and Shri Shankara Acharya of Kanchi, the then spiritual leader of South India.

When he asks Shri Shankara to be his personal tutor the reply is that his public office gives him no free time, but that he should approach "the Maharishee" (Brunton's spelling).[133] Brunton has a berth booked for his departure from India, but on being pressed by the Acharya to stay agrees to visit Ramana Maharshi. His resolve is strengthened by seeing the Acharya again in a vision and so becomes Maharshi's student for a period.

Brunton's account of his first meeting with Maharshi is memorable. At first there is no response from the master to the presence of the European – perhaps the first – amongst his devotees assembled for *darshan*. Brunton wonders if the stillness and silence is a pose; he is brimming with questions he has prepared during his journey – much as Ouspensky has questions for Gurdjieff – but has no opportunity to ask them:

> The next thought which occupies my mind, "Is this state of mystical contemplation nothing more than meaningless vacancy?" has a longer sway but I let it go for the simple reason that I cannot answer it.
> There is something in this man which holds my attention as steel filings are held by a magnet. I cannot turn my gaze away from him. My initial bewilderment, my perplexity at being totally ignored, slowly fade away as this strange fascination begins to grip me more firmly. But it is not till the second hour of the uncommon scene that I become aware of a silent, resistless change which is taking place within my mind. One by one, the questions which I have prepared in the train with such meticulous accuracy drop away. For it does not now seem to matter whether they are asked or not, and it does not seem to matter whether I solve the problems which have hitherto troubled me. I know only that a steady river of quietness seems to be flowing near me, that a great peace is penetrating the inner reaches of my being, and that my thought-tortured brain is beginning to arrive at some rest.[134]

When Brunton is finally granted the opportunity to put questions to Maharshi he cannot. It is only on a later visit that he asks: "The wise men of the West, our scientists, are greatly honored for their cleverness. Yet they have confessed that they can throw but little light upon the hidden truth behind life. It is said that there are some in your land who can give what our Western sages fail to reveal. Is this so? Can you assist me to experience enlightenment? Or is the search itself a mere delusion?" Maharshi sits for ten minutes in silence before replying: "You say I. '*I* want to know.' Tell me, who is that I?"[135] Brunton does not understand at all, asking a little later, "how long it will take to get some enlightenment with a master's help?" Maharshi replies: "It all depends on the maturity of the seeker's mind. The gunpowder catches fire in an instant, while much time is needed to set fire to the coal."

I like this answer. Clearly Rumi was like gunpowder, igniting in an instant under the contact with Shams, his teacher. Other pupils are like coal, as Maharshi says, or perhaps more like waterlogged timber. Brunton does not know what to make of the answer and goes on with further questions about the world, living, as he saw it, in critical times. (Don't we always, in all periods, think we live in critical times?) With respect to the world, Maharshi has only one thing to say: "As you are, so is the world." Unless Brunton understands himself, knows himself, all that he thinks about the world is mistaken.

Later Brunton has another dream, this time sitting in *darshan* in front of Maharshi. Brunton is small, like a child of five, and Maharshi is a great towering figure leading him up a mountain. They pass yogis of varying kinds, which they ignore. At the peak Brunton looks up at Maharshi's face:

> I become aware of a mysterious change taking place with great rapidity in my heart and mind. The old motives which have lured me on begin to desert me. The urgent desires which have sent my feet hither and thither vanish with incredible swiftness. The dislikes, misunderstandings, coldnesses and selfishness which have marked my dealings with many of my fellows collapse into the abyss of nothingness. An untellable peace falls upon me and I know now that there is nothing further that I shall ask from life.[136]

In the dream Maharshi then directs Brunton to look downwards; he sees the Western hemisphere crowded with millions of people, and Maharshi tells him that when he goes back there he will be filled with the peace

6. Instructive Negotiations

he now has, as long as he retains the understanding that he is not his body or his brain.

Maharshi remains an utter mystery to Brunton however; nothing that he knows or has learned in the West gives him any purchase on what he is experiencing. Brunton stays on, conscious that he cannot "get to grips with the man." Before he has to leave Maharshi tells him that he can make time to meditate and there is no need to give up ordinary life as Brunton insists is the teachings of the yogis. Brunton objects that if he engages with the normal work that is at the center of Western life there will be little time to meditate:

> The Maharishee seems quite unperturbed at my poser.
> "Setting apart time for meditation is only for the merest spiritual novices," he replies. "A man who is advancing will begin to enjoy the deeper beatitude, whether he is at work or not. While his hands are in society, he keeps his head cool in solitude."
> "Then you do not teach the way of Yoga?"
> "The Yogi tries to drive his mind to the goal, as a cowherd drives a bull with a stick, but on this path the seeker coaxes the bull by holding out a handful of grass!"[137]

I think this answer is most significant. It distinguishes between two approaches to the spiritual life, one of driven discipline and the other of gentle coaxing. In our examples to date it seems to me that Socrates, Shams and Maharshi believe in gentle coaxing, while Marpa and Gurdjieff believe in the stick. Maharshi adds that man's real nature is happiness; it's inborn in a man, so the search for happiness is an "an unconscious search for his true self" which is imperishable. It is just that the search is usually in the wrong place; this applies even to those we consider evil.

Maharshi's only discipline is to ask "who am I?" but the fact remains that the happiness attainable through this method – the same as Whitman's solid prizes – requires for most people a lengthy practice. We are mostly coal, if not damp logs, while the gunpowder types may even go off with a bang without any hierophant. I put Whitman in the latter category, along with Maharshi, and, as we shall see, Mother Meera. It is worth knowing that Maharshi underwent a spontaneous enlightenment at an early age which left him incapable of ordinary life to the point that he nearly died. He was rescued by priests at temple and recognized as a holy man; he then moved to his spot on the sacred mountain Arunachala and never left it. His experience was totally without system, meaning that, despite his culture, he had no direct exposure to any of the scriptures which would have offered him guidance or explanation. It was only when he was established as a guru that pupils came to him with such texts, which he discovered with interest and could confirm from his own experience. As a result Maharshi is associated with the Advaita system within Hindu thought – which most closely resembles his teachings – but is not a product of it. Through one of his pupils, H. W. L. Poonja – also known as Poonjaji – the Advaita system became popularized in the West as the neo-Advaita, a system much criticized by Andrew Cohen, despite being a pupil of Poonjaji.

Radha Mohan Lal / Irina Tweedie

If Shams, an Iranian Sufi, found a ready pupil in Rumi and effected the complete transformation of him in a short period, the example of Radha Mohan Lal, an Indian Sufi, and his western pupil Irina Tweedie, is agonizingly slow. Irina Tweedie (1907-1999) eventually became a teacher of the Naqshbandiyya-Mujaddidiya order and is known for her spiritual autobiography "Daughter of Fire" in which she details her period as a pupil of Bhai Sahib – "Elder Brother" – as her teacher was more familiarly known. Some claim that Tweedie's account, published in the 1980s, is the first detailed diary of a relationship with an Eastern teacher, but I would say that the *Ramakrishna Gospel* first published in 1942 and dealing with events a hundred years prior is a pretty detailed account of the Eastern master-disciple relationship. What Tweedie's account offers is more focused however and painfully honest of the gulf of incomprehension that her teacher had to bridge, a gulf that did not exist in the same way between Ramakrishna and his Indian pupils.

The cover of Tweedie's famous books shows a woman with intense blue eyes and rather forbidding features. While other photos show her softer side I think it fair to say that both she and her master had some "granite" in their souls as she observes of Bhai Sahib at one point. By this I mean the seriousness belonging to the spiritual path of the *will*, as in the systems of Patanjali and Gurdjieff. And here is the interesting thing about

6. Instructive Negotiations

the system of Bhai Sahib: it is a comingling of the Sufi path of the heart, or *bhakti*, with the yoga system of the head or *jnani* (in my adapted terminology). Just as in art, architecture and music, where no style on earth has not at some time fruitfully comingled with another, so in spirituality all combinations exist or are potentially there for fruitful exploration (even the largely antithetical traditions of Buddhism and Islam have a confluence in Subud, for example).

While the Sufi tradition as found in an exemplar like Rumi is about the love of God, a passionate, all-consuming love which conjures up the language of lovers and intoxication, of desperate periods of separation and longing, of union and reunion, of deeper and more permanent states of spiritual love – exactly the language that Don Cupitt found so incomprehensible – Bhai Sahib's yoga amalgam is also an *occultism*. This means that spiritual "powers" come into play along with deadly seriousness over their cultivation and uses, as detailed in great length in the later parts of the *Yoga Sutras* of Patanjali.

Personally, I am clear on this. Occult powers are not the "solid prizes of the universe" that Whitman speaks of. In the Indian system they are known as *siddhis* and are spoken out against by all the teachers I admire, including Ramana Maharshi. But Irina Tweedie arrived at the house of Bhai Sahib already a committed occultist in the school of Theosophy, an esoteric organization of wide reach in the early part of the twentieth century. Bhai Sahib agrees that they have known each other in previous lives in Tibet, the spiritual origin of much Theosophist occultism. All this is important to the perspective I am developing here on hierophancy because the very term "hierophant" is used more often within an occultist context. The master-disciple relationship in any occult tradition is, I would suggest, loaded with an extra dimension of risk down to the nature of the *siddhis* and the specific form of spiritual materialism that both teacher and pupil can fall into, though rather different to what Trungpa was warning of.

At the outset Tweedie tells us this about her spiritual diary:

> The first draft of the manuscript was begun in September 1971, in Tongue, Sutherland, Scotland, nearly ten years after having met my Revered Teacher. I could not face it before, could not even look at the entries. It was like a panic; I dreaded it. Too much suffering is involved in it;

it is written in the blood of my heart. A slow grinding down of the personality is a painful process.[138]

Suffering? A slow grinding down of the personality? Painful? Does the spiritual aspirant *have* to experience this? Tweedie has doubts of course, and these resurface many times, but as a spiritual seeker she knows what she is doing and accepts all the negatives because the positives are huge. For one, just to participate in the community around this Sufi saint would be a tremendous experience, but of course the real point was the direct teaching of Bhai Sahib. And then there is his system: he is clear that while he does the spiritual work that the seeker is incapable of, all kinds of suffering will ensue. In particular she will have to "burn" her karmic residues. Part of the process, as in Theosophy, is the submission, not just to him as an embodied teacher but also to disembodied masters, as in the training of Krishnamurti. Bhai Sahib told Tweedie: "The master must be strict, he has to be hard, because he wants the disciple to reach the high state. Absolute faith and obedience are essential; without that progress is impossible."[139]

At times it seems like Bhai Sahib is a Tantric or crazy wisdom teacher, as when he demands to know which she would choose if there were only four doors to God: one of gambling, one of drink, one of theft and one of sex. He insists that she answer this in front of a mixed audience, so she hesitantly deliberates on the first three and on pausing is not let off a reminder of the fourth. For a series of nights after that she has terrible dreams and nightmares of obscene couplings that plague her body with exhaustion and her mind with depression. It was a torture that she thought would never end, understood as a kind of spiritual power that possessed her. Slowly it subsided.[140]

The training is a progression in *love* however, a journey of the metaphysical heart which Tweedie finds hard to start with. What I find unusual in a *bhakti* or love tradition is the emphasis on *siddhis* or paranormal powers. For example Bhai Sahib claims that when young he asked an adept for the power to travel instantly from one place to another, as he had seen this adept do. He used it to surprise his father who was angry and admonished him: "Are you not ashamed of yourself? Are you after Truth or after childish play? I should never see such things again."[141] At another time he was offered the power to cure snakebites, but he rejected it saying that any *fakir* could do that; he was destined for more important powers.

In terms of locating Bhai Sahib's system I think this statement by him is significant – actually a song from his tradition:

> The world is full of beautiful things until an old man with a beard came into my life and set my heart aflame with longing and made it pregnant with Love. How can I look at the loveliness around me, how can I see it, if it hides the Face of my Lover?[142]

The "old man with a beard" would be any charismatic spiritual teacher like Shams-e Tabrizi, and the sentiment eminently recognizable from the Christian devotional mystics such as Teresa of Avila. To know God, in this system, one has to deny his creation. My question to this tradition is: why should the world – however we understand its "loveliness" – hide the Face of the Lover rather than reveal it? For it is the latter view that I ascribe to Whitman and which I believe more relevant to the spiritual life of the twenty-first century. Having said that it is interesting to note that Bhai Sahib was teaching in the middle of the twentieth century and was well aware that social change already meant that he had to interpret his system for the modern world and change some features of it.

A theme that runs through the early part of Tweedie's book is what happens to the disciple's mind in the state known as *dhyana*. This term usually means contemplation or meditation but in Bhai Sahib's yoga-oriented Sufism it has a unique character, and seems to be conflated by Tweedie – and at times by Bhai Sahib – with unconsciousness. Tweedie has a companion who is a Sorbonne-trained linguist and philosopher called "L." She raises a point about thinking, as Tweedie reports:

> A conversation began in the course of which L. was saying that the disciples of Socrates bitterly complained that they were at a disadvantage: that it is not fair to them that in his presence their mind does not work and they cannot discuss properly, as it is expected from them. Just like me, I thought.[143]

Tweedie is concerned that the master will deprive her of the capacity of thought. This is a serious issue in this type of hierophancy; at the same time it is of great interest that this conversation about Socrates in front of Bhai Sahib makes the assumption – as I do – that Socrates is a spiritual teacher and that his pupils are experiencing something of *dhyana*, a gift from the master. L. later says of this to Tweedie, "It is very bad for a philosopher not to be able to think!" They laugh at the idea that philosophers normally have to work hard to think, where now they are working hard not to. Tweedie gradually finds it harder to think about anything other than her master and immediate surroundings, but the point of *dhyana* is clear to her, as Bhai Sahib explains it:

> In our Yoga System the ultimate result is achieved in one life by Dhyana. Only one Chakra is awakened: the Heart Chakra. It is the only Yoga School, in existence, in which LOVE IS CREATED by the spiritual Teacher. It is done with Yogic Power. The result is, that the whole work of awakening, of quickening is done by one Chakra, which gradually opens up all the others.[144]

I think this is perhaps the best short summary of Bhai Sahib's system. The quieting of the mind has the purpose of letting the metaphysical heart grow as the person's center of gravity. At the same time this quieting cannot be a mere indulgence, for he says: "The time comes for some people, not for all, when the state of Dhyana becomes so sweet that they are inclined to spend too much time doing it. We are in physical bodies; we are not intended to pass our life in the unconscious state!" We note that this approach differs from the Buddha's in many ways, for example the Buddha always placed emphasis on the pupil having to do the work, and nothing is said about love at all, or *siddhis*, or chakras (according to the Buddha as represented in the Pali Canon that is).

Tweedie is resigned to the loss of mental function that accompanies the state of *dhyana*, and even jests about it when she is preparing to leave for a while. She asks Bhai Sahib if her brain will remain numb and inefficient as this may cause problems on the journey, to which he replies that he will note the dates down in his diary. She asks him: "Do you mean to say that you will note down in your diary when you have to give me back my wits?" She laughs at the idea but the guru just nods.[145]

I have only read a fifth of Tweedie's diary, but believe that my points are generally valid as I know of similar systems in some detail. That said, even the first fifth is a treasure-house of insight and I would guess that any full

6. Instructive Negotiations

reading would yield many more unexpected treasures, of especial value to those attracted to this path. I'll finish our visit to Tweedie and Bhai Sahib with one of Tweedie's assessments:

> Every Guru has only a very few "Seed-ideas" which represent the fundamental note or chord of his teaching. Only those ideas which he has absorbed lead him to Realization. He cannot give more. He will constantly manipulate those ideas which took him to the Truth, through his personal effort, and which represents a living Truth for him.[146]

I think one could say the same about most musicians, architects, or painters. Most make one fundamental creative discovery and mine it for the rest of their career; religion is no different; the Buddha is a good example. In the case of Bhai Sahib we have the confluence of two seed ideas, the first being the path of the devotional, and the second being broadly the occult. In the case of Ramakrishna, the guru is revealed to us in the lengthy diary kept by his disciple Mahendranath Gupta – or just "M" – in an intense setting similar to Bhai Sahib's. The seed idea of Ramakrishna is single (even though he explored other paths with interest) and very simple: it is devotion. His path of love resembles that of Bhai Sahib's at times, but is quite innocent of *siddhis* or any harsh discipline. Ramakrishna "samadhis" – where he becomes unconscious and has to be supported by a disciple with arms aloft and hands in ecstatic mudra form – cannot be something so different to the *dhyana* of Bhai Sahib, nor, I am convinced, so different to what overcame Socrates so often and which the citizens of Athens would even take their bedding out onto the streets to observe. But the character of Bhai Sahib's hierophancy is much removed from Ramakrishna's and a world apart from Socrates'. Bhai Sahib's path is that of the disciplinarian. The advantage for the aspirant is that this creates a clear progression in the spiritual life; the disadvantage lies in the huge potential for abuse. In this particular case both parties seem to have negotiated that successfully. While the whole context is potentially "discipleship heavy" I think that its Indian location was sufficient to provide the checks and balances necessary for good hierophancy.

Krishnamurti / Bohm and U.G.

Radha Mohan Lal was clear that the modern world required change in the way that his Sufi tradition operated. After his break with the Order of the Star, Krishnamurti was in uncharted waters but it is clear that his methods of teaching were both a reaction against the occultism of the Theosophical Society (and its methods of initiation) and a response to the modern impetus towards equality. Seekers may have sat in rows in front of him and also gained private audiences – the diaries of which are some of Krishnamurti's most revealing prose – but he was determined that nothing of the hierarchical nature of the hierophantic situation should remain. This lead to his strangely anti-guru stance and the even stranger anti-guru guru, his namesake, U. G. Krishnamurti. (We distinguish them from now on by referring to the former as "Krishnamurti" or "Jiddu" and the latter as "U. G.")

The case of Krishnamurti's dialogues with the eminent physicist David Bohm are instructive here, if not at times hilarious. Bohm and Krishnamurti had a relationship starting in 1961 that lasted twenty-five years and according to some ended in breakdown. The scientist David Peat thought that a major crisis overtook Bohm in relation to Krishnamurti in 1984, possibly because Krishnamurti began to challenge Bohm's various dependencies, particularly on him. Peat also records that Bohm was disappointed to discover that Krishnamurti apparently had an affair with the wife of his closest aide. Their lengthy dialogues form a monument to misunderstanding one could say, though only a flavor of them can be given here in some brief extracts. Krishnamurti was always critical of gurus who taught the stilling of the mind through meditation techniques such as the recitation of a mantra, insisting instead that what mattered was to become the onlooker to all arising phenomena, including thought. In this his teachings are like the Buddha's, and in the respect of a detachment that could seem almost cruel at times he also resembled that teacher.

In the middle of one particular discussion on the stilling of the mind Bohm and Krishnamurti have agreed on the distinction between thinking and "looking," the latter being this detached observation. Bohm comments:

> That is always the trouble. Everybody gets into this trouble: that he seems to be looking at everything, at his problems, saying, "Those are my prob-

lems, I am looking." But that looking is only thinking, but it is confused with looking. This is one of the confusions that arises. If you say, don't think but look, that person feels he is already looking.[147]

The problem with this statement is that it comes from the pupil, not the teacher. Krishnamurti's anti-guru stance places him in a bind, because if he thought Bohm had truly understood what he had just said and lived his life out of this insight, then Bohm would now be a master in his own right. But the conversation continues in an entirely inverted fashion:

> KRISHNAMURTI: Quite. So you see, this question has arisen and they say, "All right, then I must control thought, I must subjugate thought and I must make my mind quiet so that it becomes whole, then I can see the parts, all the fragments, then I'll touch the source." But it is still the operation of thought all the time.
>
> BOHM: Yes, that means the operation of thought is unconscious for the most part and therefore one doesn't know it is going on. We may say consciously we have realized that all this has to be changed, it has to be different.
>
> KRISHNAMURTI: But it is still going on unconsciously. So can you talk to my unconscious, knowing my conscious brain is going to resist you? Because you are telling me something which is revolutionary, you are telling me something which shatters my whole house which I have built so carefully, and I won't listen to you — you follow? In my instinctive reactions I push you away. So you realize that and say, "Look, all right, talk to your unconscious. I am going to talk to your unconscious and make that unconscious see that whatever movement it does is still within the field of time and so on." So your conscious mind is never in operation. When it operates it must inevitably either resist, or say, "I will accept"; therefore it creates a conflict in itself. So can you talk to my unconscious?
>
> BOHM: You can always ask how.
>
> KRISHNAMURTI: No, no. You can say to a friend, "Don't resist, don't think about it, but I am going to talk to you." "We two are communicating with each other without the conscious mind listening."
>
> BOHM: Yes.

Bohm is reduced to saying "yes," and in twenty-five years of such conversations he is hectored by Krishnamurti in this inverted style with little result. The problem for both here is that the assumption of symmetry is bogus. Bohm was a world-class physicist and Krishnamurti a world-class spiritual teacher, but as neither openly accepted their relationship as a hierophancy – as for example in the clear-cut discipleship between Irina Tweedie and Radha Mohan Lal – the relationship foundered in the end. There is however a considerable constituency which believes in the symmetry between the two because Bohm's scientific investigations appear to have something mystical in them, and his popular science writings – I would guess – probably outsold Krishnamurti's publications, just as Ouspensky's works probably outsold Gurdjieff's. I made my home in this popular science constituency for many years in my involvement with an organization called the Scientific and Medical Network, the British equivalent to the Institute of Noetic Sciences in America. David Peat[148] was an important member of it and his book on David Bohm seems quite determined to make Bohm the superior mind and Krishnamurti a wayward guru who subjected Bohm to harsh public discipline:

> [T]he physicist was thrown into despair. Unable to sleep, obsessed with thoughts, he constantly paced the room to the point where he thought of suicide. At one point he believed that he could feel the neurotransmitters firing in his brain. ... His despair soon reached the point where he was placed on antidepressants. ...
>
> He once wrote to [Fritz Wilhelm] that he thought that his chest pains were a result of Krishnamurti misbehaving towards him. "This problem with K is literally crushing me."

I think Bohm's problem is essentially a New Age issue. The "physics-proves-mysticism" strand of the New Age gives scientists both an excuse to talk about spirituality and their audiences the assumption that here is something genuinely new and spiritually liberating. The physicist Paul Davies once wrote that "science offers a surer path to God than religion,"[149] which I take to be a serious but entirely misguided declaration. However, the audience it appeals to is not restricted to the New Age but includes a wide range of people who need something resembling religion in their lives but believe that for them the door of religion has been slammed shut by the superior rationality emerging from the Enlightenment period.

Despite enormous regret over what the Germans call "entzauberung" – or the disenchantment of religion (as an inevitable outcome of Enlightenment advances in thought) – this group nevertheless retain a profound belief in progress. For them Bohm represents both that progress and the simultaneous re-enchantment they are looking for, while Krishnamurti represents little more than the very superstition that the Enlightenment thinkers like Voltaire set out to eradicate. If Bohm was buoyed up by a following keen to make him their guru, then his dialogues with Krishnamurti must have been nothing less than a continual humiliation for him. The rebuff was perhaps like the dismissal of Ouspensky's great philosophical works by Gurdjieff. I am also reminded of the description of Socrates by Alcibiades when the younger man describes the older man as pretending to be in love with his pupils when it was Socrates in fact that was the beloved; it was a ploy.

The relationship between U. G. and Krishnamurti seems to have foundered for entirely different reasons, though perhaps ultimately with a happier outcome. U. G. was brought up by his grandmother under whose influence he joined the Theosophical Society, placing him alongside Irene Tweedie in terms of his spiritual background. From the age of fourteen he sought enlightenment or *moksha*, though questioning all the time the validity of the term or at least its explanation by leading gurus. As Wikipedia records:

> In 1939, at age 21, [U. G.] Krishnamurti met with renowned spiritual teacher Ramana Maharshi. [U. G.] Krishnamurti related that he asked Ramana, "This thing called *moksha*, can you give it to me?" – to which Ramana Maharshi purportedly replied, "I can give it, but can you take it?" This answer completely altered [U. G.] Krishnamurti's perceptions of the "spiritual path" and its practitioners, and he never again sought the counsel of "those religious people." Later, [U. G.] Krishnamurti would say that Maharshi's answer – which he perceived as "arrogant" – put him "back on track."[150]

I find this interesting: what would one expect the answer to be? If one asks the guru, can you give me enlightenment, would one not expect the kind of answer Ramana Maharshi gave? How is that arrogance? We saw that Brunton asked something similar and was provided with the metaphor of gunpowder and coal; the same answer in different form. What should be clear however is that Jiddu Krishnamurti would probably have answered differently, conscious that Maharshi's reply instantly sets up a hierarchy, one which Jiddu rejected and which appears to have angered U. G. The latter met Jiddu through his work for the Theosophical Society and entered into a dialogue with him in 1953 which ended after seven years with much the same reaction as U. G. had to Maharshi, or Bohm to Krishnamurti. However U. G.'s life later rather bizarrely took him into Jiddu's orbit again both in London and Switzerland. Finally, in what he describes as his "calamity" he underwent an enlightenment experience in reaction to Jiddu's teachings that was amongst other things profoundly physical. After that he remained in what he describes as the "natural state" of enlightenment and began teaching it as one of the most vociferous of anti-guru gurus to date, his main point being that he had stumbled into enlightenment *in spite of* gurus like Maharshi and Jiddu Krishnamurti, not because of them (I have some sympathy to that view of course). However videos of U. G. teaching his disciples suggest a perfectly classical hierophancy to me, reminiscent perhaps of those couples who are vehemently against marriage but in practice follow all its structures.

The examples of Bohm and U. G. cannot possibly add up to a comprehensive account of Jiddu Krishnamurti's hierophancy or its legacy. There does not appear to be a successor to him; we cannot identify any pupil who could take on the mantle of the master, as we have in the case of Rumi and Shams, Ouspensky and Gurdjieff, and Irene Tweedie and Radha Mohan Lal. Instead, I would say that Krishnamurti touched on thousands of lives, including my own. He was never my guru in the sense of any private exchanges with him – that was reserved for Douglas Harding – but the few lectures I attended and above all his writings had a powerful effect on me. I *got it* – almost instantly – that any meditation technique aimed at stilling the mind would be hopeless other than serving perhaps a therapeutic function when stressed (Rajneesh had anyway prepared me for that). I *got it* that the guru cannot do the work for you, whatever Radha Mohan Lal may have told Irene Tweedie to the contrary. And above all, and this was Krishnamurti's most enduring gift to me, I got it that Nature was a site of intense spiritual experience and insight. As with all the many spiritual teachers I have encountered I have of course "filtered" out, as Whitman says, those elements of Krishnamurti's system that I do not find true to me. At the same time I am not the least concerned with his private life. If he slept with his personal assistant's wife that is a matter for the three of them; not now to my taste perhaps, but it is none of my business (for have I not done similar when young?).

Good Lance / Crow Dog

The reader may have detected by now a certain antipathy to a sub-domain of the spiritual life I call the "occult." For example, I don't believe that I have written that enthusiastically about the Theosophical Society, an organization that impinges on my account of Irene Tweedie and the two Krishnamurtis. However I am less dogmatic about this now than before, and it is a lengthy reading of the literature on the Native American religions that has changed my view. If we call the religions of indigenous peoples either shamanic or animistic, then it has long been clear to me that the occult traditions of the world – such as the Kabbalah, Theosophy or Anthroposophy – grew directly out of them. All these systems have one thing in common: a spirit world of non-physical beings and energies. (Yes, I am trained in and believe in modern physics and its implacably precise definition of physical "energy," and yes, I also experience and believe in an indefinable spiritual non-physical "energy." It's not my fault we have the same word for both.) When it comes to shamanism or animism I am fully signed up to the worldviews, practices and goals of those traditions. However I believe that in the early city-states of both East and West animism and shamanism mutated into the more learned but less experiential occultisms of astrology and alchemy and became the precursors of traditions like the Kabbalah, the many streams of the Western esoteric tradition, and the systems of spiritual teachers as far apart as Rudolf Steiner and Paramahansa Yogananda. I find myself less sympathetic to these later developments than the shamanic ground from which they sprang. For example Irene Tweedie's interest in occult powers firstly amongst the Theosophists and then in the Sufi tradition strike me as taking a direction that is at the least tangential to the quest for enlightenment, if not inimical to it. For me the occult tradition lost its grounding in Nature when it became the preoccupation of city dwellers – Ouspensky being a good example with his obsessions over the Tarot, eternal recurrence and the fourth dimension. He did not, as in the case of the artist Kandinsky, explore the roots of all this in the animist peoples of Russia at the time, such as the Tungus.

This makes the discipleship of Leonard Crow Dog (born 1942), a Lakota medicine man, to his teacher Horn Chips, of particular interest. Horn Chips was a famous medicine man or spiritual teacher in his time. If some Westerners sought out Tantric Eastern teachers in the hope of more sex, some Westerners have also sought out indigenous shamanic teachers in the hope of more drugs (for example peyote or ayahuasca), all legitimized by an aura of spirituality. While there are clearly genuine initiations of Westerners by Native Americans our example here is of native-native initiation, though during a period where the recording of such initiations was largely written either by Western-educated Native Americans or in conjunction with sympathetic Westerners. Prior to this period nothing was written and afterwards too much of the tradition was lost. In this case the book "Crow Dog: Four Generations of Sioux Medicine Men" was co-written by Crow Dog and Richard Erdoes (1912-2008), the latter having been a keen student of Native American culture and part of the American Indian Movement later notorious for armed resistance to the American state.

Crow Dog says that during certain ceremonies he can remember his birth: "When I was born I experienced earth joy, universe joy, happiness of the world. I could feel air filling my lungs, on August 18, 1942. I was born spiritually. With the gourd. The medicine man Horn Chips was shaking it."[151] Leonard Crow Dog later felt that the Great Spirit picked him out from other boys to be a "spiritual man;" he was taught initially by his father and four medicine men from the age of seven onwards, and became a medicine man in his own right at the age of thirteen, often under the guidance of a teacher known as Good Lance. From that time he experienced the "vision quest," periods of isolation, visions and spiritual learning, which I understand to be a familiar pattern amongst indigenous peoples. Elders, medicine men, shamans, or just those with the right feel for it, are aware of a child with spiritual gifts and foster them, often removing the child from the developmental stages that other children undergo. The *tulku* system in Tibet is just one rather specialized form of this early training, though belonging to a society only half-shamanic, the other half being the determinedly non-shamanic religion of the Buddha.

Crow Dog was born into a tradition that was facing annihilation from the white man, just as Tibetan Buddhism was from the Chinese. The Dalai Lama accepted from a young age that he was a *tulku*, a reincarnation of a previous lama, and found no reason to struggle against it as Chögyam Trungpa did. Similarly Crow Dog had no reason to reject his calling or his training, some of which was at the hands of disembodied teachers he names as Sitting Rock and Flying Eagle. Krishnamurti on the other hand, also initiated into an esoteric system and under the tutelage of disembodied masters, rejected the whole thing as we saw.

I don't have details of Crow Dog's training at the hands of Good Lance and other medicine men who taught him the sacred rituals, but what I do have is a composite picture of the training of shamans and medicine men across many indigenous cultures. What matters here is that the pupil is correctly divined as having the gift and that appropriate teachers are available. The spiritual system they are initiated into would have had complete cultural sanction from the tribe or larger grouping and would have been understood for a *very* long time – possibly millennia – with all the continuity that implies. It is only when modern religions such as Christianity, modern technological societies, and the globalization of spiritual knowledge emerged that these ancient forms of locally-legitimized hierophancy were lost to a market-place of competing spiritualities. I would suggest therefore that the potential for mismatch between pupil and teacher within all contemporary spiritual systems is now far higher.

What I learned from the Native American medicine men is that the occult part of their spiritual work – mainly divination and healing – segues effortlessly into the transcendent vision of spiritual development leading to what we call enlightenment. If we take Buddhism as a typical path of transcendent enlightenment, then everywhere it spread in the Far East it made accommodation with shamanism. In Tibet that accommodation was with the Bon shamanic religion (though admittedly after initial hostilities); in Japan that accommodation was made between Zen and Shinto (and admittedly tensions flare occasionally between them); and in Mongolia the nomadic herdsmen lived a life equally spread between these two religious forms. As we saw the Sufi path of Radha Mohan Lal also appears to blend comparable elements. It is not so much that paths like the Kabbalah, Theosophy, Anthroposophy and equivalent traditions native to the East are not valid spiritual systems but that the emphasis on "powers" can create additional problems for hierophancy. Enlightenment is a teaching of liberation, but the development of occult powers engenders skills no different in principal to the material skills of everyday life; some are in the service of others and some only in the service of self. I don't see how any kind of skill set is of any direct help in the search for the truth of liberation. On the other hand the possession of these skills does not *necessarily* contradict enlightenment either.

What I feel with some of the Native American medicine men is that their skill set – devoted entirely to healing – is not the point at all but rather that they often speak the language of liberation as Ramana Maharshi does, only with a different cultural inflection and with a more *via positiva* emphasis. To know the spirit world is to know more about the material world, as these two are irrevocably intertwined, and to know spirit beings is to know that they are in search of liberation just as much as embodied ones. It is clear that the Buddha was aware of spirit beings but agreed with Shankara that one had to become humanly embodied to find liberation. Now, I don't know if that is always true, or why it should be true; I just have a hunch that Shankara and the Buddha are right.

I can't recall any reference by Ramana Maharshi to disembodied beings but he did warn aspirants away from the *siddhis*. When his disciples asked him about attaining such powers – which are quite possibly the same as possessed by various medicine men – he said: "To abide firm in the Reality which is eternal is the true *siddhi*. Other attainments are all such as are possessed in dreams."[152] Given that the goal of enlightenment is to puncture all dreams it is clear to me that the *siddhis*, unless constrained by strict cultural boundaries, potentially offer the aspirant more dreaming not less. In an age of individualism too often predicated on dubious extensions of personal agency through fantasy of all types it is inevitable that many aspirants clutch at the offered "powers" as the spiritual remedy for their otherwise foundering self-esteem. What the examples of medicine men like Crow Dog show us however is that where the cultural framework remains intact for it, the development of "powers" of divination and healing become service to the community – of animals as much as people – instead of a bolster to individualism. Hierophancy operating in this indigenous context is probably not open to much abuse, though that might depend on what levels of hierarchical structure have crept into such societies (which in turn depends on what economists call the social surplus and who gets to control it).

Andrew Cohen / Michael Wombacher

The Ramakrishna Gospel is a book that probably spans many more years than the five years of Tweedie's account in her *Daugher of Fire*. The description by Michael Wombacher of a retreat with his guru Andrew Cohen covers only eleven days but is almost as weighty a tome as the other two. However I read Wombacher's account some years ago for a book review and the impact of it is long gone. I had a clear picture then of Wombacher's personal journey of discipleship with Cohen which I cannot reconstruct without re-reading the entire book. Instead I have found my notes on Day 4 of the diary which I think are sufficient to highlight some key aspects of Cohen's hierophancy.

The retreat in 2005 reads for me as something very familiar. I know Cohen's specific teachings quite well, while at the same time the format of his meditations and teachings are at heart no different from that at the feet of Ramakrishna, Gurdjieff, Bhai Sahib, or Bhagwan Shree Rajneesh. In Wombacher's case his experience of the eleven days is entirely positive and pretty typical, I would say, of most aspirants at the feet of any master. There is no trace in his account of the "paralyzing resentment" that Yenner dwells on, but then I have found no public record of Wombacher's later thoughts on Cohen.

Wombacher details not just his but other interactions between the participants of the retreat and Andrew Cohen, making this a valuable record of the master-disciple relationship. The emphasis, as Wombacher says early on, and in contrast to his former teacher, is *understanding* rather than experience. This aligns Cohen more with the Buddha, and I often find the exchanges between Cohen and his audience somewhat similar to those recorded in the Pali Canon. Despite the emphasis on understanding the eleven days would also have been a profound *experience*, because no group of seekers with their master in retreat can fail to generate a profound sense of the sacred, almost regardless of the system taught by the master.

Wombacher begins the account of Day 4 by stating that he had pretty much lost his cognitive capacity or the ability to speak on anything.[153] We have encountered this often enough by now: he could be Tweedie or any of Socrates' disciples; or for that matter any of the Buddha's. The focus of each day, beyond the meditations and chores assigned to the pupils, is the lecture by Cohen and question and answer session that follows. I find these of great interest because Cohen has to both encourage the student to see that they know nothing yet – or why would they be there? – and at the same time not discourage them. This means listening with attention to the questions, affirming what is clearly an advancing understanding and then either correcting or steering the questioner to the next necessary insight. A conversation begins on the subject of how many systems originating in India see the world as illusion, and that Cohen's is a radically different approach. One needs to see – he says – who one is "before time began," but that timeless infinite sense of Self is only the beginning for Cohen. "What do we do with it then?" is his question to the audience. My answer would be of course, "nothing." There is nobody here to do anything. It will unfold anyway. But at the heart of Andrew's teaching and his methods is the idea that "we are here to do something."[154] I find this very American and very modern, even more so when Cohen characterizes other approaches as "outdated" or "pre-modern." Where I follow him completely is over some exchanges in which he insists that at least part of the goal of the spiritual life is to escape from the conviction that there is something terribly, terribly wrong. However the idea that enlightenment elevates you to a position of ushering in the new humanity, and worse, that nothing should stand in your way, is grandiose, as we saw.

Rajneesh had a similar project, to create the "new man," as he put it. If you have low self-esteem, cannot make sense of the world around you, are prone to the view that "the system" is anyway rotten, then a guru offering firstly enlightenment as an achievement and secondly a place in history as either one of the leaders of the revolution or at least one of the chosen in its implementation, then you may be hooked. "Hooked" as in a drug – you cannot walk away. For some followers who give up career, wife and family and all their past to join a closed community, there may even be an economic reason not to walk out of the relationship with the guru if it turns abusive. I recall reading about many of Rajneesh's followers stranded in Oregon when the commune collapsed who were terrified of ordinary society and having to get a job. But the major reason I think that the aspirant clings to the guru long after the relationship turns sour is that some want the reputed status of enlightenment and the trappings of messiahood. Others simply don't want to uproot themselves from the *sangha*, their source of friendship.

I never normally use the word "ego" and particularly not a phrase like "he has a big ego." Personally I have never met a person with a big ego, or seen one on TV. Of course, some people talk incessantly about themselves, others do not. (Some people say I talk too much; well, I try not to, but if I fail, so what? How can one get through life without annoying somebody, somewhere?) What I am getting at is that if people do have a thing called "ego" then it is not a rubric by which I express my annoyance with them, or analyze them, or dismiss them. The swan is mute. The sparrow chirps all day long. Does one have a bigger ego than the other?

But in the world of Cohen and his disciples "ego" is a huge issue. It is Cohen's job, apparently, to batter down the disciple's ego. I knew one of his followers at his London center who used to tell me that she was working hard to get rid of her ego, and the discipline of living within the Cohen community was part of that process. I told her that as far as I had got to know her I couldn't spot anything overblown or at all wrong with her ego. She just shook her head. I shook mine. However if I am forced to use the language of ego I suppose that I can say this (though with reluctance): those with weak or fragile egos are attracted to the strong ego of the guru in the hope of validation. There may be a genuine search for truth in the aspirant but the truth that is avoided at all costs is this: the teacher *may* be enlightened; the teacher *may* be gifted at teaching it; *but* the teacher is human and could be wrong about almost everything other than enlightenment. What's more – if we are forced to use the language of the ego – then it *may* be true that the teacher has a massive ego, so why on earth am I supposed to jettison my own? Rajneesh said many times that to be a guru a certain aggression was needed in the temperament, or why would you bother buttonholing people in the first place? Isn't that ego?

Returning to Day 4 of Wombacher's retreat we are in a seminar room of some kind with a charged atmosphere arising from the spiritual-religious nature of the gathering, the cumulative impact of much meditation, and the charismatic leadership of Cohen. He is saying that once one discovers the unborn something changes:

> That's the exhilarating thrill in the recognition of the absolute dimension of consciousness itself. It's freedom from the ego's position that, "I have a problem, and something's wrong." That's why there's so much joy and pleasure in the experience of consciousness. It's a profound relief from the ego's heavy baggage.

Cohen's interlocutor agrees; the audience understands the point; I cannot argue with this at all, even if I would prefer for it not to be couched in terms of "ego." The conversation continues as Cohen turns to the subject of narcissism, the ugliness of the ego and so on, contrasting it with the lightness of being that dwelling on pure consciousness brings. (As an aside, in the days before I cared to read political works I was given Milan Kundera's *The Unbearable Lightness of Being*. I assumed he meant the term as Cohen intends it, but when I found that Kundera meant something more akin to shallowness I threw the book across the room.)

To be in that seminar room at that time would be to live intensely. This is not a drug, not an easy fix for a weak ego, this is spirituality in an engaged participative form, and it is transformative. All of that makes hierophancy real and worth while; this is the thesis of my book. But it doesn't make the guru *right*. Certainly not right about everything. When sitting over the years in such seminar rooms with gurus of all stripes I always kept a critical distance on every single utterance. So, I am in the presence of Cohen, imagining myself sitting with Wombacher and the others on Day 4. I really like the way he put that. He hits it on the nail there. Yup. I feel the collective energy of the group. I am not impatient for the break to come, I don't want to miss any of this. It is real, it is important. Hang on, I don't agree with this on the non-relative dimension of consciousness:

> And the degree to which it becomes the ultimate reference point for the self, one begins to consciously aspire and feel compelled to manifest that non-relative or absolute oneness in the relative world of duality and multiplicity in all its complexity. Then one becomes a conscious agent of non-

dual realization in the manifest realm, and then, instead of living for oneself, to have and to get and to become, one becomes an agent of consciousness itself.

An alternative me sits there in the seminar room ... and it is beautifully laid out, there are flowers on the podium, the air-conditioning whispers. Something else whispers to me: *yes, I want to become an agent of consciousness itself, just like the guru. I want some of that. It sounds good.*

Nope. Personally, I don't want some of that, not at least if dressed up in this particular language. But an ambitious ego does. The American ambitious ego does. I do however agree with Cohen on one thing in the above passage. If one has had a sense of the non-dual, or absolute oneness, or the non-relative, or however one wants to express it, then the question arises: does a special responsibility come with this? Should one set out to "do" something with it in the world? At times I have asked myself that question but then immediately correct myself as I have come to think that the very question is a mistake. With the separate sense of self entirely gone, one finds oneself coterminous with the whole of existence, including both fluffy bunnies and mass-murderers. I cannot "do" anything in the world because I am not *in* the world. The world is in me. And in that world there is a personality with the forenames and surname either given to me or chosen by me. And that personality has traits deeply set by nurture, nature and karma. It is going to "do" stuff anyway. If that stuff turns out to be different after enlightenment than before, then great. If it turns out to be the same as before, then great. I happen to think that enlightenment engenders a flowering of the personality, so the chances are that the stuff I do might express that. Or not. It is of no concern either way because I have faith in the totality of existence, not in its parts. To be an agent of consciousness implies duality where there is none. Stuff will happen.

From Cohen's point of view I guess that this approach is part of the "pre-modern" Advaita, the path of the non-dual and I imagine he thinks it unacceptably passive in the face of the enormous challenges facing humanity. Look at all the great men and women who have acted for change, he might argue, as Rajneesh did. Where would humanity be without them? My response is this: either somewhere else, or not. I have faith in the *whole*, not the parts. It is absurd for me to like or dislike how the universe is unfolding or to try and guide it in any way. If I can get the kids to stop squabbling in my living room that is already perhaps an interference too far, but at least it is not laughably grandiose, and, being honest, am I not doing it more for myself than the kids?

If we return to Wombacher, I don't exactly know how he responded to the statement by Cohen that we just heard regarding enlightenment, worth repeating: "Then one becomes a conscious agent of non-dual realization in the manifest realm, and then, instead of living for oneself, to have and to get and to become, one becomes an agent of consciousness itself." Given that it is impossible to convey enlightenment in words, this summary is as good as any. Having felt Andrew's presence a number of times, and that of other enlightened persons, I hear his statement as far more than the words that make it up; I hear them as authentic because I also feel the presence of the one who uttered them. But when I consider the range of possible interpretations that Wombacher and others in that air-conditioned room might make of this specific verbal construction, I am conscious that the "ego" has much to latch on to.

Cohen's hierophancy flags up for us this simple issue then: if enlightenment is cracked up as anything appealing to competitive, goal-oriented ambition, then the covenant between master and disciple has an element in its foundation likely to cause a problem.

Maharishi Mahesh Yogi / Robert Forman

I met Robert Forman at the Tucson II "Towards a Science of Consciousness" conference in 1996. I returned convinced that there could be no science of consciousness itself, though cognitive science might at least unravel the mechanics of perception and much of how the brain works. Instead I was exploring the idea of a "first-person science" – much influenced at that time by Douglas Harding – and which has no common ground with the conventional physical and biological sciences other than rigor. I gave a talk at the conference on this with the title "From Schroedinger's Cat to Krishnamurti's Dog: Mysticism as the First Person Science of Consciousness" partly based on a speculation by Krishnamurti that when he walked his dog both he and his animal were equally silent of mind.[155] It was Robert Forman who chaired my session. Afterwards I emailed him a request to read the draft of my book "Krishna, Whitman, Nietzsche, Sartre," which he agreed to for $100. However the book so enraged him – particularly over my claim to remember past lives – that he charged me $150. Needless to say the augmented payment did not produce a useful endorsement. Hence, when he published a book titled "Enlightenment Ain't What It's Cracked Up To Be," I was curious. His scholarly reputation began with his edited volume of essays on an issue in the studies of mysticism, one of the course books for my Master's degree. So what was his personal experience of enlightenment?

I think his response to being a pupil of the Maharishi Mahesh Yogi and other gurus is very Western. He began with an understanding of enlightenment as *perfection*, a goal attainable as all other goals of the highly competitive American way of life. You have to have a perfect body, a highly trained mind, a successful reputation, a beautiful house and spouse, fantastic sex and lots of money. You get all these by discipline and hard work. Why would enlightenment be any different? Here is Forman's considered opinion based on a lifetime of research and practice:

> There are such things as enlightenment, Christ Consciousness, nirvana and the like. These *are* worth working towards, *are* better to have than not. But they are not the panacea which I and so many others have staked our lives. This is the other half. Enlightenment ain't what it has been cracked up to be.[156]

I have *some* sympathy with this sentiment, but have to ask, if enlightenment is not what it has been "cracked up" to be, then "cracked up" by whom? The enlightenment market is huge and populated with as many populists, fraudsters and bunglers as any other immensely challenging field. As Forman goes on to say, being a spiritual teacher implies for many an income. A *Wall Street Journal* article in 2018 claimed that the "meditation market" was worth $1.2 billion.[157] Are teachers who are dependent on their income necessarily going to give the right hints that their "product" – enlightenment – is almost indefinable, definitely not teachable and already in the possession of the seeker? Not all of them, to be sure. Of course the real problem with enlightenment is that it is not like a banana. You cannot seek linguistic agreement on the term as you can by pointing to a curved yellow fruit.

Forman's guru, Maharishi Mahesh Yogi – about whom I know little – apparently told his followers that the Upanishads, for example, assure us: "When it [the individual soul] discovers the Atman, full of dignity and power, it is freed from all suffering." Or: "When a man knows [the infinite], he is free: his sorrows have an end ..."[158] It is true that the Buddha also taught that nirvana was the cessation of suffering. However I believe that all these systems, when examined in detail, are clear that the kind of "sorrows" and "sufferings" that end in enlightenment are not what might be commonly expected. The Buddha was clear, for example, that if you are shot in the leg with an arrow you will not be spared physical pain as an enlightened person, only the mental anguish of asking continuously "why me?" Forman and his friends understood enlightenment as perfection, however, seemingly defined not just in their terms but in terms that strike me as particularly American. "Shiny," you could say. Therefore it was disconcerting, as Forman puts it, to find that so many gurus should have feet of clay (as in the title of Anthony Storr's book on gurus), including the acquisition of Rolls Royces, sexual misbehavior and monetary greed. (For the record it seems that Maharishi Mahesh Yogi had only one Rolls Royce compared to Rajneesh's ninety-two, and that his only indulged whim was a private helicopter.)

Forman's account is honest and illuminating of much that goes on between Eastern teacher and Western pupil. I find this passage particularly relevant:

> Finding your life's work in a complex context like ours is something that our Indian teachers may not have had to confront. In India a man typically did what his father did. So did a woman. But I'm an American, and the albatross was around my neck to discover a life's task that was "right for me." What I am to believe, who I am to wed, what I am to do – these too were my choices, not my religion's, not my caste's and not my parents', and terribly complex. Perhaps closing your eyes or gaining inner quiet is just not particularly well-suited to answer such multivalent life questions. Perhaps I was looking for too much from a shift in consciousness.[159]

I think Forman is right, the "albatross" round the American neck is success and the imperative to do it "my way," all ultimately the expression of supreme individualism. In my book on American cinema I observe that

6. Instructive Negotiations

the Americans are the most Oedipal culture on earth, not so much because men want to sleep with their own mothers but because of the intense desire to compete with their fathers and by extension everybody else.[160] Yet my own observation of those that gain "inner quiet" as he puts it is that they become supremely who they are without any competitive obligation. Enlightenment is not as far as I am concerned an erasure of personality but its flowering. Worldly success is another matter of course if that is measured by populist consensus. That may take a dive on enlightenment, and that is perhaps what Forman meant when he found that his perfectly genuine shift of consciousness into an enlightened frame of being was "underwhelming." It was not going to bring the shiny rewards he must have imagined. As I recall Lao Tzu says: "Everyone else is sharp, sharp. Only I am dull, dull." I think he means that his enlightenment ended the egotistic utterances designed to impress. How can one possibly want to impress anyone any more when one sees one's identity with all that is and all sentient beings? One certainly abandons all culturally imposed goals, such as material success, reputation and "shiny" things.

What Forman went through, however, is what he calls "full catastrophe disillusionment." In the movement created by Maharishi Mahesh Yogi, named "TM" after its central practice, transcendental meditation, Forman had found a home, a *sangha*, and leaving it was traumatic. The TM movement had turned him from a "lost, confused, pot smoking, lonely and occasionally suicidal kid" into a member of something worthwhile.[161] It was a big step to leave but Forman landed up taking a PhD in religious studies and found his knowledgeable tutors devastating in their inadvertent undermining of the Maharishi. What Forman now became was a practitioner of academic thought which simultaneously ridiculed the Maharishi's claims and gave Forman the bigger picture of Hindu and Buddhist thinking on enlightenment down the ages, alongside Christian mysticism. He began to gain a broader understanding of enlightenment as a shift in consciousness that was lionized in exuberant prose but was in fact more prosaic, more like a witnessing of all phenomenon including thought and quite possibly entailing periods of pure consciousness unmarked by mental activity. But, he says, "it didn't make me chipper. It didn't end my troubles."[162] What Forman wanted and which enlightenment did not seem to provide was "an answer to our longings for personal, *individual* satisfaction."

I really can't help Forman here. No guru can help Forman here. For me the unexciting "suchness" that accompanies the shift of consciousness that Forman experienced answers everything and entirely reframes longings themselves. They do not disappear, but are placed in a context where *competition* disappears. One is as happy for another person's success as one is sorrowful for their sufferings, and should uncharitable thoughts arise one is as compassionate to the self in such failure as one is to their arising in others and what it reveals about them. What all this says about the guru-pupil relationship is that it will founder if the former appears to offer answers to longings that have nothing to do with enlightenment and if the pupil is seeking "personal, *individual* satisfaction" as demanded by Western culture with the inevitable category error around "individual." In Sankara's trilogy of good fortune – which Forman quotes – one might say that Forman had two out of the three. He had been born a human and had (possibly) found the teacher of enlightenment. But the middle step was missing or badly formed: his desire for enlightenment was weak and swamped by other desires. Hence his "full catastrophe disillusionment" was inevitable.

Mother Meera / Andrew Harvey

A few years ago I was introduced to David A. Hart, author, and something of a controversial figure after he retained his position as Anglican priest on converting to Hinduism. Our meeting over coffee and cake got off to a bad start when we disagreed over the alleged homosexuality of Ramakrishna. It became clear that for David as a gay man the saintly figure of Ramakrishna was both an exalted Hindu guru and a gay exemplar. I posited a different theory: that Ramakrishna was non-sexual, as in the remark he made once that his marriage was not consummated as "it didn't work any more" (or words to that effect). Some take this non-consummation and his intense relationship with the young male devotees around him as signs of homosexuality. I don't. Other than that David and I had much in common, and I like it, for example that Sir Mark Tully, former BBC India correspondent, wrote of one of David's books that "David Hart has now become fully multi-faith."[163] I think I was eventually forgiven our differences however and invited to Hart's leaving party as he set off to India with his young male Indian husband. Some interfaith figures in his circle were critical of this marriage, but, I suggested, given that the young man's family were now likely to disown him, better that he legally inherits from the much older David. That would give him at least some economic bulwark against traditional prejudice after his partner died.

This is by way of background to the story of Andrew Harvey's discipleship to Mother Meera which foundered over the same issue of gay marriage. Both Hart and Harvey are gay; both their paths have been intensely shaped both by Indian spirituality and their sexual orientation; and both write and pursue an interfaith existence owing much to the immense breadth and tolerance of the Indian spiritual tradition. Indian *society* on the other hand not has been tolerant of homosexuality and I bring this up here to give an example of how a deeply enlightened guru such as Mother Meera may at the same time be in possession of some rather unprogressive views.

Andrew Harvey, though English, was born in India and now describes himself as "Author, Mystic, Spiritual Teacher." He taught Shakespeare and French literature at Oxford University until the call of India – as it were – overcame academic ambition and drew him to a variety of spiritual teachers. As he says: "The academic game bored me; talk about Derrida and Deleuze seemed empty after what I had begun to learn in India; the contrast between the bloodless, sardonic world of an Ivy League university and the rapture of Pondicherry grew hallucinatory."[164] It was in 1978 near the Pondicherry ashram of Sri Aurobindo that Harvey met Mother Meera, who was to become his guru for many years until the issue of gay marriage separated them. Harvey was brought to her by a friend but was unprepared for her beauty or what would happen to him. He describes her routine of silence, holding the head and looking into the eyes of the visitor kneeling in front of her, familiar to me from my own experience decades later. He writes:

> The silence she brought with her into the room was unlike any I had ever experienced – deeper, fully of uncanny, wounding joy. I found my mind becalmed, unable to grasp at any of the thoughts that were racing through it. I had never knelt to anyone else, and I had never before seen one hu-

man being kneel to another and yet nothing in the worship that I saw before me struck me as blasphemous.[165]

Meera was seventeen at the time. A gay Oxford professor of literature – no longer metaphorically kneeling at the feet of Derrida and Deleuze – physically kneels in front of this young woman and experiences what is the essence of hierophancy, an "uncanny, wounding joy," a peace and a new relationship to thought; "knocked back" as I put it earlier, or numbed as by a stingray, to use the metaphor for Socrates. Harvey entered a period of discipleship with Meera as his guru for about fourteen years – in which time he helped put her on the world stage and make her home in Germany – only to crash out in "full catastrophe disillusionment" as Forman puts it.

A spiritual aspirant with a Romantic inclination, such as Hart and Harvey, may run into trouble with gurus if their relationship has love in the foreground. Harvey describes this love as it hits him early on in his encounter with Meera:

> The professor and I sat on the sand and talked of Plato and the vision of Love in the Symposium. He said he found Plato "repressive," a fantasist; that such love could not exist; and that a commonsense charity was more valuable than all Socrates' attempts to define a Love beyond time and space. But as he was talking I found myself filled with just that Love he said did not exist.[166]

Note that Harvey capitalizes "love" to indicate perhaps a special kind of spiritual love. At any rate we see that he is filled with it; it is a direct outcome of his contact with the young Meera. Depending on one's temperament love can be the most overpowering of feelings on contact with the guru, and at the same time it is inevitable that to some degree this love is directed *at* the guru. There is no problem with this if that love goes straight through the guru and out the other side to the infinite, to the eternal, to the Lord, or whatever we wish to name our absolute principal. But love is rather bound to stick a little on that journey, and so the person of the guru becomes as important as what they initiate in the pupil, especially perhaps to a Romantic. Catastrophe is then pretty much inevitable. Harvey meets a man he wants to marry, and Meera reacts, not out of the infinite, but out of the finite. I haven't read Harvey's book "Sun at Mid-

6. Instructive Negotiations

night: A Memoir of The Dark Night," but I don't have reason to doubt a review which quotes a message for Harvey from Mother Meera:

> Tell Andrew that he has a choice. He can either become celibate or he can get married [to a woman]. Mother prefers that you get married. When you are married, Mother wants you to write a book about how her force transformed you into a normal person, into a heterosexual. Mother says that single-sex love – man-man or woman-woman – is not good, not healthy, not wise, not in the spiritual way at all, not healthy.[167]

Harvey is plunged into turmoil, including illness and thoughts of suicide and receives death threats from loyal followers of Meera who are angered at his public doubts over her. He eventually rejects the very idea of the guru.

My take on this is as follows. Mother Meera was enlightened very young, with no effort on her part, rather like Ramana Maharshi; pure self-sparking gunpowder you could say. She found herself in her vocation as guru, that is with the role to usher in the infinite in those who come to her. But the human body is not infinite, nor is the human mind. Meera would have made sense of her situation relatively easily as her culture gave every sanction for it. She was therefore at no point at odds with her culture and had no particular reason to question the prevailing prejudice against homosexuality. Once you become a world-famous guru you do not get out much, and, despite her German location would have been insulated from the more progressive values of that country. Hence I am not surprised at her reaction, if it is recorded faithfully.

There is a broader point to be made here. Anyone attaining even a little celebrity status in any field owing to their talents in that field is under enormous temptation to make pronouncements on things far removed from their direct expertise. It is entirely possible for the greatest guru in the world to pontificate on a subject like politics with as little knowledge of the subject as the man in the pub or woman at the bus stop. I vaguely recall a comedy sketch where an Indian pundit claimed that quantum theory was Indian, and the Buddha knew all about it five thousand years ago, demonstrating an equal ignorance of science and history. Followers are easily impressed by the guru's pronouncements on such subjects, as Forman was with the Maharishi until he undertook university-level studies.

A comparison of systems

This is a good point at which to briefly triangulate the systems of the gurus just discussed with that of Whitman – as pointed out earlier, the system is bound in some degree to impact on the way that the hierophant operates. In the first instance – as Whitman has no interest in the occult and makes clear how he distances himself from Blake – his system is nothing like that of Gurdjieff, Radha Mohan Lal or the shamanic world of Crow Dog. Whitman taught no spiritual techniques that might bring occult powers or *siddhis* as did Radha Mohan Lal and the Maharishi Mahesh Yogi. Neither does Whitman's system include the devotional or *bhakti* elements found in the system of Shams and Rumi or the potential for it with Mother Meera. Whitman does not impose any kind of discipline on his followers as Cohen, Gurdjieff or Radha Mohan Lal did, and would not have dreamt of imposing anything like Marpa's punishment of Milarepa. Atonement does not exist in Whitman's system, making it far removed from the Christian tradition as we saw.

Whitman's system is as world-curious as Cohen's however, and in the sense that it celebrates all of Nature too then it has some resonance after all with the worldview of the Native Americans. In his manner however Whitman strikes me as closest to Socrates and a little similar to that of Ramana Maharshi, though their systems were *via negativa*, that is world-renouncing. What remains perhaps as the common factor in all of these teachers is that being with them is transformative, regardless of their systems. The system does however impact on *how* one spends time in the presence of the hierophant, that is on the outward form of *darshan*. That outward form may be more or less explicit in it religious nature. Krishnamurti made great efforts to rid his hierophancy of explicit religious content; Whitman simply did not have to.

7

THE HIEROPHANCY OF WALT WHITMAN

We now have a considerable number of perspectives from which to consider the hierophancy of Walt Whitman. Some preliminary points are important to make here. Firstly, although there was some faint cultural precedent for Whitman's disciples to seek religious instruction from him as a poet – perhaps beginning in the work of Blake and closer to home in the ambitions of the American Transcendentalists – Whitman was operating neither in the eastern guru framework nor in the western priestly one. His disciples had no particular expectations from him beyond what they brought themselves. Secondly, Whitman's own pronouncements as spiritual teacher are more diffuse than those of his pupils on what they received from him. Thirdly, the potentially homosexual context of utterances on both sides makes this hierophancy a case like that of Socrates, Rumi and Ramakrishna where a Freudianized interpretation rather snaps at the heels of the spiritual-religious one. All of this makes for an example of hierophancy that might on the surface seem unpromising for any aim of extracting useful or universal principles. However to counter that, Whitman appears to me to offer a spiritual teaching far more suited to the democratic age than *any* of the examples we have looked at so far.

Eros and *agape*

As so much discussion in this book is about the guru system and its origins in India it has been necessary to introduce a few additional Indian terms such as *darshan* and *sangha*. I now turn to two terms in ancient Greek to help us out in this chapter where we are faced with the issue of Whitman's alleged homosexuality, these terms being *eros* and *agape*. *Eros* means sexual love, while *agape* means love in the spiritual life. The erotic needs no explanation, but *agape* does. We have a related term "Platonic love" to mean a deep personal relationship that does not involve the erotic, but its context is not necessarily spiritual or religious. *Agape* became a Christian term meaning the highest form of love, sometimes described as the love of God for man and man for God. More broadly it includes the love that people have for each other when emptied of personal desire, as found in the members of a religious congregation, or to transpose it to the Hindu context, as found between the members of a *sangha*. Here is my testimony based on life-long experience: such love is real, deep and inexplicable. My favorite description of this non-erotic love is found in the writings of the Danish religious thinker Kierkegaard who points out that all other forms of love – particularly in the Romantic tradition – are based on *preference*.[168] When Andrew Harvey found his ideal partner and hence wanted to commit to marriage that was a love of preference. He prefers to spend time with that person above all others; marriage vows often state something to that effect. *Agape* has no such preference in it, and that is of course greatly to do with the absence of erotic feelings. There are also many such non-erotic bonds formed between individuals of all sexual orientation through contexts such as office work, farming, the army and so on where "love" is an appropriate term because it goes beyond the normal respect and trust found in friendship. Sanskrit has apparently seven different words for love to distinguish its various forms, English unfortunately only one.

If we borrow *agape* from its Christian context to mean the love between individuals bound by the common experience of anything spiritual or religious, then we have a term to describe how I see the friendships formed by Whitman. This is in contrast to Robertson who, as mentioned earlier, refers to the "erotics of discipleship" to define some of Whitman's closest friendships with men. For example he describes Whitman's friendship with William O'Conner as "chaste but erotically charged." Now, I am not sure about this. Was it chaste, as in the relationship to Socrates de-

7. The Hierophancy of Walt Whitman

scribed by Alcibiades, implying regretful, or chaste implying sublimed? Does "erotically charged" mean the raw sexual impulse or mean the sexual impulse at one or more removes, as implied by the term "sublimation," the discourse of which mostly psychologizes it as a lamentable but necessary adjustment? Or, were the men bound by the mutual recognition of something ineffable that O'Connor felt in the presence of Whitman and which we can better describe as part of some kind of hierophancy? I need to add, too, that I think it impolite to speculate about any persons, living or dead, as to whether their relationships were chaste or not. It is prurient, none of my business and irrelevant to the issue of Whitman's hierophancy. It only enters into the question of guruship in the case where the relationship is abusive, as is alleged, for example, of the founder of the Friends of the Western Buddhist Order.

Alcibiades, as we recall, described the night in bed with Socrates as no more erotically charged than when sleeping in the same bed with his father or brothers. The modern sensibility tends to equate "sleep with" and "have sex with" because modern society is wealthy enough for even the poorest to generally afford a bed of their own, either in their home or when a guest at an inn or hotel. It was not so in Whitman's time as Robertson concedes, citing the example of Abraham Lincoln as a young lawyer sharing a bed with his landlord in Illinois.[169] In the 1851 novel *Moby Dick* the protagonist Ishmael chooses one of the lower-class inns in the whaling town of Nantucket to spend the night in and is faced with the choice of a sleeping on hard wooden bench in the bar or sharing a bed with the cannibal, Queequeg. Choosing the latter, Ishmael's account includes nothing of homosexuality, or indeed any concerns about cannibalism, merely the observation that the mattress was so uncomfortable that he could not decide whether it was stuffed with crockery or corn-cobs.

Michael Robertson's account of Whitman's years in Washington, to where Whitman had moved during the Civil War so he could minister to wounded soldiers in the hospitals there, tends to the homosexual interpretation of the love between Whitman and these men.[170] Given that Robertson writes that none of the relationships with these or any other men were consummated I want to leave open the possibility that these friendships were more like Socrates' friendships, and that Alcibiades gives us an alternative explanation: that the attraction was in the first instance religious or spiritual or even moral, in other words that love here had the nature of *agape*.

We saw earlier that the modern mind, as exemplified by Don Cupitt, is baffled by the use of sexual metaphor in describing religious love. I used one of my poems to illustrate how sexual imagery comes naturally to anyone attempting to describe the intensity of spiritual experience. The reason is simple: the movement of the spiritual or religious impulse is towards union, whether with "God" or the cosmos, or the One or the All, while the movement of the sexual impulse is towards physical union; both are about union. Religious union is of an intensity far greater than physical union, but draws on erotic imagery as closest in its raw power. Here lies, I think, the major source of misunderstanding of *Leaves of Grass*, the misreading of *agape* for *eros*.

Whitman as teacher

Although we focus in this chapter more on Whitman's pupils than on Whitman himself, we first need to gather together what hints he has dropped about himself as teacher. Whitman said that he had "arrived" and was to be wrestled with as he passed because he afforded those who persevered with him the solid prizes of the universe. Any reasonable exposure to both Whitman's writings and Indian thought will convince one that these solid prizes are no less than spiritual enlightenment. In the use of "wrestled with" Whitman suggests a reluctant teacher, it is up to the pupil to force him. In other hints we see the reverse, a determined teacher who will not in fact let the pupil pass:

> You there, impotent, loose in the knees,
> Open your scarf'd chops till I blow grit within you,
> Spread your palms and lift the flaps of your pockets,
> I am not to be denied, I compel, I have stores plenty and to
>   spare,
> And any thing I have I bestow.
>
> (Song of Myself, 40)

I take "scarf'd chops" to mean the mouth of the pupil covered by a scarf; Whitman demands that he or she open the mouth and let him blow determination into it, a form of kiss perhaps. One is to open one's palms and pockets too, because he is going to give of what he has – the infinite, as I understand it – and is not to be denied. He is clear enough that his pupils have much to learn:

> Long enough have you dream'd contemptible dreams,
> Now I wash the gum from your eyes,
> You must habit yourself to the dazzle of the light and of every
>   moment of your life.
>
> Long have you timidly waded, holding a plank by the shore,
> Now I will you to be a bold swimmer,
> To jump off in the midst of the sea, and rise again and nod to me
>   and shout, and laughingly dash with your hair.
>   (Song of Myself, 46)

To "wash the gum" from the eyes of the pupil is just one expression in a line of long-standing declarations by spiritual teachers that they wish their pupils to open their eyes and see, or open their ears and hear. Whitman condemns the timidity by which people live close to the shore: he will make them bold swimmers of the sea, of the infinite. He goes on:

> I am the teacher of athletes,
> He that by me spreads a wider breast than my own proves the
>   width of my own,
> He most honors my style who learns under it to destroy the
>   teacher.
>   (Song of Myself, 46)

Whitman expresses here the start of his democratic credentials: he expects his pupils to swim further than he, and the best praise is for the pupil who destroys the teacher. This is the greatest honor that a teacher can receive, that the pupil is now an independent swimmer of the eternal and can cast off the teacher. Whether one does it with thanks or without is irrelevant. Whitman is bold as a teacher to force himself on you, but humble enough to say this, that he is: "A learner with the simplest, a teacher of the thoughtfulest …"

I have no doubt that while the genuine seeker does well to seek a teacher or guru, as Shankara says, the teacher equally seeks pupils with the capacity to learn, "athletes" as Whitman calls them, those with the strength to undergo the hardships of spiritual discovery. In his short poem "Among the Multitude" Whitman tell us of his search for pupils:

> Among the men and women the multitude,
> I perceive one picking me out by secret and divine signs,
> Acknowledging none else, not parent, wife, husband, brother,
>   child, any nearer than I am,
> Some are baffled, but that one is not — that one knows me.
>
> Ah lover and perfect equal,
> I meant that you should discover me so by faint indirections,
> And when I meet you mean to discover you by the like in you.

We may note that Jesus likewise dismissed the ties of family relationship in comparison to that which draws the master and his disciple near; he also "fished" continuously for those that would not be baffled by him. However for some commentators Whitman's greatest arrogance is indeed to compare himself with Christ:

> I discover myself on a verge of the usual mistake.
>
> That I could forget the mockers and insults!
> That I could forget the trickling tears and the blows of the
>   bludgeons and hammers!
> That I could look with a separate look on my own crucifixion
>   and bloody crowning!
>
> (Song of Myself, 38)

We saw that in the poem "To Him That Was Crucified" Whitman refers to Jesus as a dear brother and one engaged in the same work: "That we labor together transmitting the same charge and succession / We few equals indifferent of lands, indifferent of times." To say of Jesus, "we few equals" does not sit well in the Western tradition, but is perfectly normal in the guru system of the East. It is also a deeply Hindu idea that spiritual truth belongs to no specific land or era.

7. The Hierophancy of Walt Whitman

Here and there Whitman refers to his actual or potential disciples as "eleves," the French word for pupil:

> Eleves, I salute you! come forward!
> Continue your annotations, continue your questionings.
>   (Song of Myself, 38)

> Many things to absorb I teach to help you become eleve of mine;
> Yet if blood like mine circle not in your veins,
> If you be not silently selected by lovers and do not silently select lovers,
> Of what use is it that you seek to become eleve of mine?
>   (To a Western Boy)

The last short poem encapsulates some of the difficulties of interpretation we have with Whitman, bearing in mind his confession to Carpenter about hiding his true meaning. If this "western boy" is to become his pupil Whitman must teach him some preliminaries it seems, but these are not enough if the same blood does not circulate in his veins. "Do not cast pearls before swine," says Jesus, and just about every spiritual teacher I know acknowledges that the pupil has to have that opening, or crack in them, for the infinite; the same "blood" as the teacher. We saw that in Paul Brunton's account it is Shri Shankara Acharya who suggests the visit to Ramana Maharshi. What I did not add was that the Acharya had chosen one out of only two outstanding gurus to send Brunton to, the other being most likely unavailable. That in turn suggests that the Acharya had seen in Brunton an advanced capacity for spiritual instruction, otherwise there would have been hundreds of lesser teachers to choose from.

This is what I think Whitman means by silently selecting lovers or being silently selected by them: that they are also on the spiritual journey, that they form the *sangha* or spiritual community of enquirers, that they share *agape* between them, not erotic love. The potential for a homosexual interpretation remains but the word "eleve" would be odd, even if it were not for the remaining evidence of Whitman as religious teacher. An ageing queen, a satyr with endless appetite for boys does not have to teach them anything to be their lover; they are not pupils.

Whitman does not want office of any kind, least of all religious office:

> I have no chair, nor church nor philosophy;
> I lead no man to a dinner-table or library or exchange,
> But each man and each woman of you I lead upon a knoll,
> My left hand hooks you round the waist,
> My right hand points to landscapes of continents, and a plain public road.
> Not I, not any one else can travel that road for you, You must travel it for yourself.
> (Song of Myself, 46)

Again, the image of the open road is taken as a non-religious theme by the Beat Generation writers; I take it differently. Whitman's religion is of the everyday, of all the things that make a life, and for the fullness of that religion one has to be in the open, be open to what is available in the life of the city and the life of the country, not what is on offer in the confines of the monastery. Above all the "eleve" must travel that road himself or herself. Although Whitman often makes clear that he teaches only in the open air, we might take this as a metaphor once we realize that his pupils were just as likely to be engaged by his presence in a house or bar. In this poem he insists again on the open air:

> I teach straying from me, yet who can stray from me?
> I follow you whoever you are from the present hour;
> My words itch at your ears till you understand them.
>
> I do not say these things for a dollar, or to fill up the time while I wait for a boat;
> It is you talking just as much as myself, I act as the tongue of you,
> It was tied in your mouth, in mine it begins to be loosened.
>
> I swear I will never mention love or death inside a house,
> And I swear I never will translate myself at all, only to him or her who privately stays with me in the open air.
> (Song of Myself, 47)

I love this idea that Whitman teaches his pupils to "stray" from him, yet in doing so they fulfill his teachings. He is also saying that his teachings are anyway what the pupil would say if their tongue was loosened, meaning that this is not knowledge exterior to them but of their own interiority, should they look. The pupil cannot fail, either, as he explains in the last lines of "Song of Myself:" "Failing to fetch me at first keep encouraged / Missing me one place search another, I stop somewhere waiting for you."

In the Calamus poem, "Whoever you are holding me now in hand," Whitman uses the term "novitiate" in a way that I take to indicate the process of spiritual training in the disciple.

> Whoever you are holding me now in hand,
> Without one thing all will be useless,
> I give you fair warning before you attempt me further,
> I am not what you supposed, but far different.
> Who is he that would become my follower?
> Who would sign himself a candidate for my affections?
> The way is suspicious, the result uncertain, perhaps destructive,
> You would have to give up all else, I alone would expect to be
>   your sole and exclusive standard,
> Your novitiate would even then be long and exhausting,
> The whole past theory of your life and all conformity to the lives
>   around you would have to be abandon'd,
> Therefore release me now before troubling yourself any further,
>   let go your hand from my shoulders,
> Put me down and depart on your way.

What is the one thing that the novice needs, beyond the willingness to give up the "whole past theory of your life" and the conformity to the mainstream view? As Shankara says, is it not the determination for enlightenment? And I agree, that the mystic, the one who has gained the solid prizes of the universe, has had to give up all the past theories of his or her life, all the theories in fact that we are inculcated in from birth by our culture. I also like it that Whitman says "I am not what you supposed, but far different." Alcibiades says just this of Socrates as he comes to properly know the man.

I am aware of course that my interpretation here is an outlier. The mainstream view of the Calamus poems now is that they are homoerotic, an understanding won through the liberation of thought since the nineteenth century, at which time an alternative interpretation was still possible. At stake is how the above poem develops: "Here to put your lips upon mine I permit you, / With the comrade's long-dwelling kiss or the new husband's kiss, For I am the new husband and I am the comrade." What are we to make of this? Surely, many argue, this is a poem about homosexual relations. However I do not agree, because despite such imagery and more, Whitman is clear that he will not be understood, returning to the theme of the previous poem: "For all is useless without that which you may guess at many times and not hit, that which I hinted at; / Therefore release me and depart on your way." I don't think that Whitman here is making out that he is an extremely exacting gay lover and that to have physical congress with him depends on clearing some very high bar. I think he is speaking as all mystics do who engage in teaching: they know well that it takes something extremely rare for an individual to "get" what is hinted at. Tradition has it that at the point of his enlightenment the Buddha reflected that what he had attained was "deep, hard to see, hard to realize, peaceful, refined, beyond the scope of conjecture, subtle, to-be-experienced by the wise." He therefore hesitated to become a teacher as he saw that very few would understand him.[171]

There are of course many passages in Whitman's writings where he makes plain that for him religion is more important than anything and that he is here to start a new one:

> I too, following many and follow'd by many, inaugurate a religion, I descend into the arena,
> (It may be I am destin'd to utter the loudest cries there, the winner's pealing shouts,
> Who knows? they may rise from me yet, and soar above every thing.)
>
> Each is not for its own sake,
> I say the whole earth and all the stars in the sky are for religion's sake.
>
> I say no man has ever yet been half devout enough,
> None has ever yet adored or worship'd half enough,
> None has begun to think how divine he himself is, and how certain the future is.

7. The Hierophancy of Walt Whitman

> I say that the real and permanent grandeur of these States must
>   be their religion,
> Otherwise there is no real and permanent grandeur;
> (Nor character nor life worthy the name without religion,
> Nor land nor man or woman without religion.)
>
> 8
>
> What are you doing young man?
> Are you so earnest, so given up to literature, science, art, amours?
> These ostensible realties, politics, points?
> Your ambition or business whatever it may be?
>
> It is well — against such I say not a word, I am their poet also,
> But behold! such swiftly subside, burnt up for religion's sake,
> For not all matter is fuel to heat, impalpable flame, the essential
>   life of the earth,
> Any more than such are to religion.
>
> (Starting From Paumanok vs. 7 and 8)

Whitman entreats you to share with him two greatnesses, Love and Democracy, but there is a third, more important:

> My comrade!
> For you to share with me two greatnesses, and a third one rising
>   inclusive and more resplendent,
> The greatness of Love and Democracy, and the greatness of Religion.
>
> (Starting From Paumanok, v. 10)

If Whitman's principal preoccupation is religion, and he is teacher of a new religion, fit for the emerging democracy of America, then who are his principal disciples? In Michael Robertson's book they appear in this order: William O'Connor, John Burroughs, Anne Gilchrist, Richard Maurice Bucke, John Addington Symonds, Edward Carpenter, Oscar Wilde and Horace Traubel. Robertson's work is pretty comprehensive of these individuals – and others – but he is interested everywhere in the sexual and romantic connections between Whitman and these admirers to the point, I have to admit, that it pains me. Instead we are interested here in how they received Whitman as spiritual teacher, and what we find is some variety, all instructive of the situation of hierophancy, though perhaps not one we normally recognize as such.

Horace Traubel

One of Whitman's biographers cites the American critic Paul Zweig as saying in his book on Whitman that "The nineteenth century transposed the religious quest for salvation into a variety of secular idioms."[172] This sentiment sums up my own response to the three-volume diary kept by Horace Traubel of the last years of Whitman: it is secular; it is not a picture of anything we normally call "religious." While Nambiar wrote "Whitman was Traubel's Guru" we have to say that daily life with Whitman was nothing like that of daily life with an Indian guru like Ramakrishna, for example. There are no outward religious forms or symbols. Yet to immerse oneself in Traubel's recorded conversations with Whitman is not ultimately so different to immersing oneself in Ramakrishna's conversations with his disciple Mahendranath: there is for me an equal sense of *darshan*. Zweig's point holds throughout Traubel's diaries however because it is an entirely secularized version of *darshan* where the secular idiom is literature. As we saw, Whitman asserted: "The priest departs, the divine literatus comes."

Horace Traubel was a teenage boy when he first met Whitman in 1873, the poet then laid low by a stroke and staying with his brother George in Camden, New Jersey. Traubel became Whitman's literary secretary and when he was in his final years kept a diary of their exchanges covering the years 1888 to Whitman's death in 1892, three volumes of which were published. Robertson tells us: "Like all the disciples, Traubel was a spiritual seeker, but whereas the others promoted a highly individualistic, anti-institutional spirituality, he had a mania for organizing."[173] One has to hunt through the three volumes for that sense of spiritual seeking and the answering of it by Whitman, but the clues are all there.

While Whitman's preoccupation and conversation as portrayed in Traubel's diaries are literary, Whitman is scathing of art for art's sake, always making the point that his poetry serves a religious purpose. Style is secondary. Neither was Whitman in favor of any organization for promoting his work; he remained an individualist and anticlerical. He says for example: "Now, I never object to a man—any kind of a man—but I object to a priest—any kind of a priest. The instant a priest becomes a man I am on his side—I no longer oppose him."[174]

What I really get from the Traubel diaries is the impression of an unshakeable generosity of spirit in Whitman that only the word "religious" – or if you hate that word, then "spiritual" – will do. Ramakrishna lived in a temple on the banks of the Ganges devoted to the Hindu goddess Kali and his devotees were steeped in the sacred traditions. In contrast Whitman's circle, present in his small house in Camden, included only an old couple who acted as housekeepers and later a male nurse, regular visits from Traubel, and less frequent but greatly welcomed visits from a wide range of close friends and admirers, particularly Richard Maurice Bucke, who was also his doctor. Whitman's conversations are more like the "down time" of gurus such as Mother Meera or Krishnamurti. The themes are mostly literary, such as the disputed authorship of the Shakespeare plays, sometimes political, sometimes regarding controversies in science. But pervading all of them is a faith in life, in ordinary people and a refusal to criticize persons. Traubel tells us: "W. will not talk persons in his censure. He says he will talk persons only in his love."[175]

It is often assumed that religion means a belief in the afterlife. Whitman makes it clear to Traubel that he does not believe death is the end: "I believe in immortality, and by that I mean identity. I know I have arrived at this result more by what may be called feeling than formal reason—but I believe it: yes, I know it. I am easily put to flight, I assure you, when attacked, but I return to the faith, inevitably—believe it, and stick to it, to the end."[176] Traubel records another conversation on this theme with a friend called Moorhouse:

> W. speaking of the idea of immortality, of the "fact" as he prefers to call it, added: "When I say immortality I say identity—the survival of the personal soul—your survival, my survival."
>
> Moorhouse: "It could not be otherwise with a man of your optimism. It would be impossible for a man of your optimism to have any other belief."

> To which W. replied: "Optimism—pessimism: no one word could explain, enclose, it. There is more, much more, to be canvassed than is included in either word, in both words. I am not prepared to admit fraud in the scheme of the universe—yet without immortality all would be sham and sport of the most tragic nature. I remember, also, what Epictetus said: What is good enough for the universe is good enough for me!—immortality for the universe, immortality is good enough for me!"[177]

For me these can only be the words of a spiritual teacher: "I am not prepared to admit fraud in the scheme of the universe." As Traubel observes, Whitman regards this immortality as a fact, and, as Whitman responds to Moorhouse's point, it is not a matter of mere optimism. Also significant in this passage is the fact that Whitman draws on *The Enchiridion* by Epictetus, a book that Traubel often finds Whitman reading and in which he has inscribed his name. After mentioning this, Traubel records the scene that night:

> W. was very affectionate in his manner tonight. "Come here, Horace," he said. I went over. He took my hand. "I feel somehow as if you had consecrated yourself to me. That entails something on my part: I feel somehow as if I was consecrated to you. Well—we will work out the rest of my life-job together: it won't be for long: anyway, we'll work it out together, for short or long, eh?" He took my face between his hands and drew me to him and kissed me. Nothing more was then said. I went back to my chair and we sat in silence for some time.[178]

I have deliberately quoted this extract to show how easily the Whitman material can be interpreted in one of two ways. There is the homosexual interpretation, based on the use of word "affection" and the physical contact between the men, the taking of a hand and a kiss. For example Mitchell Santine Gould published an essay in the journal *Quaker History* practically declaring that Whitman had learned his gay sexual permissiveness from the Quaker reformer Elias Hicks, and further implying that the *Moby Dick* characters Ishmael and Queequeg sleeping together in Quaker Nantucket was an example of Quaker gay love.[179] Gould also suggests that Traubel was "a devotee who was arguably Whitman's greatest lover." I make a different interpretation of the above scene. For me Whitman understands Traubel to be an "eleve" or disciple, and is grateful to him for consecrating his life to not just Whitman the teacher, but also his "life-job." The latter term is also illuminating: Whitman is telling us that he regards *Leaves of Grass* as part of a life-long sacred project; if Traubel as pupil has consecrated himself to Whitman, then Whitman must consecrate himself as hierophant to Traubel. Yes, there are none of the outward signs of the sacred as there would have been in Ramakrishna's Kali temple, but here is the inward sense of the sacred. Crucially, I suggest that the love between them is *agape* not *eros*.

The diaries make clear that Whitman is not here to extol only the great heroes of the religious life – or even those not so clearly religious such as Epictetus – as Whitman's complaint about the special status of Jesus' crucifixion points to. He suggests to Traubel that Thoreau had an "inability to appreciate the average life" and concludes:

> That, after all, is my message—what I am here for—what I am to testify. I am not a witness for saviors—exceptional men: for the nobility—no: I am a witness for the average man, the whole.[180]

Whitman is using religious language: "witness" and "testify" are terms that readily come to the lips of Quakers. References to them crop up regularly in his conversations, for example in this exchange (Whitman speaking first):

> "Did you know (but I guess you did not) that when I was a young fellow up on the Long Island shore I seriously debated whether I was not by spiritual bent a Quaker?—whether if not one I should not become one? But the question went its way again: I put it aside as impossible: I was never made to live inside a fence."
>
> "If you had turned Quaker would *Leaves of Grass* ever have been written?"
>
> "It is more than likely not—quite probably not—almost certainly not. I guess you are right, Horace: you have hit the nail on the head. We must go outside the lines before we can know the best things that are within."[181]

When Whitman refers to the "fence" he means the famous Quaker "hedge" which they place between themselves and the rest of the world. He would indeed have chafed at such restrictions in that historical period. Elsewhere he comments: "Too much is often said—perhaps even by me—

about my Quaker lineage."[182] Despite that, in Whitman's last book, an anthology of poems and prose pieces, he published not one but two essays on key Quakers: firstly on the founder, George Fox and secondly on the great American Quaker reformer of his day, Elias Hicks. The book is called *November Boughs* and much conversation between Whitman and Traubel is about this last effort, a considerable trial for the ailing poet. At one point Traubel has been reading Whitman's essay on George Fox, which concludes with this passage:

> What is poor plain George Fox compared to William Shakespeare—to fancy's lord, imagination's heir? Yet George Fox stands for something too—a thought—the thought that wakes in silent hours—perhaps the deepest, most eternal thought latent in the human soul. This is the thought of God, merged in the thoughts of moral right and the immortality of identity. Great, great is this thought—aye, greater than all else.[183]

Traubel reads that passage and raises it with Whitman:

> I had been stirred by the last paragraph of the Fox. "It's splendid: perfect strength and eloquence—you never went higher than that."
>
> W. exclaimed: "Ah! You find that all there—just as you say it? I am glad—glad: there is at least that much to it all. I have never made any full statement on religion in any of my writings but I have always intended to."
>
> "But your whole book is religion. We do not want the figures for it. We are satisfied with the spirit."
>
> "You say that, too? Well—maybe, maybe. No doubt I have said enough on the subject—said really all there was in me to say: a few figures more would not have helped. In the days when I was planning to write and deliver lectures I designed one lecture at least on religion—indeed, collected a great mass of material for it. I never felt as though the discussion of religion should be left to the priests: it never seemed to me safe in their hands."[184]

In this extract we see that Traubel tells Whitman that his whole book – meaning *Leaves of Grass* – is religion. Whitman thinks that he could have not said more, and I think he is right. No essays on the subject of religion could match the unique insights in *Leaves*, nor could the scholarly marshalling of arguments that essay-writing entails have possibly matched the spontaneous urgency of the poems written in the peak of his health and during a period that can only be described as one of revelation. At the same time note again Whitman's instinctive anticlericalism: he does not think religion is safe in the hands of the priests.

The central point of *Leaves* however is always the body, even if it is a book of religion. Whitman tells Traubel: "After the long period in which the other view was upheld—the contempt of the body, the horrible, narrow, filthy, degenerate, poisonous, distaste expressed in ascetic religions for the physical man—I confess that even materialism is a relief, like a new day, like sunlight, like beauty—yes, like truth itself."[185] We note that Whitman says "even" materialism; it suggests perhaps that to swing from the extreme of asceticism to the extreme of materialism might be a relief but no advance.

We learn much about Whitman from Traubel's diaries, but let us return to Traubel himself. When Nambiar concluded that Whitman was Traubel's guru he was drawing on a chapter in Bucke's *Cosmic Consciousness* where various minor examples of illumination are described. Bucke has a section on Traubel which is in answer to Bucke's questioning him on his spiritual life. Bucke records Traubel as saying: "You are quite familiar with the path of my spiritual development – with the course taken by my mental self in arriving at its present state. You know I have come to my own, whatever that may be, mostly by immediate contact with experience rather than through books, ..."[186] Traubel mentions Emerson, Carlyle and Hugo as important to his early reading and adds that he cannot recall a time when *Leaves of Grass* was unknown to him. He says: "But previous to May, 1889, I do not seem to have got that (in a sense) final grasp of its mystery which now imparts to it its primary and supernatural significance." It was this event that Nambiar quotes, a moment leaning on the railings of a ferryboat when Traubel "lost this world for another, and in the anguish and joy of a few minutes saw things heretofore withheld from me revealed."

Traubel continues:

> Those who have had such an encounter will understand what this means, others will not, or will perhaps only realize it by intimation. I could not separate the physical and spiritual of that moment. My physical body

went through the experience of a disappearance in spiritual light. All severe lines in the front of phenomena relaxed. I was one with God, Love, the Universe, arrived at last face to face with myself. I was sensible of peculiar moral and mental disturbances and readjustments. There was an immediateness to it all – an indissoluble unity of the several energies of my being in one force. I was no more boating it on a river than winging it in space or taking star leaps, a traveler from one to another on the peopled orbs.[187]

This is a classic description of an enlightenment experience. It is comparable to Rumi's experience with Shams, Brunton's experience with Ramana Maharshi, Irina Tweedie's experience with Radha Mohan Lal, or Andrew Harvey's experience with Mother Meera. Given that Traubel and Harvey are both literary types the comparison is pertinent; both use literary flights to describe their experience. Nambiar is also rightly taken with Traubel's description of how Whitman spots the aftermath, an exalted state that Traubel cannot hide. Traubel says he has been wondering all day if he were not crazy; Whitman assures him that he is finally sane. This scene reminds me a little of the moment when the Egyptian hierophant Hermes (Egyptian name Thoth) teaches his son Tat on Mount Sinai. It is unusual for a son to be the disciple of his father but it works out in this instance. Rather like Brunton in front of Ramana Maharshi, young Tat is overwhelmed by a cosmic experience, similar also to how Traubel describes it.[188] Like Traubel he asks his guru if he is going mad; like Whitman Thoth replies no, you are finally sane.

John Burroughs

John Burroughs was a naturalist and writer though he earned his living for while as a federal bank examiner before he had the means to establish a farm for himself. Unlike Whitman who needed the bustle of city life Burroughs preferred a rural setting where he planted fruit bushes including grapes, baskets of which he would send to the poet in old age. Burroughs was well-known in his day for his Nature writings and literary criticism and spent time with personalities of his era including Theodore Roosevelt, John Muir, Henry Ford, Harvey Firestone, and Thomas Edison. Muir is significant here because I regard him, like Burroughs, as a Nature mystic as well as a Nature writer. However Burroughs was more famous in his day, his Nature writings finding their way into the school curriculum of just about every district in America.[189]

Burroughs describes how he found *Leaves of Grass* fascinating but puzzling to start with. He writes:

> My absorption of Emerson had prepared me in a measure for Whitman's philosophy of life, but not for the ideals of character and conduct which he held up to me, ... Whitman was Emerson translated from the abstract into the concrete. There was no privacy with Whitman; he never sat me down in a corner with a cozy, comfortable shut-in feeling, but he set me upon a hill or started me upon an endless journey.[190]

Burroughs first met Whitman in 1863, after which he made this assessment: "he was so sound and sweet and gentle and attractive as a man, and withal so wise and tolerant, that I soon came to feel the same confidence in the book that I at once placed in its author." Burroughs became convinced that Whitman represented a new type of man – an astonishing remark considering how in general Burroughs is careful and reserved in his prose. He is clear: no person had afforded him more of the "solid prizes of the universe" than Whitman, citing those exact words.[191] He also tells us that his book on Whitman is no dispassionate view; if it is one-sided it is because he loves him. Yet another homosexual declaration? I do not think so: again this is *agape*, not *eros*. Burroughs speaks of Whitman as "benignant" – a wonderful term – and suggests that "even his literary friends often sought his presence less for conversation than to bask in his physical or psychical sunshine ..."[192]

Burroughs knew Whitman best during the period when they were both in Washington, from 1863 to 1873, after which Burroughs would visit Whitman about once a year in Camden. After his last visit, not long before Whitman's death, he records:

> When I last saw him (December 26, 1891), though he had been very near death for many days, I am sure I had never seen his face so beautiful. There was no breaking-down of the features, or the least sign of decrepitude, such as we usually note in old men. The expression was full of pathos, but it was as grand as that of a god. I could not think of him as near death, he looked so unconquered.[193]

Unconquered. This is an important assessment for me, bearing in mind my earlier remarks as to whether Whitman's system, a revelation that crowded on him when young and fit, would survive disability and old age. It seems it did, although Whitman's confession to Traubel that he was easily "put to flight" in his belief in immortality rather humanizes the "unconquered." Burroughs was impressed, too, by the remark made by Moncure D. Conway, a minister in various faiths, a freethinker, abolitionist and biographer, regarding the face of Whitman in death: "It is the face of an aged loving child. As I looked, it was with the reflection that, during an acquaintance of thirty-six years, I never heard from those lips a word of irritation, or depreciation of any being. I do not believe that Buddha, of whom he appeared an avatar, was more gentle to all men, women, children, and living things."

Burroughs records a number of such impressions made on people by Whitman, this one from a visiting Scottish doctor:

> But it was not in any one of these features that his charm lay so much as in his *tout ensemble*, and the irresistible magnetism of his sweet, aromatic presence, which seemed to exhale sanity, purity, and naturalness, and exercised over me an attraction which positively astonished me, producing an exaltation of mind and soul which no man's presence ever did before. I felt that I was here face to face with the living embodiment of all that was good, noble, and lovable in humanity.[194]

Perhaps because he was a Nature writer Burroughs wrote a lot about Whitman's appearance, saying for example that it had "none of the eagerness, sharpness, nervousness, of the modern face. It had but few lines, and these were Greek." The general tone of Burroughs' prose is of his era and of an outlook long abandoned in materialist modernity. No modern writer could be imagined producing a statement like this for example: "Whitman's absolute faith in himself was a part of his faith in creation. He felt himself so keenly a part of the whole that he shared its soundness and excellence; he must be good as it is good."[195] This correlates well with what Whitman told Traubel, that he was "not prepared to admit fraud in the scheme of the universe."

The following remark on detachment also stands well with what Whitman himself says about being "apart from the pulling and hauling":

7. The Hierophancy of Walt Whitman

> Then Whitman had a curious habit of standing apart, as it were, and looking upon himself and his career as of some other person. He was interested in his own cause, and took a hand in the discussion. From first to last he had the habit of regarding himself objectively. On his deathbed he seemed to be a spectator of his own last moments, and was seen to feel his pulse a few minutes before he breathed his last.[196]

Burroughs is considered to have become an atheist in later years or possibly a pantheist – radically different positions from my perspective – but he made this religious assessment of Whitman:

> It is hardly necessary to say that the religion which Whitman celebrates is not any form of ecclesiasticism. It was larger than any creed that has yet been formulated. It was the conviction of the man of science touched and vivified by the emotion of the prophet and poet. As exemplified in his life its chief elements were faith, hope, charity. Its object was to prepare you to live, not to die, and to "earn for the body and the mind what adheres and goes forward, and is not dropped by death."[197]

Burroughs is quoting a line from verse 12 of "Starting from Paumanok" which confirms again that Whitman believed in some form of immortality for the self. In addition Burroughs is every bit as anticlerical as Whitman, happy to declare that Whitman is effectively saying to the priests "your day is done."

Burroughs always remained important to Whitman. We know this because Whitman tells Traubel in 1888 that if Traubel were to write to Burroughs: "Make it plain to him always that he is eminently present to me always here: no matter what happens, remains vitally with me, sharing my life."[198] Whitman includes him in his "New Guard," those who have faith in *Leaves of Grass* – or "men affiliated through thick and thin" as Whitman describes his followers – listing them as Dowden, Rossetti, O'Connor, Burroughs, Symonds, Rhys, Noel, and elsewhere making similar lists that include Burroughs.[199] At another point he tells Traubel: "John was with the original *Leaves of Grassers*—in the first rank (the body guard)—has never wavered that I know of."[200] However Whitman is occasionally exercised in this last period that Burroughs is not quite the same as when they were in Washington together, finding it difficult to write to him for example.[201]

I think this raises an important issue in good hierophancy. Burroughs feels a life-long debt to Whitman as his teacher, and honors him as he can. Those solid prizes of the universe that Burroughs now owns were afforded by Whitman. But it is not so much that Burroughs has "spread a wider breast" than Whitman or that he has learned to "destroy the teacher," but that his spiritual center of gravity lies a little to the left or right of Whitman's. The clues to this are found in remarks by Whitman such as this: "John is a wood wizard: things come out of their holes—present themselves—ask for orders—when John goes into the woods."[202] Or this about Burroughs, that he is: "so calm, so poised, so much at home with himself, so much a familiar spirit of the forests."[203] Whitman can see the difference of temperament between them when he says:

> He is a child of the woods, fields, hills—native to them in a rare sense (in a sense almost of miracle). My own favorite loafing places have always been the rivers, the wharves, the boats—I like sailors, stevedores. I have never lived away from a big river. ... John's faithfulness, affection, are beyond question. Our relations with each other have always been comradely—largely and directly personal.[204]

Whitman is again most perceptive when he says: "Outdoors taught Burroughs gentle things about men—it had no such effect on Thoreau."[205] What I get from all this but have not been able to directly correlate in writings by or about Burroughs is that he is far closer to the shamanic Native American sensibility than Whitman, far more of an animist, and that the hierophancy between Horn Chips and Crow Dog may have been his truer spiritual milieu. That the wild should teach Burroughs "gentle things about men" is absolutely right, this is the impression I have from all hunter-gatherer or animist cultures.

Perhaps this thought from Whitman wraps it up: "Burroughs could not help but be what he is: the factor in him which provides for that sort of life is the primitive—the wild man, the woods man, the man of flint and skins, born over again into an age of more sophisticated ideals."[206] I have personally grappled with this all my life, reconciling my shamanic instincts – which I feel are "born over again" from the ancient past – with an age of more sophisticated ideals. I don't actually see those ideals as more sophisticated, just different, part of irrevocable change, true, but not of "progress." Hence I am deeply with Burroughs here.

The guru may be of the first order, but he or she will always operate within their own spiritual system, which cannot by the nature of things be complete. The good hierophant may have some instinct, as Whitman does here, that a pupil belongs to a subtly different spiritual universe, even if they cannot enter it themselves. Crucially, the good hierophant makes no move to prevent the pupil from entering it.

John Addington Symonds

John Addington Symonds (1840-1893) was an English poet, literary critic and cultural historian, known for his work on the Renaissance. Included by Whitman as one of his "Leaves of Grassers," Symonds was indeed an enthusiast for Whitman's work though he never visited him. He was one of the most eminent men of letters in his day to endorse Whitman, especially in his book *Walt Whitman: a Study*. Typical for much of the response to Whitman, the Symonds' book approaches the question of Whitman's religious thought via literary writings, in this case that of Victor Hugo. Declaring that there were analogies between the spirits of the two great men, Symonds goes on to explore their differences. He writes of Whitman:

> Every detail of the world endowed with life, with shape, contained for him God, was a microcosm of the whole, an apparent and ever-recurring miracle. Upon abstractions he refused to dwell, because (without having perhaps appropriated the Hegelian philosophy) he regarded the concrete as the ultimate reality, the self-effectuation of the Idea, while the abstract remains mere gaping void.[207]

Symonds adds: "For him Soul was the most etherealised, the least palpable and visible, yet the most formative and durable element in everything that is. He clung to the belief in immortality." I think these lines are a fair assessment of Whitman's spiritual-religious system, couched in the language of the day. Symonds' chapter on Whitman's religious thought comes early in his book and I find little to argue with in it; Symonds' treatment could be pretty much substituted for my own (indeed the whole book could stand for much in my account of Whitman). He finishes the chapter with an account of how Whitman, his "master," had transformed him. I copy here the greater part of it, simply as the best account of the hierophancy-at-a-distance between them:

> In bounden duty toward Whitman, I make this personal statement; for had it not been for the contact of his fervent spirit with my own, the pyre ready to be lighted, the combustible materials of modern thought awaiting the touch of the fire-bringer, might never have leapt up into the flame of life-long faith and consolation. During my darkest hours, it comforted me with the conviction that I too played my part in the illimitable symphony of cosmic life. When I sinned, repined, sorrowed, suffered, it touched me with a gentle hand of sympathy and understanding, sustained me with the strong arm of assurance that in the end I could not go amiss (for I was part, an integrating part of the great whole); and when strength revived in me, it stirred a healthy pride and courage to effectuate myself, to bear the brunt of spiritual foes, the slings and arrows of outrageous fortune. For this reason, in duty to my master Whitman, and in the hope that my experience may encourage others to seek the same source of inspiration, I have exceeded the bounds of an analytical essay by pouring forth my personal confession.[208]

As a disciple Symonds describes himself here as a "pyre ready to be lighted." In a materialist, modernist, sexualized, atheistic, psychologized world that "pyre" is understood by many as purely homosexual. A little more broadly it might also be understood as literary, in a Romantic mode. Neither of these interests me; instead I think of Ramana Maharshi's remark to Paul Brunton in answer to how long might it take for him to become enlightened. Maharshi used the metaphor, not of a pyre, but of gunpowder and coal, the former lighting up in an instant with a mere spark, the latter taking much more coaxing. Symonds is clearly of the readily combustible type, perhaps to Whitman like Rumi to Shams.

Let us look in turn at how Whitman regarded Symonds. Traubel writes:

> Talked an hour or more about Symonds. W. very frank, very affectionate.
>
> "Symonds is a royal good fellow—he comes along without qualifications: just happens into the temple and takes his place. But he has a few doubts yet to be quieted—not doubts of me, doubts rather of himself.

7. The Hierophancy of Walt Whitman

One of these doubts is about Calamus. What does Calamus mean? What do the poems come to in the round-up? That is worrying him a good deal—their involvement, as he suspects, is the passional relations of men with men—the thing he reads so much of in the literatures of southern Europe and sees something of in his own experience. He is always driving at me about that: is that what Calamus means?—because of me or in spite of me, is that what it means? I have said no, but no does not satisfy him. But read this letter—read the whole of it: it is very shrewd, very cute, in deadliest earnest: it drives me hard—almost compels me—it is urgent, persistent: he sort of stands in the road and says: 'I won't move till you answer my question.'"[209]

Whitman is clear: Symonds has taken his place in the temple, meaning in the spiritual life of the followers of *Leaves of Grass*. Reading Symonds' book on Whitman I have to agree: the Englishman is a disciple of Whitman's as much as any follower of an Eastern guru. But Whitman is conscious of Symonds' preoccupation and answers no, the Calamus poems are not poems of the "passional relations of men with men." Whitman goes on: "My first instinct about all that Symonds writes is violently reactionary—is strong and brutal for no, no, no." However Whitman qualifies this, leaving the door open for different or nuanced interpretations. I am not against any of these interpretations as long as they are not magnified to the point that the spiritual Whitman is eclipsed. Whitman may well have been gay and if gay men, historically and still under the burden of much misunderstanding and sometimes cruel prejudice or repression, take him as an icon of gay pride, why should I argue with that? It is when that eclipses what I feel is far more important that I murmur: "by the way he was also a buddha." I am sure for example that when Whitman compares Symonds to the Irish critic Edward Dowden he is talking in spiritual terms: "Dowden does not melt himself and melt me, as Symonds does: he is more stiffly literary: but he comes dangerously near to our standard."[210] "Melt" could mean anything; perhaps homosexual love, perhaps literary ecstasy, or, in my preferred interpretation, the spiritual closeness of master and disciple.

Whitman is conscious of Symonds' delicate constitution – he had several nervous breakdowns – calling him "overbred," but declares "yet he has remained human, a man, in spite of all."[211] This is Whitman's generosity: to see qualities that transcend class and culture in someone who a man of his American vigor and temperament might easily call decadent. Whitman follows this remark with another expression of irritation at Symonds over his homosexual interpretations of Calamus. He thinks that Traubel might be wondering why he doesn't shut him up with a direct answer. Tellingly Trauble says: "I think your silence might lead him to suppose there was a nigger in your wood pile." Whitman jokes about this and then points out that in the old letter they are discussing Symonds address him as "Sir," not yet "Master." Whitman dislikes both but is clear: he loves Symonds. Comparing him again with Dowden, he finds in Symonds no presence of the qualifying no in Dowden. He was sorry that he had never actually met Symonds, mentioning later that his greatest regret in not travelling to Europe was the missed opportunity to see him.[212] This is a significant point in much of Whitman's hierophancy: it was as much by exchange of letter as by physical presence. The following, part of his conversation with Traubel, makes the point: "I am always strangely moved by a letter from Symonds: it makes the day, it makes many days, sacred."[213]

Symonds' book can almost be summed up by his opening words:

> The world has lost another good and great man. Walt Whitman died in March 1892 at Camden, New Jersey, U.S.A., after a lingering and painful illness, which terminated in distressing debility, borne by him with serenity and fortitude. A spiritual force has been resumed through his death into the occult stock of universal energy; and it is too early as yet to sum up any final account of his achievement as the teacher of a new way of regarding life, the prophet of a democratic religion, and the poet of a revolutionary school.[214]

Much in this paragraph is obscure to the modern mind, though we can note how Symonds regards Whitman as the prophet of a religion that has as its chief characteristic democracy. Obscure to many perhaps, but meaningful to me, is his curious comment: "A spiritual force has been resumed through his death into the occult stock of universal energy." I think this true at the death of all living things but perhaps of particular significance for the great spiritual teachers. To my mind they color eternity more strongly than most, though I have to concede that I first learnt this idea from Rajneesh. Whitman's unique contribution is well stated by Symonds: "The body has therefore a mystic value for Whitman, not merely because of its exceeding beauty and delightfulness, but also because it is verily the temple of the divinest of all things we know, the human soul."[215]

Edward Carpenter

The story of Edward Carpenter's discipleship to Walt Whitman is also equally open to a homosexual, literary or spiritual interpretation. Additionally socialism enters the story, as it should, because of Whitman's ever-present linkage between comradeship and democracy. Like Symonds, Carpenter (1844-1929) was an English literary figure and homosexual, differing in that he twice visited Whitman and was politically active on the left. Like Symonds, Carpenter wrote a book, *Days With Walt Whitman*, about the poet he admired, though this time based on his visits. Carpenter was an eminent man of his day, friendly in person or by correspondence with such figures as Rabindranath Tagore, Annie Besant, Isadora Duncan, Havelock Ellis, Mahatma Gandhi, Keir Hardie, Jack London, William Morris and John Ruskin. Unlike Burroughs and Symonds, he travelled to India and his exposure to Eastern thought enabled him to place Whitman's teachings in a wider spiritual context.

After Carpenter's first visit to Whitman in 1886 he wrote:

> Meanwhile in that first ten minutes I was becoming conscious of an impression which subsequently grew even more marked — the impression, namely, of an immense vista or background to his personality. If I had thought before (and I do not know that I had) that Whitman was eccentric, unbalanced, violent, my first interview produced quite a contrary effect. No one could be more considerate, I may almost say courteous; no one could have more simplicity of manner and freedom from egotistic wrigglings; and I never met anyone who gave me more the impression of *knowing what he was doing* than he did. Yet away and beyond all this I was aware of a certain radiant power in him, a large benign affluence and inclusiveness, as of the sun, which filled out the place where he was — yet with something of reserve and sadness in it too, and a sense of remoteness and inaccessibility.[216] (Carpenter's emphasis)

As a socialist Carpenter was moved to find that Whitman was treasured by the working people they encountered when crossing by ferry to Philadelphia. As he says: "we were before long quite besieged." Carpenter reports that one working man who had not seen Whitman for a while had tears in his eyes. Whitman was not well enough then to walk far so they used the tramcars for much of their outing, giving Carpenter the opportunity to see city life through Whitman's eyes. Whitman also introduced him to the Gilchrists, who at that time lived not far away from Whitman and in whose house they kept "a kind of prophet's chamber for him there, always ready" as Carpenter put it. He later caught up with Whitman at a friend's house in the countryside near the creek that Whitman liked to bathe in. Carpenter observed this at the evening meal:

> When we went in to dinner Mr. Stafford was already seated; I think he was about to say grace. Walt, with greater grace, stood for a moment bending over him from behind, and clasped Stafford's head in his great hands; then passed on in silence. What a large sweet presence — so benign, yet so determined! [217]

This is an interesting picture. Whitman holds the head of a friend, perhaps as Mother Meera does, a laying on of hands, a spiritual transmission, or just an expression of grace and compassion. It does not belong to ordinary discourse one has to say, either in the giving or the receiving. Carpenter accounts for the determination in Whitman by adding: "... no rough draft of his character would be complete which did not take into account the strong Quaker element of obstinacy which existed in him ..."[218]

We see that Carpenter is no more fooled by mere literary expression than Whitman:

> Literary persons, as a rule, write over their own heads; they talk a little bigger than themselves. But Whitman seemed to fill out "Leaves of Grass," and form an interpretation of it. I began to see that all he had written there was matter of absolute personal, experience—that you might be sure that what was said was meant.[219]

When Carpenter says that literary persons "write over their own heads" he could have been Gurdjieff teasing Ouspensky over his *Tertium Organum*. Earlier I reproduced a passage in which Whitman confided to Carpenter that he hid his spiritual truths, upon which Carpenter suggested that "probably we had something yet to learn from India in these matters." Whitman was not so sure about that, but it remains a useful feature of the discipleship of Carpenter to Whitman that Carpenter could so readily draw on India's spiritual traditions. He made direct analogies in the Appendix to his book between passages from *Leaves of Grass* and passages from the Upanishads, Buddhist texts, the *Bhagavad Gita*, the *Tao Teh Ching*, and the New Testament. Carpenter also presents an interesting comparison between Whitman and an Indian seer that probably sums up his attitude to both Whitman and *Leaves*.

> I have two portraits — photographs — which I am fond of comparing with each other. One is of Whitman, taken in 1890; the other, taken about the same time and at the same age (seventy years), is of an Indian Gnani or seer. Both are faces of the highest interest and import; but how different! That of Whitman deeply lined, bearing the marks of life-long passion and emotion; aggressive and determined, yet wistful and tender, full of suffering and full of love, indicating serenity, yet markedly turbid and clouded, ample in brow and frame and flowing hair, as of one touching and mingling with humanity at all points — withal of a wonderful majesty and grandeur, as of the great rock (to return always to that simile) whose summit pierces at last the highest domain.
>
> The other portrait, of a man equally aged, shows scarcely a line on the face; you might think for that and for the lithe, active form that he was not more than forty years old; a brow absolutely calm and unruffled, gracious, expressive lips, well-formed features, and eyes — the dominant characteristic of his countenance — dark and intense, and illuminated by the vision of the seer. In this face you discern command, control, gentleness, and the most absolute inward unity, serenity, and peace; no wandering emotions or passions flit across the crystal mirror of the soul; selfhood in any but the highest sense has vanished — the self has, as it were, returned to its birthplace — leaving behind the most childlike, single-hearted, uncensorious, fearless character imaginable.
>
> Yet just here one seems to miss something in the last character — the touch of human and earthly entanglement. Here is not exactly the great loving heart which goes a few steps on the way with every child of man; here is not the ample-domed brow which tackles each new problem of life and science. Notwithstanding evident signs of culture and experience in the past, notwithstanding vast powers of concentration in any given matter or affair when necessary, the face shows that the heart and intellect have become quiescent, that interest in the actual has passed or is passing away.[220]

I think this passage is so important that I also quote it in full in my book *Secularism* as one of the best illustrations of the difference between the two spiritual paths I term *via positiva* and *via negativa*. Carpenter is talking about an "Indian Gnani or seer" – in my terminology simply a *jnani* – whose identity we do not know. It could well describe Ramana Maharshi, but he was born in 1879, too late for the photographs that Carpenter was contemplating. Carpenter's trip to India is detailed in his travelogue, *From Adam's Peak to Elephanta: Sketches in Ceylon and India*. However a chapter in which he describes coming across a great sage does not record an immediate discipleship as with Paul Brunton to Ramana Maharshi. Like Brunton, he is however aware that the sage or *jnani* has an intensity of inner life unmatched by interest in the outer world.

Carpenter has a section in his book on Whitman called "Whitman as Prophet" in which he says: "In the Vedic scriptures, and, in lineal succession from these, in the Buddhist and Platonist and Christian writings, in the Taoists of China, the Mystics of Egypt, the Sufis of Persia, the root is to be found—and is clearly distinguishable—the very same from which 'Leaves of Grass' has sprung."[221] Carpenter goes on to cite passages from the Hindu, Buddhist, Taoist and Christian scriptures to support that idea. However he does not follow up on his insight when comparing the *jnani* with Whitman, that Whitman appears to hold detachment from the world in extraordinary balance with his love for it.

Whitman told Traubel: "Carpenter is a man of means on whom his estate sits lightly: is intensely interested in the radical problems: is of a religious nature—not formally so, but in atmosphere."[222] In this entry in Traubel's diary we see more of Whitman's high regard for Carpenter:

> W. today gave me a Carpenter letter, saying of it: "It is beautiful, like a confession: it was one of Carpenter's first letters. I seem to get very near to his heart and he to mine in that letter: it has a place in our personal history—an important place. Carpenter was never more thoroughly Carpenter than just there, in that tender mood of self-examination. Introspection! I am afraid of it, generally: just enough of it is good, too much of it is disease: most people don't stop with just enough. Carpenter is a thoroughly wholesome man—alive, clean, from head to foot."[223]

In turn, the following letter from Carpenter reflects the debt he has to Whitman:

> Will it ever be that human love—strong to meet with adventurous joy all chance and change—will cease to be a mere name? that men will "understand"—eat of the tree of knowledge of good and evil, and so be immortal? How strange it is! I know that it must be, I see it everywhere—in face after face in the streets, in the sound of men's voices and in their silence—clear, unmistakable, as if just about to be disclosed, the divine "everywhere-equal" life; and yet the children die, hardly knowing what they have sought yet knowing that they have not found it, and their dreams fade away, and to long suffering succeeds rest, and still the distance remains immeasurable. All is resumed. As soon as I remember what the end is—however great the distance—I do not doubt. It is quite true—even as it is truly present with us now underlying all thought and these words. Dear friend, you have so infused yourself that it is daily more and more possible for men to walk hand in hand over the whole earth.[224]

I like it that Carpenter talks about the "divine everywhere-equal life," juxtaposing it with the perception he had in common with Marx and Engels that children were dying from working-class poverty – indeed as a "man of means" Carpenter was perhaps rather like Engels, only having in addition a profound religious optimism. The "divine everywhere-equal life" appears to me both the epitome of Whitman's teaching and also the extension by Carpenter of it into the realms of socialism where Whitman did not exactly venture.

Anne Gilchrist

Anne Gilchrist pursued an interesting negotiating strategy with her hierophant: she tried to marry him. I have some sympathy with this as, long before I met my wife, I entertained similar ideas about Mother Meera. We are creatures of imagination, and when our religious sensibilities are triggered by the hierophant our romantic inclinations may follow. My idle speculations were not serious however and anyway I believe she had taken a German husband of convenience in order to stay in the country, a ploy that I understand but do not terribly like: I am old-fashioned about marriage.

Gilchrist had fallen in love with an imaginary man as conjured up through reading *Leaves of Grass*, an imaginary man not so different perhaps to the one whose portrait I paint in this book. By this I mean that however much Whitman tells us that to hold his book is to hold the man, and however much research we may do into the life of a person we have never met, the flesh-and-blood person is not recoverable in the slightest (though I hope that what we learn about hierophancy more than makes up for it). Gilchrist was a determined Victorian widow however and packed up her home and children to cross the Atlantic in pursuit of her husband-to-be. The fantasy did not survive the first few minutes of meeting him, it seems. Remarkably, however, Whitman and Gilchrist formed such a deep friendship that the old poet became a regular visitor to her home. He became an honorary family member for whom they reserved a room – Carpenter's "prophet's chamber" – with a stove and a supply of oak for burning. When Gilchrist's circumstances changed she moved back to England, a great loss to Whitman's social life.

But how do we chart the course of the hierophancy between them? Gilchrist is the classic case of a person who comes to a spiritual teacher through their writings. This requires the easy distribution of the printed word and the widespread fostering of literacy, such as found in the modern world. I doubt, for example, that many people became Buddhists via the written word for at least five hundred years after the Buddha's death, not at least until the oral tradition began to appear in writing. Gilchrist was steeped in the ambience of Blake's work – her husband was the key Victorian biography of Blake – and found that Whitman spoke to her, partly because his work is suffused at every point with a respect for women's capacities almost unknown in that era, and partly because of the spiritual content.

Gilchrist first read *Leaves of Grass* in the expurgated edition published in England in 1868. This was edited by William Michael Rossetti (1829-1919) an English writer and critic who was one of the founders of the Pre-Raphaelites, and who was later able to lend Gilchrist the complete edition. Gilchrist's correspondence with him forms a document called "A Woman's Estimate Of Walt Whitman,"[225] her name being originally suppressed on the advice of Rossetti. One can immediately see in the letters that Whitman has had a profound effect on her, for example she writes early on: "There is nothing in him that I shall ever let go my hold of. For me the reading of his poems is truly a new birth of the soul." She observes quite acutely that the poems are vital; they had grown; they were not made. Gilchrist is conscious of Whitman's detractors, both literary and moral, but declares:

> And I know that poetry must do one of two things,—either own this man as equal with her highest, completest manifestors, or stand aside, and admit that there is something come into the world nobler, diviner, than herself, one that is free of the universe, and can tell its secrets as none before.

Poetry, it seems, *has* eventually owned Whitman as one of its greats, but has not, perhaps cannot, grant that there is something bigger than poetry which Whitman brings into the world. Poets who enjoy the "chill and faded beauty of the past" do not make Gilchrist happy, she tells Rossetti, but Whitman's works grasps immediate reality. Her response to it was to be electrified, and, as we saw, ultimately led her to take the extraordinary step of moving to Philadelphia. Gilchrist completed her husband's seminal work, *The Life of William Blake*, and so would have had extensive knowledge of Blake's thinking and spiritual significance. Her approach to the Calamus poems is of a woman's sympathy for friendship amongst men, touched too that Whitman nursed so many dying soldiers. The generally held view of the Calamus poems today is expressed in Wikipedia's entry on the subject: "Most critics believe that these poems are Whitman's clearest expressions in print of his ideas about homosexual love." In contrast Gilchrist's assessment of them acknowledges only what we call *agape* and nothing of *eros*.

Gilchrist seems to lack any trace of Victorian prudery, and writes to Rossetti after reading the unexpurgated version that, "I saw at a glance that it was not, as men had supposed, the heights brought down to the depths, but the depths lifted up level with the sunlit heights, that they might become clear and sunlit too." In our post-Freudian world it is easy to overlook how significant that statement was in her era.

Whitman in turn was greatly appreciative of her "Woman's Estimate."[226] As a literary figure like Andrew Harvey, Gilchrist was perhaps drawn to the silence in Whitman's presence, the kind of silence that makes the mere presence of the guru so efficacious in the spiritual life, the basis of *darshan*. Unlike Harvey she maintained good relations with her guru and unlike Alcibiades with Socrates she was not at all rueful of her spurned romantic advances. If Gilchrist, like Symonds, was looking for the flame that would ignite her – whether coal, or pyre or gunpowder in our various metaphors – it is interesting to speculate whether the preparatory work for Whitman's spark had been done in part by William Blake. Even if Whitman is clear where he and Blake differ, he would, I imagine, allow him into the company of the "divine literatus," the hierophancies of which follow such a different course to that of the priest.

Richard Maurice Bucke

We can now turn to the pivotal figure of Richard Maurice Bucke (1837-1902). He was a Canadian psychiatrist whose life was profoundly impacted by Whitman and who provided me with so much spiritual impetus, both in the understanding of Whitman and in the wider field. I will now quote in full the passage where he describes how he gradually came to understand *Leaves of Grass*:

> At first as I read, it seemed to me the writer was always on the point of saying something which he never actually said. Page after page seemed equally barren of any definite statement. Then after a time I found that a few lines here and there were full of suggestion and beauty. Gradually these bright spots, as I may call them, grew larger, more numerous and more brilliant, until at last the whole surface was lit up with an almost unearthly splendor.[227]

I find this an accurate description of my own encounter with many sacred texts. It is a process of gradual attunement and it does not work for everything. For example, though I imagine it true for millions who read the Bible or the Koran, neither of those have ever lit up for me in this way. As discussed earlier, Bucke's encounters with Whitman – both through *Leaves* and in person – led to his book on "cosmic consciousness" of which he thought Whitman the prime exemplar. Bucke insisted that Whitman visit him in London, Ontario, so he could write a book about him, much to Whitman's protestations. As in the book by Burroughs, Bucke says at the outset: "I make no pretence that they are other than from a friendly point of view."[228] Where Burroughs is measured in his assessment of

Whitman, Bucke throws all caution to the winds, an approach that led the Oxford scholar of mysticism R. C. Zaehner to call him fatuous and silly.[229] For example Bucke says of Whitman:

> According to the poet himself, he has lived a common life; and this is true, not in the sense that it has been like other lives, but that other lives in future are to be like it, and that his life is to be the common property of humanity. For this man, who has absorbed the whole human race, will, in the future, in turn, be absorbed by each individual member of the race who aspires to attain complete spiritual growth.[230]

It is an extraordinary claim, that Whitman is the template for future humans, the template for those who want "complete spiritual growth." It fits of course with Bucke's evolutionary point of view, but it does not fit my perception that people like Whitman are no more common now than in the past, nor are likely to be in the future. Bucke's other main preoccupation is what he terms "moral elevation," the subject of one of his other books, the theme that runs alongside evolution in his book on Whitman, and a term that he applies in the greatest order to Whitman. Isn't this all too much? While Robertson does not regard Buck as fatuous or silly he does suggest that Bucke is painting a messianic view of the poet and was "promoting Walt Whitman as the greatest religious figure in history."[231] He adds that Bucke's book on Whitman is nothing more than an exercise in hero-worship, and provides details of Bucke's career in Victorian psychiatry that might easily lead the modern reader to view Bucke with contempt, a view that I believe should be resisted however.

Twenty years ago I read Bucke's book on Whitman in the old Round Reading Room at the British Library; today I am as moved by my downloaded version as then. It is of a piece with the accounts by Traubel, Burroughs and Carpenter; it records in simple language Bucke's observation of Whitman in varied circumstances and with many other people; and it conveys Bucke's own personality and of course the period he lived in and which shaped him. When immersed in the Whitman literature of the period and in the intellectual climate of that period I see nothing to justify the cynicism of such modern writers as Robertson. Nor does the term "sycophancy" cover Bucke's enthusiasm. He is clear-eyed enough to quote this for example, from a woman who knew him: "Mr. Whitman was not a smooth, glib, or even a very fluent talker." It is passages more like the following which suggest hero-worship or naivety to the modern mind – Bucke is commenting about Whitman's ministrations to dying soldiers: "I believe, knowing Walt Whitman as I do, and having some knowledge of medicine, that the man did possess an extraordinary power, by which he must have been able in many cases to turn the scale in favor of life, when without him the result would have been death."[232] Bucke tells us that Whitman's health was broken on the wards, the doctors there putting it down to "hospital malaria," eventually leading to the stroke that paralyzed him. How medically accurate any of this is, I do not know. Here is another passage from Bucke's book that is hostage to the fortune of modern skepticism:

> No description can give any idea of the extraordinary physical attractiveness of the man. I do not speak now of the affection of friends and of those who are much with him, but of the magnetism exercised by him upon people who merely see him for a few minutes or pass him on the street.[233]

It is a passage like this perhaps that leads Robertson to insist that there was an "unacknowledged homoerotic attraction" between the two men, going on to cite another passage supporting the idea, in which Bucke describes the impact that meeting Whitman had on a friend who had been reading *Leaves*: "but shortly after leaving, a state of mental exaltation set in, which he could only describe by comparing to slight intoxication by champagne, or falling in love!" Bucke writes that the state lasted about six weeks and left a permanent change in the mind of this person.[234] Robertson claims that in fact "this person" was Bucke himself.

When I wept over the death of Rajneesh it was not because of a homoerotic relationship. It was because of a special kind of love that the guru engenders. Thousands who have attended *darshan* with Mother Meera, for example, have known it, as have those at the feet of the other gurus discussed here. However what makes Whitman important to me is the lack of classical guru-disciple context. There is nothing explicitly elevated or exotic with Whitman. This passage from Bucke's book on Whitman is a clue:

> Walt Whitman, in my talks with him at that time, always disclaimed any lofty intention in himself or his poems. If you accepted his explanations

they were simple and commonplace. But when you came to think about these explanations, and to enter into the spirit of them, you found that the simple and commonplace with him included the ideal and the spiritual. So it may be said that neither he nor his writings are growths of the ideal from the real, but are the actual real lifted up into the ideal.[235]

Whitman is not Ramakrishna in the Kali temple; his pupils are not worshippers; his conversation is not about the goddess, devotion, avatars or sacred ritual. Whitman is a guru of an entirely different type. As Bucke records, Whitman was clear that he had no experiences that were particularly religious, never felt the need for spiritual regeneration or to be "saved," had no fear of hell and above all had no "distrust of the scheme of the universe."[236] All this suggests to me that what Whitman has to teach us – as his eleves – is eminently compatible with the modern world and its democratic tenor. I agree with Bucke when he says in one of his letters that we injure Whitman if we think him a mere literary figure, even if of the standing of Samuel Johnson, Tennyson, Victor Hugo or Goethe, and that we should reach instead for comparisons with the Buddha, Jesus and Zoroaster.[237] Buck writes:

> What the Vedas were to Brahmanism, the Law and the Prophets to Judaism, the Avesta and Zend to Zoroastrianism, the Kings to Confucianism and Taoism, the Pitakas to Buddhism, the Gospels and Pauline writings to Christianity, the Quran to Mohammedanism, will *Leaves of Grass* be to the future of American civilization.[238]

I am comfortable with Bucke's assessment of where *Leaves of Grass* stands in relation to the world's sacred texts, but observe that his futurology is not so sound. American civilization now is no more patterned on *Leaves* than when Whitman wrote it. I sometimes see Bucke to Whitman a little like Ouspensky to Gurdjieff or even Bohm to Krishnamurti. Bucke and Ouspensky were not so much literary figures as dabbling in the science of their day and had profound convictions about the nature of the universe they wanted to convey and with a considerable audience. It is not of course scientific in any modern sense to apply evolutionary ideas to the spiritual development of mankind, but Bucke's work prefigures much of the New Age and also the "evolutionary enlightenment" of Andrew Cohen. While one can find *some* support for such ideas in *Leaves of Grass* a careful reading of it and the conversations between Traubel and Whitman show as much contradiction of them. David Bohm was of course an entirely modern physicist by profession, but his obsessions were possibly as unscientific as those of Bucke and Ouspensky. Bucke's futurological obsessions entirely survived his hierophancy with Whitman, where those of Bohm and Ouspensky seemed to cause more serious problems.

8

NEGOTIATING THE HIEROPHANT

We can now bring together the two themes in this book, firstly that of Whitman's hierophancy and secondly our composite picture of the guru-disciple relationship through history. While we have examined many possible reasons for skepticism towards the hierophantic relationship my closing remarks will emphasize the positive.

While studying for my Master's in mysticism I purchased a book called "Half Way up the Mountain." It is potentially a useful survey of spiritual teachers and their shortcomings, making the general claim that too many hierophants start teaching before they are ready.²³⁹ One of my tutors asked my opinion of it. "By the timid, for the timid," was my instant response. This book, in contrast, is not for the timid. If one thinks of motor-racing for example, it is clear that both the risks and the rewards are high and definitely not an occupation for the faint-hearted. In my opinion, the life of a spiritual seeker involves far greater risks and rewards than merely losing one's life. What is at stake, as Whitman puts it, are the solid prizes of the universe, not just a large ornate silver cup, fame and money. Those are, in spiritual terms, not solid at all. My attitude to this has not changed in forty years and led me to rather upset my friends who were Andrew Cohen disciples as mentioned earlier. I cannot avoid it that in my opinion it is better to have gone through the high points with Cohen and crashed than not to have had exposure to him at all. Of course I might have a different opinion if I had engaged more closely with Rajneesh; in his case my involvement had pretty much ended by the time his community crashed.

In a recent discussion with Quakers some points from an article by a leading contemporary Quaker, a former anarchist named Ben Pink Dandelion, were raised. We should engage in "radical spirituality" he suggested, something I could sign up to easily. However a lady present shook her head. She had been to India a number of times, followed gurus and practiced Buddhism, she said, and it had put her in a mental hospital. No, radical spirituality was not for her.

I respect this lady's sentiment. Even the innocuous-sound "mindfulness," deriving from Buddhist tradition but shorn of all the normal trappings of hierophancy, has been criticized for its dangers. I know a peer in the House of Lords partly responsible for setting up the "Mindfulness All-Party Parliamentary Group" which introduces the practice to British politicians.[240] The UK National Health Service and many other public and private organizations have shown an interest in it, but there is now a growing literature on the negative effects, including panic, depression, pain and anxiety.[241] However I know from my own spiritual journey that no amount of such literature, or any other warnings, would have halted my explorations. I continued at each stage because I had to. Already deeply curious before I arrived at the Rajneesh ashram I then found the ground completely cut away from under me. There was nothing solid, I realized, to my life. I faced an existential challenge in many ways, but most profoundly from the *being* of Rajneesh, and by extension from the being of all the spiritual teachers. When I look at the list of spiritual teachers covered in this book, including Socrates, Rumi, Ramana Maharshi, Gurdjieff, Krishnamurti, Andrew Cohen, Mother Meera and most definitely Walt Whitman, each stand as the same existential challenge, just presented on a different wavelength as it were.

Whatever risks arose in following the hierophants I encountered, one thing is clear to me: such individuals are mostly not going to take advice from the seeker. It is up to the seeker to negotiate the hierophants as they loom in one's life. A clear picture of the hierophant is impossible, because by definition they represent the unknown. A clear picture of the seeker is all that can guide one, and that is a picture of risk, the greatest of which is total mental collapse. This is nothing like "full catastrophe disillusion-

8. Negotiating the Hierophant

ment" where the pupil walks away from the teacher with anger, bitterness and cynicism. All of that is perfectly survivable. In contrast mental breakdown in the modern world has pretty much only one destination: medication, and that can be for life. That it may be a spiritual-led breakdown as opposed to a psychological breakdown is a distinction pursued only by a few, notable amongst which is Natalie Tobert, a Western expert on the Indian system of mental healthcare which often is rather good at distinguishing a spiritual crisis from the ordinary type, and prescribing different kinds of intervention accordingly.[242]

To enter a hierophancy with a spiritual teacher is not for the timid therefore; neither is it for the sycophant. Of course nobody judges themselves as sycophantic, but one can have a clear eye for how much adulation for the teacher goes on in the *sangha*. This is a very difficult judgment: how much does the teacher encourage blind praise? How much does the hierarchy indulge in such praise and encourage new entrants to join in? I don't think that the guru system in India is much inclined to foster sycophancy because devotion to the guru is better understood as impersonal. In the transition to the individualistic West the broader context was lost and so the risks are greater of unquestioning admiration. I saw this at the Friends of the Western Buddhist Order and to a lesser extent with the Andrew Cohen *sangha*; all I can suggest is to keep some sense of proportion.

Spiritual materialism

The most important question the seeker can ask of themselves as they "wrestle" with the hierophants placed in their way by the universe is this: have I succumbed to spiritual materialism? Let us look at how Trungpa, who coined the term, defines it. He starts with:

> There are numerous sidetracks which lead to a distorted, ego-centered version of spirituality; we can deceive ourselves into thinking we are developing spiritually when instead we are strengthening our egocentricity through spiritual techniques. This fundamental distortion may be referred to as *spiritual materialism*.[243] (Trungpa's emphasis.)

This is good as far as it goes, but takes us to ego again. More usefully Trungpa says that ego merely *imitates* true spirituality, and he also provides us with a relevant metaphor. Consider the relationship between the ruler of a state and its head of church, he says. If there appears to be some conflict between policy and morality, the head of the church can always work out some justification to allow the ruler to go ahead with a clear conscience. So it is with us internally; our spirituality can serve the ego in the same way.[244] In a more concrete sense the ego wants "a higher, more spiritual, more transcendent version of knowledge, religion, virtue or judgment," meaning that it makes one feel special. Trungpa saw this when Tibetan Buddhism was new in America and his pupils liked to bathe in the cachet of "ancient wisdom." He makes clear that the wisdom he offered was not ancient at all, it was just plain wisdom, real experience, perennial. But Trungpa's analysis keeps coming back to ego. My take on this is, why should the aspirant accept they have a big ego where Trungpa does not? He sure looks full of himself, as does Cohen and most of the other gurus discussed here. Hence I am not sure that the question of ego is so useful. But crucially Trungpa says this: "The very notion that we will *get* something from the guru – happiness, peace of mind, wisdom, whatever it is we seek – is one of the most difficult preconceptions of all."[245] I think he is right. For me a good hierophancy is not really a giving and receiving, even if I have used those words from time to time, rather it is a kind of resonance where what is buried in the disciple begins to twang, like a guitar string in a powerful audio field. The string is not directly plucked; it resonates. The vessel is not filled from without but from within.

Looking at the master-disciple relationships we examined in Chapter 6, we can ask: what did Alcibiades *want* from Socrates? What did Rumi *want* from Shams? What did Ouspensky *want* from Gurdjieff? And so on. To start with we need to think of what people want from any relationship, whether business partnerships, ordinary friendship, romantic involvement, or the hierophantic relationship. In the first instance there has to be a *chemistry*. There has to be a mutual attraction which is not loaded at all with the sense of advantage. What do I *want* from my wife? To even ask that question implies that something has gone wrong. We resonate with each other, that is the basis of our relationship. What do I *want* from the guru? This should equally be wrong. Resonance is what counts.

8. Negotiating the Hierophant

When it came to Alcibiades it seems he wanted sex from Socrates. There was a chemistry there, but the younger man had misinterpreted it, had confused *agape* with *eros*, and came away rueful but in awe of the older man. When there is either no cultural support for the spiritual teacher or the pupil wants fulfillment of a material desire, then such misunderstandings can arise. As far as I know with Andrew Cohen and his pupils the misunderstanding of sexuality did not arise; the chemistry was hierophantic or nothing. Another profound misunderstanding we explored was between Jiddu Krishnamurti and David Bohm where neither was prepared to admit the master-disciple context of their relationship. The example of Gurdjieff and Ouspensky is also interesting: we can ask whether Ouspensky mostly considered his quest to be one of knowledge and philosophy, despite Gurdjieff continuously mocking him for it. The pupil can therefore be looking for entirely the wrong thing. It is down to the teacher to understand all those misplaced desires as mirages and keep directing the pupil to the solid prizes. It is also down to the teacher to resist the perennial sycophancy of some seekers who, in their weakness, only want to lean on the strong.

More usually, it strikes me, the pupil can be looking for roughly the right thing, as Trungpa explains, but is searching in the wrong place for it. I have an analogy for this. Imagine a vast ice-sheet, the topology of which is so subtly marked out in low light and snowstorms that the novice has lost all bearings. The master points in the direction of the one fishing-hole, and off rushes the pupil, missing it by a few yards, or a few miles, it makes no difference, landing up as far away as when they started. The Master miraculously appears at the new spot and points to the fishing-hole again, using directions that apparently contradict the previous ones. The somewhat chastened student rushes off with marginally less confusion, only to miss it again. Rinse and repeat. Sometimes the student finds the hole by accident, obtains a lovely fish, and then cannot find it again for years. In this metaphor the student and master are talking roughly the same language, but the sheer subtlety of the terrain confounds the student. More importantly it is the *desire* for something tantalizing and remote that confuses them, hence they keep rushing off. The fishing hole is actually where they stand. (Agreed, this metaphor does not work perfectly: in real life you cannot stand over a hole in the ice without falling in. With enlightenment, maddeningly, you can and do.)

But what do pupils desire above all? What is it that leads to the relationship with the master breaking down? And why am I blaming only the pupil? I think it is partly down to the issue of *permanence*, which one seeks in marriage for example. When a romantic relationship is right for both partners then a faithfulness unto death is no social construct but a natural and wonderful thing as Whitman observes in his oft-used phrase "well-married." We now include in this all kind of gender-fluid combinations, and are confident that Mother Meera is wrong to confine it to that of a man and a woman. But for the master this is not the case: the master has to be promiscuous; the master cannot shelter the pupil under his or her wing for ever. A productive hierophancy is when the pupil both enters and leaves the relationship at the right time. However, some pupils do stay their entire lives. Generally they become aides rather than seekers and historical examples might include the Buddha's cousin Ananda, Krishnamurti's housekeeper Rajogapal, and the close confidantes of Mother Meera. Also of interest are the married partners, for example Damema, the wife of Marpa; Julia Ostrowskaya, wife of Gurdjieff; Margaret Fell, who married George Fox in his old age; and the delightful wife of Andrew Cohen, who I have met but unfortunately forgotten the name of. How do they negotiate their hierophants? The question may not be so relevant to the general path of hierophancy, beyond this observation: the spouse of the guru may well be part of the hierarchy and may have to be negotiated with for access to the hierophant. It may be of interest to note that Marpa's wife seemed to form the "good cop" role against her husband's "bad cop" style of teaching when it came to poor Milarepa, often comforting the young aspirant after yet another devastating humiliation delivered by the master.

The desire for the pupil to stay for ever with the master is clearly a potential form of spiritual materialism. The antidote is the realization that the arrangement must be temporary. Of course if it is your fate to marry him or her then that is great, but at the same time it probably means it is not your fate to be a successful seeker.

We can turn now to the other major desires that Trungpa was aware of in his pupils and which are obstacles to successful hierophancy. The example of Robert Forman and his "full catastrophe disillusionment" with the entire process of hierophancy, if not enlightenment itself, is instructive. He said: "But I'm an American, and the albatross was around my neck to discover a life's task that was 'right for me.'" His point was that he had to remain *in charge* of his life, and what he had been promised by his guru was that when he discovered the Atman he would be full of dignity and power and freed from suffering. Forman hadn't spotted the thing about him not existing as a him anymore, as not existing as a separate entity with dignity and power and freedom separate from the dignity and power and freedom of the cosmos. He was an American over-achiever by culture, so why should he not have *personal* cosmic dignity and power and freedom? If we have to use the terminology of the ego, then it illustrates Trungpa's point well: Forman was intent on strengthening his egocentricity through spiritual techniques. I think the fact that he saw the albatross of self-definition as also one of *complexity* is also revealing: complexity is a gratifying challenge where simplicity is not. He could not step out of his culture which declares the American as not only destined for success but to have a cosmic life task as a beacon to others, often described as American exceptionalism, where it is the nation's destiny to be the "city on the hill," the light of which will illuminate the world. I am not picking on Americans here: each culture has its more or less modest version of the same thing, though couched in different terms. The hierophant has to dismantle all this culturally-ingrained sense of achievement, the relishing of complexity, and the gratification of personal agency in the pupil. That is often a painful process.

If we look at the case of Michael Wombacher, then what he wanted from his guru Andrew Cohen again had parameters set out by the guru, but potentially misinterpreted by the ego (if we must use that word). Cohen was not using the traditional Hindu language of Atman and Brahman and so on, but was transposing it into the culture of American ambition. As we examined earlier, Cohen says of enlightenment: "Then one becomes a conscious agent of non-dual realization in the manifest realm, and then, instead of living for oneself, to have and to get and to become, one becomes an agent of consciousness itself." The very word *agent* triggers the response that Forman made in recognizing his "albatross" – the desire to achieve something in the manifest world, something unique to his own individuality. How wonderful to be the agent of consciousness itself! James Bond, we may recall, was also an agent. This is much grander however. As painted by Cohen, his successful pupils were to be the advance wave of a new humanity, charged with being revolutionaries – actually "evolutionaries" in Cohen's terminology – for the brave new world. Enlightenment is being cracked up here to look most enticing.

The master can, therefore, contribute to spiritual materialism in their languaging of the goal. Rajneesh often said that spiritual teachers had to invent "devices" so that the student would be drawn to them in the first place and then stay long enough to learn something. How consciously or unconsciously this is done I am not sure, but it is not difficult, for example, to take Andrew Cohen's teachings and strip out everything that looks superficially attractive, while yet retaining his core teaching on enlightenment. One could rewrite his statement quoted above in this way: "Nondual realization in the manifest realm means that instead of living for oneself, to have and to get and to become, one simply becomes consciousness itself and lives for the whole." The meaning remains the same but it is stripped of its grandiose language. Such a move would possibly undermine Cohen's efforts to distance his work from classical enlightenment which he sees as irredeemably passive. However, such a move would do nothing to undermine the tangible *chemistry* that arises between him and the seekers drawn to him, apart perhaps from those like Forman whose personal ambition needs to be flattered. I think the same is true with Rajneesh. How consciously did he invent the devices present in his teachings? Was he actually serious about the "new man"? One could ask the same of Gurdjieff, and of course with Richard Maurice Bucke as a disciple of Whitman. Bucke thought that Whitman was the precursor of the "new man," though a careful reading of *Leaves of Grass* shows Whitman to be saying no such thing.

Whether the teacher invents something grandiose, or whether the pupil imagines it, such promises must inevitably lead to spiritual materialism and the potential for Forman's "full catastrophe disillusionment." It doesn't have to however, if the hierophancy is based on a genuine chemistry. In such a case the disciple stays long enough to outgrow their illusions.

The inverse of spiritual materialism must be the yearning to suffer at the hands of the master. Milarepa entered his discipleship with a direct and explicit sense of guilt and the need for atonement. We may be alarmed at how gleefully Marpa seems to have obliged Milarepa in dishing out punishment, but the hierophancy worked for both of them. Many people live with a more diffuse sense of guilt or have hidden needs for atonement and stick with abusive masters for no obvious reason. What they *want* from the master is forgiveness, which again is something that cannot be given or received but must resonate as an inner freedom under the force field of the master's inner freedom.

Finally I want to touch on what I think is the most dangerous of spiritual materialisms: the quest for occult powers, or *siddhis*. The discipleship of Irina Tweedie to Radha Mohan Lal is our best example of a hierophancy predicated on occult powers. Tweedie had immersed herself in occult practices and doctrines via the Theosophists, and much of her experiences with Lal are couched in those terms. However Radha Mohan Lal gave the example of the occult power of instant travel as a warning against spiritual materialism: when he had practiced this as a young man his father had rebuked him for it. Nevertheless he sought and practiced occult powers where these could be used in the service of others. However for some I would suggest that initiation into such powers is not in the service of the greater good, but in the service of individual gratification or even revenge. Although I think the example of Milarepa does stray into mythology, his acquisition of *siddhis* led to the classic actions of the black magician, a figure reviled in all folk traditions. The subsequent work needed to undo the spiritual harm to himself was colossal, as we saw.

Whether the healing experienced in the presence of a man like Jesus, Gurdjieff or Whitman is down to benign occult powers I do not know, but I cannot see how the discipline of acquiring them is at all congruent with enlightenment. I once taught some modules in a postgraduate course on spiritual development and met a mature student who was a spiritualist medium. As I got to know him I understood two things about him: firstly that his mediumship was a genuine service to his spiritualist community, and secondly that he was content with this level of spiritual development. Occult powers are not *in themselves* dangerous, any more than powers in the political realm. They tend to corrupt if the wielder of that power is corruptible, that is all. If one believes that the spiritual gifts of a trained medicine man like Crow Dog are occult powers, then it is clear that his training was all about their service to the community. But for millions of spiritual seekers with low self-esteem and a chip on their shoulders, the avenue of spiritual powers can be tempting. A genuine master knows this, though might possibly dangle such things in front of the student as a device. We saw that Ouspensky was much occupied by all things occult; Gurdjieff would humor him sometimes just to cheer him up. The true teacher works with the material at hand, but I have to admit I prefer Ramana Maharshi's clear-cut advice to entirely avoid *siddhis*. Just for once my preference here also aligns itself with modernity, which is of course skeptical about their very existence.

Some seekers have a one-to-one relationship with their teacher without entering into spiritual community or *sangha*, Milarepa seeming to be an example of this. Similarly the transmission between Shams and Rumi seems to be one-to-one. But more often a seeker joins a spiritual community built up around the master, in which case negotiating the hierophant involves negotiating the hierarchy. For example a man like Sangharakshita, founder of the Friends of the Western Buddhist Order, put huge energies into shaping his *sangha*, indeed much that is positive in *sangha* life I learned from his community and its hierarchy. Here then is a second level of chemistry: do you feel at home in the spiritual community you have chosen? If so their looms the second level of spiritual materialism: does your desire that the comforts of this community be permanent outweigh your desire for enlightenment? It is often more shattering to leave the community than the guru.

Discipleship heavy, discipleship light

Crucially, can you bring humor, lightness and love into your search? When I first came across the *Gospel of Thomas* – one of the Nag Hammadi texts discovered in 1945 – I was taken with saying 90: "My yoke is easy, my Lordship gentle." I later found that Jesus says something similar in the canonical gospels:

> Come to me, all you who are weary and burdened, and I will give you rest. Take my yoke upon you and learn from me, for I am gentle and humble of

8. Negotiating the Hierophant

heart; and you will find rest. For my yoke is easy, and my burden is light. (Matthew 11:29-30).

These sayings are an interesting proposition in hierophancy, amounting to the offer of "discipleship light." For some seekers this is simply impossible. We cannot imagine Milarepa, Irina Tweedie, or P. D. Ouspensky taking their discipleship in a light manner, whatever the offer from their masters. But Rumi's discipleship to Shams was light, however intense, and Crow Dog would have studied in all solemnity but would no doubt also have enjoyed a joke and some horseplay with his teachers.

What factors make a discipleship "heavy?" I think these are important to understand because they change the way we negotiate the entire world of hierophancy. The first factor must be one's sense of guilt, whether explicit or diffuse, whether truly held or whether culturally imposed. A spiritual path of atonement will throw up entirely different problems with the guru because it opens up the possibility of abuse. It is interesting that a brigand called Angulimāla came to the Buddha with far more blood on his hands than when Milarepa approached Marpa. How historical either stories are is a matter of interpretation of course but in the case of Angulimāla no abusive penances were demanded of him by the Buddha. In theory Jesus' path as a path of atonement also require no humiliation, only the gentle "yoke" of devotion, but later on the priests of the Christian tradition turned all that into something much darker.

Guilt for former crimes may be absent, but the seeker may feel entirely inadequate in the face of spiritual teachings while at the same time gripped by a deadly seriousness in mastering their content. I think this more common and part of where Cohen went wrong with his students. To the extent that they perceived themselves as inadequate "transformative evolutionaries" or inadequate "agents of consciousness in the manifest world," they would submit to various indignities at the hands of Cohen. In other spiritual communities the task of handing out indignities can pass to senior members of the hierarchy and become entrenched in the life of the *sangha*; before long the hierarchy may embody abuse more than it embodies *agape*.

So is the guru system, in travelling from the East to the West, bound to move from discipleship light to discipleship heavy? I think so, unfortunately, and Andrew Cohen's example is instructive of what can go wrong.

This is only a personal impression of course, but I always felt that Cohen's Jewish background hauled in much that is absolutist from the Western monotheist traditions. Absolutism is probably stronger in Christianity and Islam than in Judaism, but the problem remains: monotheism is not an inherently pluralist doctrine. I explore this at length elsewhere,[246] but we do not need to go into the history of it much to see that a hierophant in the Western context can absorb that rather absolutist mindset. If it is an Eastern guru operating in the West, like Trungpa, then it is the Western pupils that will bring that discipleship heavy with them, and if it is a Western guru like Cohen operating out of an Eastern tradition then, although such a teacher may understand their Western pupils better, the chances are doubled of a hierophancy that can tip into abuse. Cohen seems to have understood some of this when he wrote in his letter of apology, as we saw, about the "rocky legacy of eastern Enlightenment coming to the psychologically informed West." However I don't think the problem lies in the West being psychologically informed but about a Western heritage of abusive Christianity.

This is where I think it useful to consider the "counter-religion of the West" as I put it, broadly the stream of religious ideas called Neoplatonism. It was always abused rather than abusing and its history makes its adherents anticlerical, just like Whitman. Putting it another way, if teacher and pupil have their religious center of gravity in the Hellenic rather than the Hebraic tradition, then they are instinctively anticlerical and – which is just as important – instinctively pluralist. At the same time this tradition is inclined to find both the sciences and the arts intimately linked to their enquiry into truth. The Greek mindset, then, may well a better home for discipleship light; Whitman's hierophancy is a supreme illustration of that.

Negotiating the Hierophant

We can now pull together the major issues in negotiating the hierophant, ahead of asking what the special case of Walt Whitman teaches us. We can do this under three headings: (1) spiritual chemistry vs. spiritual materialism. (2) negotiating the guru vs. negotiating the *sangha*, and (3) discipleship heavy vs. discipleship light. We assume that somehow the seeker has avoided a hierophant who is leading the pupils to a terrible disaster, a de-

8. Negotiating the Hierophant

bacle, or even embarrassment, at least for now. It is a matter of ongoing negotiation, though of course "negotiation" is not what takes place on the surface at all, rather it is the inner reality of the pupil confronted with the impossible. What the pupil does by way of negotiating is more the sort you do when encountering a wild beast guarding the only drinking hole in a desert – or guarding a fishing hole in the ice. The desire of the pupil for the "water" – or for the "fish" – of enlightenment overcomes the fear of the beast, so you cannot run away. You stay and negotiate with your own fears and desires.

Basing one's discipleship on a positive feeling for the spiritual chemistry with one's teacher means one approaches the hierophant in the right way, I would suggest. Spiritual materialism means one approaches the hierophant in the wrong way. The negotiation then is about knowing that the chemistry is right and surviving the blows to the ego that come from the false desires that constitute spiritual materialism. Deep down one has to know that one loves the guru for some mysterious reason, perhaps termed "enlightenment," but because one's understanding of it is bound to be wrong, one may desire the wrong things. Perhaps one is only attracted by something as simple as the boundless confidence of the teacher, or something darker such as magical powers. Also crucial is that staying with the hierophant does not become in itself a piece of spiritual materialism or just a plain comfort. Unless the negotiation involves making a break at some point then one has failed to negotiate the hierophant.

I do believe that there is only one thing better than good family life, and for sure when family life goes wrong one is terribly hurt. The one better thing is good *sangha*, spiritual community. It is a wonderful thing in itself, and there is the problem for the seeker: you can make your home there. In Buddhist terms one can take the three "jewels" on offer, the Buddha, his teachings and his community, and simply buy into only the third, the community. The Buddha, or whoever the hierophant of the community happens to be, will probably be remote and surrounded by the upper echelon of devotees, while the teachings are anyway impenetrable, but here is a group of people you like to be with as an alternative if family or sexual relationships break down, or if you are alienated from mainstream communities. During the time I spent in the *sangha* of the Friends of the Western Buddhist Order (FWBO) I came to realize that, yes, they did *sangha* beautifully, but it was no place for a seeker. As just one symptom of that, I found it impossible to engage anyone in a conversation about enlightenment, that being (a) only for the Buddha, or (b) not for this lifetime. My negotiation with the FWBO was simple: I enjoyed hanging out there but I wasn't signing up. In any case its hierophant, Sangharakshita, was to my mind not enlightened, nor did he claim to be.

If one does sign up to a hierophant with a sizeable *sangha* then, as pointed out earlier, one's negotiations may be more with the *sangha* hierarchy or order members than with the hierophant. I have also pointed out that a residential *sangha* is similar to other elective communities; a study of how they fall apart should be sobering. Some outright negotiation may be possible of course, but it is also the case that, out of sight of the hierophant, the order members may be pursuing distinctly unenlightened practices. If the master dishes out humiliations and ordeals to students that is one thing and one hopes that they are done with utmost compassion and with direct pedagogic intent and outcome. However, members of the hierarchy may be tempted to throw their weight around in imitation of the master without understanding anything of the proper dynamics of teaching. Worse, as in the case of Rajneesh, the master may appoint power-hungry individuals in full knowledge of the chaos that they will inflict. Negotiating all this needs a clear eye.

Finally, all of this can be heavy, man, or light. If you have a deep sense of guilt and are looking for atonement then the chances are your discipleship will be heavy. And of course it depends enormously on the master.

The hierophancy of Walt Whitman

We have seen that what in the East was generally discipleship light became discipleship heavy in the West, for reasons outlined above. It is here, I think, that the hierophancy of Walt Whitman is so instructive. While he had some awareness of the East, and Eastern thinkers lionized him, he was profoundly American and profoundly modern. As a spiritual teacher one could say that his was hierophancy so light as to have almost escaped historical attention. Whitman admitted that he was like a "furtive old hen" in hiding his truths like eggs in a hedgerow. Yet I believe that his example holds the promise of a Western guruship that is home-grown and worka-

8. Negotiating the Hierophant

ble. Crucially, Whitman was not a Christian. He tells us that he toyed for a while with the idea of becoming a Quaker – perhaps the least Christian of all Christian churches – but rejected it as too restricting. More than that his anticlericalism was deeply held and did not take much to provoke. All this means that the context within which he impacted upon his pupils had none of the landmarks of conventional religion, as had been understood for two thousand years in the West. More bluntly, Whitman's religion was not Judeo-Christian but Greek; not Hebraic but Hellenic. It belongs to philosophy, literature, and science, and not to the piety of the Virgin Mary or the horrors of the Inquisition. At the same time it was uniquely his own, uniquely American, and uniquely democratic. There was also nothing in it to foster sycophancy, even if some have effectively accused disciples like Bucke of it.

If we look at the six disciples of Whitman explored in Chapter 7 we see that all of them belong to the spheres of philosophy, literature, and science, and not to the sphere of Christian religion. On a daily basis their spiritual interactions with Whitman seem mostly literary, tinged with forward-looking interest in the emerging sciences and democratic reforms of their day. However, to twenty-first century eyes that forward-looking optimism may seems naive. As atheism hardened since Whitman's day, literature has become only escapism; actual science has become the mistrusted realm of the "expert;" democracy appears to have been commandeered by corporate wealth; Christianity flourishes relatively unchanged in its bunker; and "spirituality" talked about only by New Age types. Philosophy too has become a shrunken discipline of arid logic and linguistic naval-gazing. All this makes it hard to understand Whitman as religious and having as a major influence the Greek "philosopher" Epictetus, especially as those exploring Whitman's legacy seem determined to focus on a matter utterly irrelevant to his own stated goals regarding *Leaves of Grass*, his alleged homosexuality.

However I would argue that a closer examination of the hierophancy of Walt Whitman offers us exactly what the twenty-first century needs in negotiating the guru, wherever they emerge and in whatever system they teach. His ideas were far ahead of his time, which is why Romain Rolland called him a "Precursor." Whitman is answering at the deepest level the question in his pupils, "how should I be?" It is not asked or answered in a devotional context; no saint or God is elevated for worship here, however much the pupils of Whitman loved him. It is not asked or answered in such a way as to encourage spiritual materialism. It is not asked or answered in terms of occult powers. Above all Whitman's "lordship" is light, his yoke is gentle. It is discipleship light, not discipleship heavy. Whitman answers his pupils as an equal, yet without for example the convolutions that ultimately made barren the hierophancy between Krishnamurti and Bohm. Indeed when we look at the high drama of hierophancy in some of the examples of Chapter 6 in contrast to the exchanges between Whitman and his pupils we find in those examples the potential for both spiritual materialism and abuse. The whole Gurdjieff hierophancy was based on an impossibly high bar set by the master, which arose out of occult traditions not that different to those pursued by Irina Tweedie. Krishnamurti made valiant attempts to escape the deadly seriousness of those traditions but Bohm still foundered. Robert Forman's "full catastrophe disillusionment" owed much to spiritual materialism fostered by the Eastern exoticism of what was promised him. Andrew Harvey's equivalent disaster was down to culture clash. In all those cases the East did not travel well at all. And in Cohen's case his – possibly quite unconscious – Old Testament and teleological outlook prevented the natural playfulness and pluralism of his teacher's Hindu tradition coming to the fore. I am sure, had Whitman contemplated the two Buddhist examples of a murderer attaining enlightenment, he would have preferred the story of the Buddha and the brigand Angulimāla to the story of Marpa and Milarepa. Why should hierophancy involve digging ditches to be filled or building houses to be demolished, however penitent the pupil? Whitman understood evil as much as he understood good but he would have advocated a path of human dignity not humiliation. If a system of spiritual instruction requires the denigration or even degradation of the pupil then Whitman would have wanted no part in it. His eleves were to be elevated not cast down.

However, as I suggested in the case of Burroughs, Whitman's system was not sufficiently animist for him, and it would be foolish to claim Whitman's system as complete. Whitman also has an optimism about the future we cannot wholly share with him now. When he says "None has begun to think how divine he himself is, and how certain the future is," we can agree with the first half but not the second. The future does not look at all certain to us, indeed all that is certain is that profound change is coming. Whitman's system is therefore not necessarily to be adopted wholesale along with his methods of hierophancy. Instead I offer – elsewhere – my own system as filling in just those gaps that Burroughs perhaps had to fill in for himself and just those gaps that would make it relevant to an *uncertain* future.[247] However, regardless of the system – and even if it fulfils the bulk of our spiritual needs – it is the methods of hierophancy that Whitman embodies, his benignancy, that are his real legacy.

Go, seeker, go

I conclude by saying to the seeker, go for it. I only agree with the statement that enlightenment is not all it is cracked up to be because there are many teachers who "crack it up" all wrong. In reality it is far more than anyone can imagine. It takes nothing from one's personality or individuality or destiny: it is the flowering of all those things. I hope the examples in this book are some kind of useful guidance, though I do not expect the seeker to avoid all the pitfalls explored here. The one thing seekers cannot afford however is modern cynicism, as they are heading out on a path pretty much in the opposite direction of the mainstream. I just hope that a Whitman-like figure looms ahead of them, forbidding, yes, but a figure of benignity, and are better prepared by this book for a hierophancy that avoids all trace of abuse. Whoever the hierophant is, their system will not be complete, that is an impossibility, but the relationship is more important than the bits that are missing; they can be filled in elsewhere. This *is* a democratic age, and while the hierophant will probably not be negotiated with directly by the pupil, the pupil has the right to negotiate with themselves as to how they respond. And as Whitman says, the pupil proves the master by spreading a wider breast. Of course when Whitman adds: "He most honors my style who learns under it to destroy the teacher," he means only destroy the teacher *as hierophant*. In that moment, when the seeker becomes the finder, both hierophant and sycophant disappear and become lovers – by which I mean just friends and democrats.

BIBLIOGRAPHY

Allen, G.W. *The Solitary Singer: A Critical Biography of Walt Whitman*, Chicago: University of Chicago Press, 1985

Bellin, H. F. and Ruhl, D. (Eds.), *Blake and Swedenborg: Opposition is True Friendship*, New York: Swedenborg Foundation, 1985

Bennett, J., *Witness (2nd Ed.)*, Wellingborough: Turnstone Press, 1983

Bharati, Agehananda, *The Light at the Centre: Context and Pretext of Modern Mysticism*, Santa Barbara: Ross-Erikson, 1976

Brunton, Paul, *A Search in Secret India*, York Beach, Maine: Samuel Weiser, Inc. 1970

Bucke, R.M., *Walt Whitman*, Philadelphia: David McKay, 1883

Burroughs, John, *Whitman: A Study*, Boston and New York: Houghton, Mifflin and Company, 1896

Callow, Philip, *Walt Whitman: From Noon to Starry Night*, London: Allison & Busby, 1992

Caplan, Mariana, *Halfway Up the Mountain: the Error of Premature Claims of Enlightenment*, Prescott, Arizona: Hohm Press, 1999

Carpenter, Edward, *Days with Walt Whitman*, London: George Allen, 1906

Chandmal, Asit, *One Thousand Moons: Krishnamurti at Eighty-Five*, New York: Abrams, 1985

Chari, V.K. *Whitman in the Light of Vedantic Mysticism*, Lincoln: University of Nebraska Press, 1976

Crow Dog, Leonard, and Erdoes, Richard, *Crow Dog: Four Generations of Sioux Medicine Men*, New York: HarperPerennial, 1996

Cupitt, Don, *Mysticism After Modernity*, Oxford: Blackwell Publishers, 1998

Dawkins, Richard, *Unweaving the Rainbow*, London: Penguin, 1998

Davies, Paul, *God and the New Physics*, London: Penguin, 1990

Feuerstein, Georg, *Holy Madness: The shock tactics and radical teachings of crazy-wise adepts, holy fools, and rascal gurus*, London: Arkana, 1990

Forman, Robert, *Enlightenment Ain't What It's Cracked Up To Be: A Journey of Discovery, Snow and Jazz in the Soul*, Washington: O Books, 2011

Gabb, W.J., *The Goose is Out: A Zen Pilgrim's Progress*, 58 Eccleston Square, London: The Buddhist Society, 1944

Gould, Mitchell Santine, "Walt Whitman's Quaker paradox" in *Quaker History*, V. 96, 1 (Spring 2007): pp. 1-23

Gregory, John, *The Neoplatonists: A Reader*, London and New York: Routledge, 1999

Hart, David A., *The Unification of World Faith: The Challenge of Sun Myung Moon*, Thiruvananthapuram: Om Books, 2007

Hartmann, de, Thomas and Olga, *Our Life with Mr Gurdjieff*, London: Arkana, 1992

Harvey, Andrew, *Hidden Journey*, London: Rider, 1991

Hayes, Will, *Walt Whitman: The Prophet of the New Era*, 1921

Heelas, Paul, *The New Age*, Oxford and Malden: Blackwell Publishers, 1996

Hermes Trismegistus (Trans. Walter Scott), *Hermetica*, Solos Press, 1997

Hourihan, Paul, *Mysticism in American Literature: Thoreau's Quest and Whitman's Self*, Redding: Vedantic Shores Press, 2004

Hutchinson, George B., *The Ecstatic Whitman: Literary Shamanism and the Crisis of the Union*, Ohio State University Press (Jun. 1986)

James, W. *The Varieties of Religious Experience*, Middlesex, England: Penguin Books, 1986

Jefferies, R. *The Story of My Heart*, London: MacMillan St Martin's Press, 1968

King, Mike, *Secularism: The Hidden Origins of Disbelief*, Cambridge: James Clarke & Co., 2007

King, Mike, *Enigma's Coda*, London: Stochastic Press, 2016

King, Mike, *Luminous: The Spiritual Life on Film*, London: Stochastic Press, 2018

King, Mike, *The American Cinema of Excess: Extremes of the National Mind on Film*, London: Stochastic Press, 2016

King, Mike, *Mountain Calls*, London: Stochastic Press, 2017

Kierkegaard, S., *The Essential Kierkegaard*, Princeton, New Jersey: Princeton University Press, 1990

Krishnamurti, J., *The Awakening of Intelligence*, London: Victor Gollancz, 1973

Kuebrich David, "Literary Shamanism & the Crisis of the Union, [review]," in *Walt Whitman Quarterly Review*, Volume 5 | Number 3 (1988)

Kuebrich, David, *Minor Prophecy: Walt Whitman's New American Religion*, John Wiley & Sons, 1990

Mercer, Dorothy, "Walt Whitman on Reincarnation" in *Vedanta and The West*, IX Nov/Dec 1946

Bibliography

Muir, John, *Letters to a Friend, 1866-1879*, Boston and New York: Houghton Mifflin Company, 1915

Naifeh, S. and Smith, G.W., *Jackson Pollock: An American Saga*, London: Pimlico, 1992

Nambiar, O.K. *Maha Yogi: Walt Whitman: New Light on Yoga*, Bangalore: Jeevan Publications, 1978

Nanamoli, Bhikku, and Bhodi, Bhikku, *The Middle Length Discourses of the Buddha: a New Translation of the Majjhima Nikaya*, Boston: Wisdom Publications, 1995

Needleman, Jacob, *The Heart of Philosophy*, London, Melbourne and Henley, Routledge and Kegan Paul, 1983

Ouspensky, P. D., *In Search of the Miraculous: Fragments of an Unknown Teaching*, Arkana, 1987

Ouspensky, P. D. *Tertium Organum: A Key to the Enigmas of the World*, New York: Alfred A. Knopf, 1947

Osborne, Arthur, *Ramana Maharshi and the Path of Self-Knowledge*, Maine: Samuel Weiser, 1970

Palmer, Martin and Elizabeth Breuilly (Eds.) *The Book of the Chuang Tzu*, London: Penguin Arkana, 1996

Pirsig, Robert M., *Lila: An Enquiry into Morals*, London: Black Swan, 1991

Plato, *Protagoras and Meno*, Penguin Books, Middlesex, England, 1981

Plato (Trans. Walter Hamilton), *The Symposium*, Harmondsworth: Penguin, 1951

Plato (Trans. Walter Hamilton), *Phaedrus and Letters VII and VIII*, Harmondsworth: Penguin, 1973

Possamai, Adam (Ed.), *Handbook of Hyper-real Religions*, Leiden, Boston: Brill, 2012

Prabhavananda, Swami, and Christopher Isherwood (Eds.) *Shankara's Crest-Jewel of Discrimination*, Hollywood, California: Vedanta Press, 1975

Rajneesh, B.S., *Krishna: The Man and His Philosophy*, Oregon: Rajneesh Foundation International, 1985

Rajneesh, B.S., *The Book of the Secrets Vol. 2*, New York, Hagerstown, San Francisco, London: Harper Colophon, 1979

Rawlinson, Andrew, *The Book of Enlightened Masters: Western Teachers in Eastern Traditions*, Chicago and La Salle, Illinois: Open Court, 1997

Robertson, Michael, *Worshipping Walt: The Whitman Disciples*, Princeton University Press, 2010

Rolland, Romain, *Prophets of the New India*, London, Toronto, Melbourne, Sidney: Cassell and Co., 1930

Rumi, Jelaluddin (trans. A.J.Arberry), *Mystical Poems of Rumi - Vol. 1*, Chicago and London: The University of Chicago Press, 1968

Rumi, Jelaluddin (trans. Edmund Helminski), *The Ruins of the Heart*, Putney: Threshold, 1981

Sachitanandan, V. *Whitman and Bharati: A Comparative Study*, The MacMillan Company of India Ltd., Bombay, Calcutta, Delhi, Madras, 1978

Storr, Anthony, *Feet of Clay: A Study of Gurus*, London: HarperCollins Publishers, 1997

Swinburne, Algernon Charles, *William Blake: A Critical Essay*, London: John Camden Hotten, 1868

Symonds, John Addington, *Walt Whitman: a Study*, London: John C. Nimmo, 1893

Thoreau, Henry, *Walden and Other Writings*, Bantam, 1962

Tobert, Natalie, *Cultural Perspectives on Mental Wellbeing: Spiritual Interpretations of Symptoms in Medical Practice*, London and Philadelphia: Jessica Kingsley Publishers, 2017

Traherne, Thomas, *Centuries of Meditations*, Fintry: Shrine of Wisdom; 2002

Traherne, Thomas, *Selected Poems and Prose*, London: Penguin, 1991

Traubel, Horace, *With Walt Whitman in Camden, Vol. 1*, Boston: Small, Maynard & Company, 1906

Traubel, Horace, *With Walt Whitman in Camden, Vol. 2*, New York: Mitchell Kennerley, 1915

Traubel, Horace, *With Walt Whitman in Camden, Vol. 3*, New York: Mitchell Kennerley, 1914

Trungpa, C., *Cutting Through Spiritual Materialism*, Boston and London: Shambhala, 1987

Tucker, Mike, *Dreaming with Open Eyes: the Shamanic in 20th C Art and Culture*, London: Aquarian/HarperSanFrancisco, 1992

Tweedie, Irina, *Daughter of Fire: A Diary of a Spiritual Training with a Sufi Master*, Inverness, California: The Golden Sufi Centre, 1995

Whitman, Walt, *Leaves of Grass*, Oxford University Press, Oxford, New York, 1990

Whitman, Walt, *Leaves of Grass: The First (1855) Edition*, (Penguin Classics), Kindle Edition

Whitman, Walt, *Specimen Days*, London: The Folio Society, 1979

Whitman, Walt (Ed. Edwin Haviland Miller), *The Correspondence*, New York: New York UP, 1961

Whitman, Walt (Ed. Clarence Gohdes and Rollo G. Silver), *Faint Clews & Indirections: Manuscripts of Walt Whitman and His Family*, Durham: Duke UP, 1949

Whitman, Walt (Ed. Horace Traubel), *An American Primer*, Boston: Small, Maynard, 1904

Wombacher, Michael, *11 Days at the Edge*, Findhorn: Findhorn Press, 2008

Wordsworth, William, *Poetical Works*, Oxford: Oxford University Press, 1990

Xenophon (Trans.: Hugh Tredennick and Robin Waterfield), *Conversations of Socrates*, London: Penguin, 1990

Yenner, William, *American Guru: A Story of Love, Betrayal and Healing, Former Students of Andrew Cohen Speak Out*, Rhinebeck, New York: Epigraph Books, 2009

Zaehner, R.C., *Drugs, Mysticism and Make-Believe*, Collins, London 1972

REFERENCES

1. Tarkovsky, Andrei, *Sculpting in Time*, Faber and Faber, 1989, p. 226
2. Prabhavananda, Swami, and Christopher Isherwood (Eds.) *Shankara's Crest-Jewel of Discrimination*, Hollywood, California: Vedanta Press, 1975, p. 33
3. King, Mike, *Secularism: The Hidden Origins of Disbelief*, Cambridge: James Clarke & Co., 2007, p. 25
4. O'Brien, Elmer (Trans.), *The Essential Plotinus*, Indiana: Hackett Publishing Company, 1964, p. viii
5. http://www.jnani.org/mrking/writings/essays/other/whitman-headless.html
6. https://whitmanarchive.org/criticism/disciples/tei/anc.00170.html
7. Whitman, Walt, *Leaves of Grass: The First (1855) Edition* (Penguin Classics), Kindle Edition, p. xi
8. Whitman, Walt, *Leaves of Grass: The First (1855) Edition* (Penguin Classics), Kindle Edition, pp. xi-xii
9. Whitman, Walt, *Leaves of Grass: The First (1855) Edition* (Penguin Classics), Kindle Edition, p. xii
10. Whitman, Walt, *Leaves of Grass: The First (1855) Edition* (Penguin Classics), Kindle Edition, p. xiv
11. Kuebrich David, "Literary Shamanism & the Crisis of the Union, [review]," in *Walt Whitman Quarterly Review*, Volume 5 | Number 3 (1988), p. 27
12. Tucker, Mike, *Dreaming with Open Eyes: the Shamanic in 20th C Art and Culture*, London: Aquarian/HarperSanFrancisco, 1992
13. Kuebrich, David, *Minor Prophecy: Walt Whitman's New American Religion*, John Wiley & Sons, 1990, p.2
14. Kuebrich, David, *Minor Prophecy: Walt Whitman's New American Religion*, John Wiley & Sons, 1990, p. 3
15. Kuebrich, David, *Minor Prophecy: Walt Whitman's New American Religion*, John Wiley & Sons, 1990, p. 12
16. Robertson, Michael, *Worshipping Walt: The Whitman Disciples*, Princeton University Press, 2010, p.13
17. Robertson, Michael, *Worshipping Walt: The Whitman Disciples*, Princeton University Press, 2010, p. 6
18. http://www.jnani.org/mrking/writings/post2000/Hourihanintro.htm
19. Hourihan, Paul, Mysticism in American Literature: Thoreau's Quest and Whitman's Self, Redding, Vedantic Shores Press, 2004, p.78
20. Hourihan, Paul, *Mysticism in American Literature: Thoreau's Quest and Whitman's Self*, Redding: Vedantic Shores Press, 2004, p. 83
21. Hourihan, Paul, *Mysticism in American Literature: Thoreau's Quest and Whitman's Self*, Redding: Vedantic Shores Press, 2004, p.87
22. Hourihan, Paul, *Mysticism in American Literature: Thoreau's Quest and Whitman's Self*, Redding: Vedantic Shores Press, 2004, p.91
23. Burroughs, John, *Whitman: A Study*, Boston and New York: Houghton, Mifflin and Company, 1896, p. 24
24. Burroughs, John, *Whitman: A Study*, Boston and New York: Houghton, Mifflin and Company, 1896, p.41
25. Burroughs, John, *Whitman: A Study*, Boston and New York: Houghton, Mifflin and Company, 1896, p. 35
26. Burroughs, John, *Whitman: A Study*, Boston and New York: Houghton, Mifflin and Company, 1896, p. 36
27. Bucke, R. M. *Walt Whitman*, Philadelphia: David McKay, 1883, p. 40
28. Bucke, R. M. *Walt Whitman*, Philadelphia: David McKay, 1883, p. 42
29. Carpenter, Edward, *Days with Walt Whitman*, London: George Allen, 1906, p. 43
30. Whitman, Walt, *Leaves of Grass: The First (1855) Edition* (Penguin Classics), Kindle Edition, p. 25
31. Xenophon (Trans.: Hugh Tredennick and Robin Waterfield), *Conversations of Socrates*, London: Penguin, 1990, "The Dinner Party" 2.19, p. 234
32. Bucke, R. M. *Walt Whitman*, Philadelphia: David McKay, 1883, p. 42
33. James, W. *The Varieties of Religious Experience*, Middlesex, England: Penguin Books, 1986, p.87
34. Mercer, Dorothy, "Walt Whitman on Reincarnation" in *Vedanta and The West*, IX Nov/Dec 1946
35. Rolland, Romain, *Prophets of the New India*, London, Toronto, Melbourne, Sidney: Cassell and Co., 1930, p.273
36. Rolland, Romain, *Prophets of the New India*, London, Toronto, Melbourne, Sidney: Cassell and Co., 1930, p. 285

37. Nambiar, O.K. *Maha Yogi: Walt Whitman: New Light on Yoga,* Bangalore: Jeevan Publications, 1978, p. iii
38. Chandmal, Asit, *One Thousand Moons: Krishnamurti at Eighty-Five,* New York: Abrams 1985, p. 21
39. Nambiar, O.K. *Maha Yogi: Walt Whitman: New Light on Yoga,* Bangalore: Jeevan Publications, 1978, p. 30
40. Nambiar, O.K. *Maha Yogi: Walt Whitman:New Light on Yoga,* Bangalore: Jeevan Publications, 1978, p. 236
41. https://www.theosophical.org/publications/quest-magazine/1346
42. Traubel, Horace, *With Walt Whitman in Camden, Vol. 1,* Boston: Small, Maynard & Company, 1906, p. 119
43. Chari, V.K. *Whitman in the Light of Vedantic Mysticism,* Lincoln: University of Nebraska Press, 1976
44. Allen, G.W. *The Solitary Singer: A Critical Biography of Walt Whitman,* Chicago: University of Chicago Press, 1985
45. Sachitanandan, V. *Whitman and Bharati: A Comparative Study,* Bombay, Calcutta, Delhi, Madras: The MacMillan Company of India Ltd., 1978
46. Cupitt, Don, *Mysticism After Modernity,* Oxford: Blackwell Publishers, 1998, p. 45
47. Nanamoli, Bhikku, and Bhodi, Bhikku, *The Middle Length Discourses of the Buddha: a New Translation of the Majjhima Nikaya,* Boston: Wisdom Publications, 1995, 70.21, p. 582
48. Bucke, R. M. *Walt Whitman,* Philadelphia: David McKay, 1883, p. 196
49. Traubel, Horace, *With Walt Whitman in Camden, Vol. 1,* Boston: Small, Maynard & Company, 1906, p. 103
50. Robertson, Michael, *Worshipping Walt: The Whitman Disciples,* Princeton University Press, 2010, p.17
51. Thoreau, Henry, *Walden and Other Writings,* Bantam, 1962, p. 280
52. Thoreau, Henry, *Walden and Other Writings,* Bantam, 1962, p.86
53. https://whitmanarchive.org/published/LG/1856/poems/34
54. Bucke, R. M. *Walt Whitman,* Philadelphia: David McKay, 1883, 197
55. Whitman, Walt, *Specimen Days,* London: The Folio Society, 1979, p. 240
56. Bucke, R. M. *Walt Whitman,* Philadelphia, 1883, p. 61
57. Whitman, Walt, *Specimen Days,* London: The Folio Society, 1979, p. 118
58. Callow, Philip, *Walt Whitman: From Noon to Starry Night,* London: Allison & Busby, 1992, p. 242
59. Thoreau, Henry, *Walden and Other Writings,* Bantam, 1962, p. 16
60. Jefferies, R. *The Story of My Heart,* London: MacMillan St Martin's Press, 1968
61. Jefferies, R. *The Story of My Heart,* London: MacMillan St Martin's Press, 1968, p. 56
62. Jefferies, R. *The Story of My Heart,* London: MacMillan St Martin's Press, 1968, p. 17
63. Muir, John, *Letters to a Friend, 1866-1879,* Boston and New York: Houghton Mifflin Company, 1915, (letter of 1873)
64. Whitman, Walt (Ed. Edwin Haviland Miller), *The Correspondence,* New York: New York UP, 1961, vol. 5, p. 95.
65. Traherne, Thomas, *Selected Poems and Prose,* London: Penguin, 1991
66. Wordsworth, William, 'The Prelude' in *Poetical Works,* Oxford: Oxford University Press, 1990, verses 356 - 380, p. 460
67. Traherne, Thomas, *Centuries of Meditations,* Fintry: Shrine of Wisdom; 2002, p. x
68. Traherne, Thomas, *Selected Poems and Prose,* London: Penguin, 1991, p. 194
69. Dawkins, Richard, *Unweaving the Rainbow,* London: Penguin, 1998, p. 17
70. Swinburne, Algernon Charles, *William Blake: A Critical Essay,* London: John Camden Hotten, 1868, p. 300.
71. Whitman, Walt (Ed. Clarence Gohdes and Rollo G. Silver), *Faint Clews & Indirections: Manuscripts of Walt Whitman and His Family,* Durham: Duke UP, 1949, p. 53
72. Bellin, H. F. and Ruhl, D. (Eds.), *Blake and Swedenborg: Opposition is True Friendship,* New York: Swedenborg Foundation, 1985, p.105
73. https://whitmanarchive.org/criticism/disciples/gilchrist/works/anc.02116.html
74. Cited in Naifeh, S. and Smith, G.W., *Jackson Pollock: An American Saga,* London: Pimlico, 1992, p. 337
75. Pirsig, Robert M., *Lila: An Enquiry into Morals,* London: Black Swan, 1991, p. 44-62
76. Burroughs, John, *Whitman: A Study,* Boston and New York: Houghton, Mifflin and Company, 1896, p. 51
77. Whitman, Walt (Ed. Horace Traubel), *An American Primer,* Boston: Small, Maynard, 1904, p. 18
78. Robertson, Michael, *Worshipping Walt: The Whitman Disciples,* Princeton University Press, 2010, p. 20
79. Rajneesh, B.S., *Krishna: The Man and His Philosophy,* Oregon: Rajneesh Foundation International, 1985, p.6
80. https://www.constitution.org/jl/tolerati.htm

References

81. Gregory, John, *The Neoplatonists: A Reader*, London and New York: Routledge, 1999, p. 180
82. https://www.osv.com/Article/TabId/493/ArtMID/13569/ArticleID/10336/What-is-a-Spiritual-Director.aspx
83. King, Mike, *Enigma's Coda*, London: Stochastic Press, 2016
84. Gabb, W.J., *The Goose is Out: A Zen Pilgrim's Progress*, 58 Eccleston Square, London: The Buddhist Society, 1944, p. 28
85. Palmer, Martin and Elizabeth Breuilly (Eds.) *The Book of the Chuang Tzu*, London: Penguin Arkana, 1996, p. 64
86. Feuerstein, Georg, *Holy Madness: The shock tactics and radical teachings of crazy-wise adepts, holy fools, and rascal gurus*, London: Arkana, p. 55
87. Storr, Anthony, *Feet of Clay: A Study of Gurus*, London: HarperCollins Publishers, 1997, pp. 23-43
88. Bennett, J., *Witness (2nd Ed.)*, Wellingborough: Turnstone Press, 1983, p. 243
89. Chandmal, Asit, One Thousand Moons: Krishnamurti at Eighty-Five, New York: Abrams, 1985, p. 9
90. https://en.wikipedia.org/wiki/U._G._Krishnamurti
91. Feuerstein, Georg, *Holy Madness: The shock tactics and radical teachings of crazy-wise adepts, holy fools, and rascal gurus*, London: Arkana, p. 73
92. Feuerstein, Georg, *Holy Madness: The shock tactics and radical teachings of crazy-wise adepts, holy fools, and rascal gurus*, London: Arkana, 1990, p.72
93. https://emilymrutherford.com/2011/07/21/adventures-in-the-archives-or-in-which-professional-homosexuality-takes-a-new-turn/
94. Feuerstein, Georg, *Holy Madness: The shock tactics and radical teachings of crazy-wise adepts, holy fools, and rascal gurus*, London: Arkana, p. 74
95. https://en.wikipedia.org/wiki/Sogyal_Rinpoche#Abuse_allegations
96. Rawlinson, Andrew, *The Book of Enlightened Maste:, Western Teachers in Eastern Traditions*, Chicago and La Salle, Illinois: Open Court, 1997
97. Bharati, Agehananda, *The Light at the Centre: Context and Pretext of Modern Mysticism*, Santa Barbara: Ross-Erikson, 1976
98. Rajneesh, B.S., *The Book of the Secrets Vol. 2*, New York, Hagerstown, San Francisco, London: Harper Colophon, 1979
99. Feuerstein, Georg, *Holy Madness: The shock tactics and radical teachings of crazy-wise adepts, holy fools, and rascal gurus*, London: Arkana, p.65
100. Possamai, Adam (Ed.), *Handbook of Hyper-real Religions*, Leiden, Boston: Brill, 2012
101. Heelas, Paul, *The New Age*, Oxford and Malden: Blackwell Publishers, 1996, p. 137
102. https://en.wikipedia.org/wiki/Operation_Snow_White
103. Yenner, William, *American Guru: A Story of Love, Betrayal and Healing, Former Students of Andrew Cohen Speak Out*, Rhinebeck, New York: Epigraph Books, 2009, p. 1
104. Yenner, William, *American Guru: A Story of Love, Betrayal and Healing, Former Students of Andrew Cohen Speak Out*, Rhinebeck, New York: Epigraph Books, 2009, p. 30
105. https://www.andrewcohen.com/open-letter/
106. https://en.wikipedia.org/wiki/Abbey_Arts_Centre
107. https://www.andrewcohen.com/open-letter/
108. http://www.stochasticpress.com/papers/SocratesMystic.html
109. Plato (Trans. Walter Hamilton), *The Symposium*, Harmondsworth: Penguin, 1951, p. 103
110. Plato (Trans. Walter Hamilton), *The Symposium*, Harmondsworth: Penguin, 1951, p. 101
111. Plato (Trans. Walter Hamilton), *The Symposium*, Harmondsworth: Penguin, 1951, p. 102
112. Needleman, Jacob, *The Heart of Philosophy*, London, Melbourne and Henley, Routledge and Kegan Paul, 1983, p. 35
113. Plato (Trans. Walter Hamilton), *The Symposium*, Harmondsworth: Penguin, 1951, p. 110
114. Plato (Trans. Walter Hamilton), *The Symposium*, Harmondsworth: Penguin, 1951, p. 111
115. Plato (Trans. Walter Hamilton), *Phaedrus and Letters VII and VIII*, Harmondsworth: Penguin, 1973, p. 46
116. Plato, *Protagoras and Meno*, Penguin Books, Middlesex, England, 1981, p.127
117. Robertson, Michael, *Worshipping Walt: The Whitman Disciples*, Princeton University Press, 2010, p.25
118. King, Mike, *Luminous: The Spiritual Life on Film*, London: Stochastic Press, 2018, p. 168
119. Trungpa, C., *Cutting Through Spiritual Materialism*, Boston and London: Shambhala, 1987, p. 38
120. http://www.bbc.com/culture/story/20140414-americas-best-selling-poet

121. Rumi, Jelaluddin, *The Ruins of the Heart* (trans. Edmund Helminski) Putney: Threshold, 1981, p.10

122. Rumi, Jelaluddin (trans. A.J.Arberry), *Mystical Poems of Rumi – Vol. 1*, Chicago and London: The University of Chicago Press, 1968, p. 5

123. Rumi, Jelaluddin (trans. Edmund Helminski), *The Ruins of the Heart*, Putney: Threshold, 1981, p. 23

124. http://www.khamush.com/divani_shams.htm

125. Ouspensky, P. D., *In Search of the Miraculous: Fragments of an Unknown Teaching*, Arkana, 1987, p. 44

126. Ouspensky, P. D., *In Search of the Miraculous: Fragments of an Unknown Teaching*, Arkana, 1987, p. 65

127. Ouspensky, P. D., *In Search of the Miraculous: Fragments of an Unknown Teaching*, Arkana, 1987, p. 58

128. Ouspensky, P. D., *In Search of the Miraculous: Fragments of an Unknown Teaching*, Arkana, 1987, p. 20

129. Ouspensky, P.D., *Tertium Organum: A Key to the Enigmas of the World*, New York: Alfred A. Knopf, 1947, p. 236

130. Ouspensky, P. D., *In Search of the Miraculous: Fragments of an Unknown Teaching*, Arkana, 1987, p. 251

131. Hartmann, de, Thomas and Olga, *Our Life with Mr Gurdjieff*, London: Arkana, 1992, p. 178

132. Brunton, Paul, *A Search in Secret India*, York Beach, Maine: Samuel Weiser, Inc. 1970, p. 194

133. Brunton, Paul, *A Search in Secret India*, York Beach, Maine: Samuel Weiser, Inc. 1970, p. 130

134. Brunton, Paul, *A Search in Secret India*, York Beach, Maine: Samuel Weiser, Inc. 1970, p. 141

135. Brunton, Paul, *A Search in Secret India*, York Beach, Maine: Samuel Weiser, Inc. 1970, p. 144

136. Brunton, Paul, *A Search in Secret India*, York Beach, Maine: Samuel Weiser, Inc. 1970, p. 152

137. Brunton, Paul, *A Search in Secret India*, York Beach, Maine: Samuel Weiser, Inc. 1970, p. 157

138. Tweedie, Irina, *Daughter of Fire: A Diary of a Spiritual Training with a Sufi Master*, Inverness, California: The Golden Sufi Centre, 1995, p. ix

139. Tweedie, Irina, *Daughter of Fire: A Diary of a Spiritual Training with a Sufi Master*, Inverness, California: The Golden Sufi Centre, 1995, p. 120

140. Tweedie, Irina, *Daughter of Fire: A Diary of a Spiritual Training with a Sufi Master*, Inverness, California: The Golden Sufi Centre, 1995, p. 113

141. Tweedie, Irina, *Daughter of Fire: A Diary of a Spiritual Training with a Sufi Master*, Inverness, California: The Golden Sufi Centre, 1995, p. 123

142. Tweedie, Irina, *Daughter of Fire: A Diary of a Spiritual Training with a Sufi Master*, Inverness, California: The Golden Sufi Centre, 1995, p. 87

143. Tweedie, Irina, *Daughter of Fire: A Diary of a Spiritual Training with a Sufi Master*, Inverness, California: The Golden Sufi Centre, 1995, p. 34

144. Tweedie, Irina, *Daughter of Fire: A Diary of a Spiritual Training with a Sufi Master*, Inverness, California: The Golden Sufi Centre, 1995, p.55

145. Tweedie, Irina, *Daughter of Fire: A Diary of a Spiritual Training with a Sufi Master*, Inverness, California: The Golden Sufi Centre, 1995, p. 72

146. Tweedie, Irina, *Daughter of Fire: A Diary of a Spiritual Training with a Sufi Master*, Inverness, California: The Golden Sufi Centre, 1995,, p. 132

147. Krishnamurti, J., *The Awakening of Intelligence*, London: Victor Gollancz, 1973, p. 536

148. see this web page: http://www.strippingthegurus.com/stgsamplechapters/krishnamurti.html

149. Davies, Paul, *God and the New Physics*, London: Penguin, 1990, p. ix and p. 229

150. https://en.wikipedia.org/wiki/U._G._Krishnamurti

151. Crow Dog, Leonard, and Erdoes, Richard, *Crow Dog: Four Generations of Sioux Medicine Men*, New York: HarperPerennial, 1996, p. 71

152. Osborne, Arthur, *Ramana Maharshi and the Path of Self-Knowledge*, Maine: Samuel Weiser, 1970, p. 153

153. Wombacher, Michael, *11 Days at the Edge*, Findhorn: Findhorn Press, 2008, p. 148

154. Wombacher, Michael, *11 Days at the Edge*, Findhorn: Findhorn Press, 2008, p. 151

155. http://www.jnani.org/mrking/writings/asats/catdog.html

156. Forman, Robert, *Enlightenment Ain't What It's Cracked Up To Be: A Journey of Discovery, Snow and Jazz in the Soul*, Washington: O Books, 2011, p.2

157. https://www.wsj.com/articles/headspace-vs-calm-the-meditation-battle-thats-anything-but-zen-11544889606

References

158. Forman, Robert, *Enlightenment Ain't What It's Cracked Up To Be: A Journey of Discovery, Snow and Jazz in the Soul*, Washington: O Books, 2011p. 8
159. Forman, Robert, *Enlightenment Ain't What It's Cracked Up To Be: A Journey of Discovery, Snow and Jazz in the Soul*, Washington: O Books, 2011, p. 46
160. King, Mike, *The American Cinema of Excess: Extremes of the National Mind on Film*, London: Stochastic Press, 2016, p. 78
161. Forman, Robert, *Enlightenment Ain't What It's Cracked Up To Be: A Journey of Discovery, Snow and Jazz in the Soul*, Washington: O Books, 2011, p. 48
162. Forman, Robert, *Enlightenment Ain't What It's Cracked Up To Be: A Journey of Discovery, Snow and Jazz in the Soul*, Washington: O Books, 2011, p.78
163. Hart, David A., *The Unification of World Faith: The Challenge of Sun Myung Moon*, Thiruvananthapuram: Om Books, 2007
164. Harvey, Andrew, *Hidden Journey*, London: Rider, 1991, p. 30
165. Harvey, Andrew, *Hidden Journey*, London: Rider, 1991, p.33
166. Harvey, Andrew, *Hidden Journey*, London: Rider, 1991, p. 40
167. http://www.ralphmag.org/CA/harvey-meera.html
168. Kierkegaard, S., *The Essential Kierkegaard*, Princeton, New Jersey: Princeton University Press, 1990, p. 280
169. Robertson, Michael, *Worshipping Walt: The Whitman Disciples*, Princeton University Press, 2010, p. 214
170. Robertson, Michael, *Worshipping Walt: The Whitman Disciples*, Princeton University Press, 2010, p. 51
171. Ariyapariyesana Sutta, https://www.accesstoinsight.org/tipitaka/mn/mn.026.than.html
172. Callow, Philip, *Walt Whitman: From Noon to Starry Night*, London: Allison & Busby, 1992
173. Robertson, Michael, *Worshipping Walt: The Whitman Disciples*, Princeton University Press, 2010, p. 239
174. Traubel, Horace, *With Walt Whitman in Camden, Vol. 1*, Boston: Small, Maynard & Company, 1906, p. 144
175. Traubel, Horace, *With Walt Whitman in Camden, Vol. 1*, Boston: Small, Maynard & Company, 1906, p. 14
176. Traubel, Horace, *With Walt Whitman in Camden, Vol. 1*, Boston: Small, Maynard & Company, 1906, p. 110
177. Traubel, Horace, *With Walt Whitman in Camden, Vol. 1*, Boston: Small, Maynard & Company, 1906, p. 148
178. Traubel, Horace, *With Walt Whitman in Camden, Vol. 1*, Boston: Small, Maynard & Company, 1906, p. 207
179. Gould, Mitchell Santine, "Walt Whitman's Quaker paradox" in *Quaker History*, V. 96, 1 (Spring 2007): 1-23
180. Traubel, Horace, *With Walt Whitman in Camden, Vol. 1*, Boston: Small, Maynard & Company, 1906, p. 230
181. Traubel, Horace, *With Walt Whitman in Camden, Vol. 2*, New York: Mitchell Kennerley, 1915, p. 19
182. Traubel, Horace, *With Walt Whitman in Camden, Vol. 1*, Boston: Small, Maynard & Company, 1906, p. 77
183. https://www.bartleby.com/229/5022.html
184. Traubel, Horace, *With Walt Whitman in Camden, Vol. 2*, New York: Mitchell Kennerley, 1915, p. 63
185. Traubel, Horace, *With Walt Whitman in Camden, Vol. 2*, New York: Mitchell Kennerley, 1915, p. 168
186. Bucke, R.M., *Walt Whitman*, Philadelphia: David McKay, 1883, p. 345
187. Bucke, R.M., *Walt Whitman*, Philadelphia: David McKay, 1883, p. 346
188. Hermes Trismegistus (Trans. Walter Scott), *Hermetica*, Solos Press, 1997, p. 97
189. Robertson, Michael, *Worshipping Walt: The Whitman Disciples*, Princeton University Press, 2010, p. 38
190. Burroughs, John, *Whitman: A Study*, Boston and New York: Houghton, Mifflin and Company, 1896, p. 3
191. Burroughs, John, *Whitman: A Study*, Boston and New York: Houghton, Mifflin and Company, 1896, p. 5
192. Burroughs, John, *Whitman: A Study*, Boston and New York: Houghton, Mifflin and Company, 1896, p. 52
193. Burroughs, John, *Whitman: A Study*, Boston and New York: Houghton, Mifflin and Company, 1896, p. 53
194. Burroughs, John, *Whitman: A Study*, Boston and New York: Houghton, Mifflin and Company, 1896, p. 56
195. Burroughs, John, *Whitman: A Study*, Boston and New York: Houghton, Mifflin and Company, 1896, p. 94
196. Burroughs, John, *Whitman: A Study*, Boston and New York: Houghton, Mifflin and Company, p. 96

197. Burroughs, John, *Whitman: A Study*, Boston and New York: Houghton, Mifflin and Company, p. 258
198. Traubel, Horace, *With Walt Whitman in Camden*, Vol. 3, New York: Mitchell Kennerley, 1914, p. 28
199. Traubel, Horace, *With Walt Whitman in Camden*, Vol. 3, New York: Mitchell Kennerley, 1914, p. 66
200. Traubel, Horace, *With Walt Whitman in Camden*, Vol. 1, Boston: Small, Maynard & Company, 1906, p. 348
201. Traubel, Horace, *With Walt Whitman in Camden*, Vol. 2, New York: Mitchell Kennerley, 1915, p. 9
202. Traubel, Horace, *With Walt Whitman in Camden*, Vol. 2, New York: Mitchell Kennerley, 1915, p. 43
203. Traubel, Horace, *With Walt Whitman in Camden*, Vol. 2, New York: Mitchell Kennerley, 1915, p. 71
204. Traubel, Horace, *With Walt Whitman in Camden*, Vol. 2, New York: Mitchell Kennerley, 1915, p. 343
205. Traubel, Horace, *With Walt Whitman in Camden*, Vol. 1, Boston: Small, Maynard & Company, 1906, p. 231
206. Traubel, Horace, *With Walt Whitman in Camden*, Vol. 1, Boston: Small, Maynard & Company, 1906, p. 278
207. Symonds, John Addington, *Walt Whitman: a Study*, London: John C. Nimmo, 1893, p. 14
208. Symonds, John Addington, *Walt Whitman: a Study*, London: John C. Nimmo, 1893, p. 35
209. Traubel, Horace, *With Walt Whitman in Camden*, Vol. 1, Boston: Small, Maynard & Company, 1906, p.73
210. Traubel, Horace, *With Walt Whitman in Camden*, Vol. 1, Boston: Small, Maynard & Company, 1906, p. 122
211. Traubel, Horace, *With Walt Whitman in Camden*, Vol. 1, Boston: Small, Maynard & Company, 1906, p. 202
212. Traubel, Horace, *With Walt Whitman in Camden*, Vol. 1, Boston: Small, Maynard & Company, 1906, p. 388
213. Traubel, Horace, *With Walt Whitman in Camden*, Vol. 2, New York: Mitchell Kennerley, 1915, p. 276
214. Symonds, John Addington, *Walt Whitman: a Study*, London: John C. Nimmo, 1893, p. 1
215. Symonds, John Addington, *Walt Whitman: a Study*, London: John C. Nimmo, 1893, p. 48
216. Carpenter, Edward, *Days with Walt Whitman*, London: George Allen, 1906, p. 5
217. Carpenter, Edward, *Days with Walt Whitman*, London: George Allen, 1906, p. 15
218. Carpenter, Edward, *Days with Walt Whitman*, London: George Allen, 1906, p. 21
219. Carpenter, Edward, *Days with Walt Whitman*, London: George Allen, 1906, p. 31
220. Carpenter, Edward, *Days with Walt Whitman*, London: George Allen, 1906, p. 49
221. Carpenter, Edward, *Days with Walt Whitman*, London: George Allen, 1906, p. 49, p.77
222. Traubel, Horace, *With Walt Whitman in Camden*, Vol. 1, Boston: Small, Maynard & Company, 1906, p. 104
223. Traubel, Horace, *With Walt Whitman in Camden*, Vol. 1, Boston: Small, Maynard & Company, 1906, p. 158
224. Traubel, Horace, *With Walt Whitman in Camden*, Vol. 3, New York: Mitchell Kennerley, 1914, p. 415
225. https://whitmanarchive.org/criticism/disciples/gilchrist/works/anc.02116.html
226. Bucke, R.M., *Walt Whitman*, Philadelphia: David McKay, 1883, p. 31
227. Bucke, R.M., *Walt Whitman*, Philadelphia: David McKay, 1883, p. 176
228. Bucke, R.M., *Walt Whitman*, Philadelphia: David McKay, 1883, p. 7
229. Zaehner, R.C., *Drugs, Mysticism and Make-Believe*, Collins, London 1972, p. 60 and p. 63
230. Bucke, R.M., *Walt Whitman*, Philadelphia: David McKay, 1883, p. 8
231. Robertson, Michael, *Worshipping Walt: The Whitman Disciples*, Princeton University Press, 2010, p. 99
232. Bucke, R.M., *Walt Whitman*, Philadelphia: David McKay, 1883, p. 35
233. Bucke, R.M., *Walt Whitman*, Philadelphia: David McKay, 1883, p. 50
234. Bucke, R.M., *Walt Whitman*, Philadelphia: David McKay, 1883,p. 50
235. Bucke, R.M., *Walt Whitman*, Philadelphia: David McKay, 1883, p. 51
236. Bucke, R.M., *Walt Whitman*, Philadelphia: David McKay, 1883, p. 61
237. cited in Robertson, Michael, *Worshipping Walt: The Whitman Disciples*, Princeton University Press, 2010, p. 127
238. Bucke, R.M., *Walt Whitman*, Philadelphia: David McKay, 1883, 185
239. Caplan, Mariana, *Halfway Up the Mountain: the Error of Premature Claims of Enlightenment*, Prescott, Arizona: Hohm Press, 1999
240. https://www.themindfulnessinitiative.org.uk/about/mindfulness-appg

241. https://www.theguardian.com/lifeandstyle/2016/jan/23/is-mindfulness-making-us-ill

242. Tobert, Natalie, *Cultural Perspectives on Mental Wellbeing: Spiritual Interpretations of Symptoms in Medical Practice*, London and Philadelphia: Jessica Kingsley Publishers, 2017

243. Trungpa, C., *Cutting Through Spiritual Materialism*, Boston and London: Shambhala, 1987, p. 3

244. Trungpa, C., *Cutting Through Spiritual Materialism*, Boston and London: Shambhala, 1987, p. 13

245. Trungpa, C., *Cutting Through Spiritual Materialism*, Boston and London: Shambhala, p. 31

246. King, Mike, *Secularism: The Hidden Origins of Disbelief*, Cambridge: James Clarke & Co., 2007

247. King, Mike, *Mountain Calls*, London: Stochastic Press, 2017

INDEX

Advaita, 50, 52, 111, 132, 151
agape, 161, 162, 164, 167, 175, 179, 193, 203, 209
Alcibiades, 81, 112-116, 126, 141, 163, 169, 194, 202, 203
Allen, Gay Wilson, 15, 50, 92
animism, 17, 38, 73, 143, 182, 214
Anthroposophy, 143, 146
ashram, 2, 8, 9, 13, 50, 100, 101, 102, 128, 157, 200
atheism, 7, 36, 55, 69, 74, 117, 181, 184, 213
atonement, 52, 72, 111, 117, 207, 209, 212
Aurobindo, Sri, 93, 157
Ayengar, B. K. S, 7
Balsekar, Ramesh, 95
Bennett, John G., 86, 115
Bhagavad Gita, 16, 46, 50, 55, 57, 71, 189
bhakti, 51, 52, 121, 133, 134, 160
Black Elk, 73
Blake, William, 16, 23, 24, 55, 64, 68, 69, 70, 71, 72, 73, 102, 120, 160, 161, 192, 193, 194
Bohm, David, 88, 89, 138-140, 142, 197, 203, 214
Bon (religion), 117, 145
Brunton, Paul, 128-131, 141, 167, 178, 184, 190
Bucke, Richard Maurice, 2, 3, 7, 13, 16, 23, 24, 25, 27, 28, 29, 31, 44, 46, 47, 58, 60, 68, 171, 173, 177, 194-197, 206, 213
Buddha, the, 6, 7, 9, 14, 32, 36, 42, 43, 52, 77, 88, 89, 104, 107, 110, 117, 136, 137, 138, 145, 146, 147, 148, 154, 159, 170, 180, 192, 197, 204, 209, 211, 214
Burroughs, John, 58, 72, 171, 178-182, 187, 194, 195, 214
Burroughs, William, 15
Carlyle, Thomas, 35, 56, 57, 177
Carpenter, Edward, 29, 167, 171, 187-192, 195
Caussade, Jean Pierre de, 82
Chari, V. K., 46, 50
Christ, Jesus, 7, 19, 36, 42, 52, 54, 81, 83, 88, 104, 119, 153, 166, 167, 175, 197, 207, 208, 209
Christianity, 3, 6, 7, 17, 24, 31, 35, 36, 42, 52, 53, 54, 55, 64, 66, 67, 68, 72, 74, 76, 79, 83, 98, 121, 135, 145, 155, 160, 162, 190, 197, 209, 210, 213

Cohen, Andrew, 9, 42, 95, 96, 106, 107, 108, 109, 110, 111, 128, 132, 147-152, 160, 197, 199, 200, 201, 202, 203, 204, 205, 206, 209, 214
Cosmic Consciousness, 2, 13, 24, 177
Cowley, Malcolm, 16, 17, 24
Crow Dog, 73, 143-146, 160, 182, 207, 209
cult, 8, 42, 98, 99, 103, 107
Cupitt, Don, 51, 133, 164
darshan, 14, 51, 83, 93, 129, 130, 160, 162, 172, 194, 196
Darwin, Charles, 34, 44, 76, 125
Deism, 35, 53
democracy, 1, 19, 75, 115, 161, 165, 171, 186, 187, 197, 213, 215
Descartes, René, 3, 7, 78, 79, 80
discipleship light, 6, 208, 209, 210, 212, 214
Eckhart, Meister, 32, 34, 81
Eliade, Mircea, 18
Emerson, Ralph Waldo, 21, 23, 35, 46, 55, 56, 57, 58, 177, 179
Enlightenment, European, 4, 7, 55, 74, 76, 111, 140, 146, 153, 155, 206, 210
enlightenment, spiritual, 2, 7, 9, 27, 28, 34, 77, 85, 86, 89, 90, 92, 93, 95, 96, 107, 109, 110, 112, 117, 121, 130, 131, 141, 143, 145, 146, 148, 149, 151, 152, 153, 154, 155, 156, 164, 169, 170, 178, 197, 204, 205, 206, 207, 208, 211, 212, 214, 215
Enneads, 13
eros, 162, 164, 175, 179, 193, 203
Feuerstein, Georg, 86, 91, 92, 93, 94, 102, 103
Forman, Robert, 152-156, 158, 159, 205, 206, 214
Fox, George, 176, 204
Freud, Sigmund, 3, 4, 34, 44, 46, 76, 77, 102, 105
Gabb, W. G., 85
Gilchrist, Anne, 23, 70, 71, 171, 191, 192, 193
Ginsberg, Allen, 15, 92
Good Lance, 143-145
Gurdjieff, G. I., 13, 79, 83, 84, 86, 87, 90, 92, 93, 96, 102, 108, 114, 115, 123-129, 131, 132, 140, 141, 142, 147, 160, 188, 197, 200, 202, 203, 204, 206, 207, 214
guru, 1, 2, 5, 6, 7, 8, 9, 10, 12, 15, 16, 18, 47, 48, 50, 52, 58, 74, 79, 81, 82, 83, 89, 90, 91, 92, 95, 97, 98, 99, 104, 107, 108, 112, 123, 128,

Index

132, 136, 137, 138, 139, 140, 141, 142, 147, 148, 149, 150, 151, 154, 156, 157, 158, 159, 161, 166, 172, 177, 178, 183, 185, 193, 196, 197, 199, 201, 202, 204, 205, 208, 209, 210, 211, 213
Harding, Douglas, 8, 9, 13, 14, 90, 92, 95, 96, 100, 106, 108, 142, 152
Harlan, James, 22, 54
Hart, David A., 156-158
Harvey, Andrew, 93, 95-97, 156, 157, 158, 159, 162, 178, 193, 214
hatha yoga, 8
Hicks, Elias, 174, 176
hierophancy, 2, 26, 48, 82, 98, 111, 112, 117, 118, 119, 121, 123, 125, 128, 133, 135, 137, 140, 142, 145, 146, 147, 150, 152, 158, 160, 161, 163, 172, 182, 184, 186, 192, 198, 199, 200, 201, 202, 204, 206, 207, 209, 210, 212, 213, 215
hierophant, 1, 3, 6, 12, 14, 67, 70, 74, 77, 79, 81, 84, 86, 89, 90, 94, 96, 97, 98, 102, 104, 105, 106, 110, 115, 116, 120, 123, 131, 133, 160, 175, 178, 183, 191, 199, 200, 204, 205, 208, 210, 211, 212, 215
Hinduism, 2, 46, 47, 50, 53, 103, 121, 132, 155, 156, 162, 166, 173, 190, 205, 214
Hourihan, Paul, 16, 19, 20, 21, 24, 31, 33, 34
Hutchinson, George, 16, 17, 18, 24
Huxley, Aldous, 17, 18, 86, 88
individualism, 4, 55, 70, 75, 76, 77, 78, 146, 154, 173
Islam, 6, 99, 119, 121, 123, 133, 210
James, William, 42, 43, 77
Jefferies, Richard, 58, 61, 62, 73
jnani, 51, 52, 133, 190
Kabbalah, 143, 146
karma, 16, 38, 118, 151
Kerouac, Jack, 15
Kierkegaard, Søren, 162
Krishnamurti, Jiddu, 8, 47, 83, 88, 89, 104, 138, 142, 203
Krishnamurti, U. G., 89, 138, 141, 142
Kuebrich, David, 16, 17, 18, 24
Lal, Radha Mohan (Bhai Sahib), 132-138, 140, 142, 145, 147, 160, 178, 207
Leaves of Grass, 13, 16, 19, 21, 22, 23, 25, 27, 29, 33, 46, 47, 50, 54, 56, 57, 59, 71, 164, 175, 176, 177, 179, 181, 183, 185, 188, 189, 190, 192, 194, 197, 206, 213
Leibniz, Gottfried Wilhelm, 78, 79, 80
Lewis, C. S., 14
Lincoln, Abraham, 23, 163

Liquorman, Wayne, 95, 96
Locke, John, 77
Maharaj, Nisargaddata, 95
Maharishi Mahesh Yogi, 152-155, 159, 160
Maharshi, Ramana, 14, 95, 106, 128-133, 141, 146, 159, 160, 167, 178, 184, 190, 200, 208
Marpa (Lotsawa, Marpa), 110, 117, 118, 131, 160, 204, 207, 209, 214
Marx, Karl, 34, 44, 76, 191
Marxism, 72
master, 1, 2, 6, 7, 8, 11, 13, 14, 56, 80, 85, 92, 96, 106, 108, 110, 111, 112, 114, 115, 116, 117, 120, 121, 123, 124, 125, 127, 129, 130, 132, 133, 134, 135, 139, 142, 147, 152, 166, 184, 185, 202, 203, 204, 206, 208, 212, 214, 215
Mercer, Dorothy, 46
Milarepa, Jetsun, 110, 117, 118, 160, 204, 206-209, 214
moksha, 7, 141
Mother Meera, 9, 83, 93-96, 131, 156-160, 173, 178, 188, 191, 196, 200, 204
Muir, John, 58, 63, 73, 178
mysticism, 7, 17, 19, 24, 27, 29, 31, 32, 33, 34, 36, 47, 50, 58, 61, 62, 63, 65, 66, 67, 69, 70, 81, 96, 113, 121, 122, 123, 135, 140, 153, 155, 169, 170, 179, 186, 195, 199
Nambiar, O. K., 2, 47-50, 172, 177, 178
Native Americans, 72, 73, 143, 144, 145, 146, 160, 182
Nature mystic, 58, 63, 73
Nausea, 16
Needleman, Jacob, 114
Neoplatonism, 24, 72, 78, 80, 210
New Age, 24, 78, 79, 104, 128, 140, 197, 213
Newton, Sir Isaac, 80
Nietzsche, Friedrich Wilhelm, 16, 38, 127, 152
O. K. Nambiar, 2, 47, 48-50, 172, 177, 178
O'Connor, William Douglas, 15, 22
occult, 51, 61, 88, 125, 126, 133, 137, 143, 145, 160, 186, 207, 214
Orage, A. R., 79, 84, 128
Ouspensky, P. D., 123-129, 140, 141, 142, 143, 188, 197, 202, 203, 208, 209
Pali Canon, 42, 136, 147
Parsons, Tony, 9, 95, 96, 121
Patanjali, 71, 125, 132, 133
perennial philosophy, 17, 18
Plato, 80, 112, 115, 116, 158, 190
Plotinus, 3, 7, 13, 24, 76, 79, 80, 127
Poonjaji, W. L., 95, 106, 111, 132
Pythagoras, 7, 79, 80

227

Quaker, 53, 174, 175, 188, 200, 213
quintessence, 30, 32, 36, 37
Rajneesh, Bhagwan Shree, 3, 4, 7, 8, 9, 12, 13, 14, 52, 71, 76, 77, 83, 84, 89, 90, 91, 92, 93, 96, 98, 99-106, 108, 109, 111, 112, 113, 121, 128, 142, 147, 148, 149, 151, 154, 186, 196, 199, 200, 206, 212
Ramakrishna, 12, 13, 16, 19, 47, 52, 117, 132, 137, 147, 156, 161, 172, 173, 175, 197
Rawlinson, Andrew, 86, 95
reincarnation, 14, 16, 39, 43, 46, 70, 84, 91, 103, 104, 118, 145
religion, 15, 18, 33, 41, 42, 44, 51, 53, 55, 68, 70, 72, 74, 75, 76, 77, 78, 80, 81, 83, 90, 103, 107, 117, 137, 140, 145, 154, 168, 170, 171, 173, 176, 177, 181, 186, 202, 213
Rinpoche, Sogyal, 92
Robertson, Michael, 16, 18, 19, 24, 55, 75, 117, 162, 163, 171, 172, 195, 196
Rolland, Romain, 46, 213
Rumi, Jalāl ad-Dīn Muhammad, 119-123, 130, 132, 133, 142, 160, 161, 178, 184, 200, 202, 208, 209
samadhi, 48, 101
sangha, 42, 50, 149, 155, 162, 167, 201, 208, 209, 210, 211, 212
Sartre, Jean-Paul, 16, 152
science, 29, 30, 55, 59, 69, 78, 99, 103, 104, 124, 125, 140, 152, 159, 171, 173, 181, 189, 197, 213
Scientology, 103, 104, 105
Sebald, W. G., 9
sexuality, 3, 10, 28, 51, 76, 77, 91, 92, 93, 134, 144, 153, 159, 163, 203
shamanism, 17, 40, 85, 109, 143, 145
Shams-e Tabrizi, 119-123, 130, 131, 132, 135, 142, 160, 178, 184, 202, 208, 209
Shankara, 5, 7, 12, 52, 102, 111, 129, 146, 166, 167, 169
siddhi, 51, 133, 134, 136, 137, 146, 160, 207, 208
socialism, 43, 44, 72, 90, 187, 191
Socrates, 7, 13, 24, 32, 79, 80, 112-116, 124, 126, 131, 135, 137, 141, 148, 158, 160, 161, 162, 163, 169, 194, 200, 202, 203
Spinoza, Baruch, 3, 7, 24, 78, 79, 80
spiritual advisor, 7, 74, 81, 82
spiritual director, 81, 82, 83
spiritual liberation, 5, 6, 7, 77, 90, 146, 169
spiritual materialism, 91, 117, 133, 201, 204, 206, 207, 208, 210, 211, 214

spiritual teacher, 1, 2, 3, 4, 5, 6, 7, 9, 12, 13, 19, 33, 41, 42, 50, 68, 69, 74, 77, 79, 81, 83, 84, 88, 89, 94, 95, 96, 97, 99, 106, 108, 109, 111, 116, 118, 119, 121, 128, 135, 136, 140, 141, 143, 144, 153, 157, 161, 165, 167, 172, 174, 186, 192, 199, 200, 201, 203, 206, 212
St John of the Cross, 7, 20
Storr, Anthony, 86, 154
Sufism, 8, 119, 121, 132, 133, 134, 135, 138, 143, 145
supernatural, 43, 118, 177
Suzuki, T. D., 85
Swedenborg, Emanuel, 70
sycophancy, 1, 6, 195, 201, 203, 213
sycophant, 1, 201, 215
Symonds, John Addington, 171, 181, 183-187, 194
Tantra, 66, 90, 91, 92, 134, 144
Tao, 33, 85, 103, 190, 197
Tarkovsky, Andrei, 4
Tarot, 125, 126, 144
Tennyson, Lord Alfred, 63, 197
Teresa of Avila, 7, 20, 31, 135
Theosophy, 49, 88, 89, 104, 126, 133, 134, 138, 141, 142, 143, 146, 207
Thoreau, Henry David, 16, 19, 21, 46, 50, 55, 56, 60, 61, 175, 182
Thus Spake Zarathustra, 16
Traherne, Thomas, 44, 64, 66-68, 72, 73, 82
Transcendentalists, American, 16, 46, 55, 68, 72, 161
Traubel, Horace, 2, 47, 48, 50, 171, 172-178, 180, 181, 184, 186, 190, 195, 198
Trungpa, Chögyam, 83, 90-93, 96, 102, 117, 133, 145, 201, 203, 204, 210
Tucker, Mike, 17
Tweedie, Irina, 132-136, 140, 141, 142, 143, 147, 148, 178, 207, 209, 214
Unitarianism, 55, 56
Upanishads, 16, 50, 154, 189
Vedanta Society of Los Angeles, 46, 83
via negativa, 14, 52, 160, 190
Vivekananda, 46, 53, 83
Wilde, Oscar, 21, 23, 171
Wombacher, Michael, 106, 147, 148, 150, 152, 205
Wordsworth, William, 66, 67
Yellow Tail, 73
Yenner, William, 106, 107, 108, 147
yoga, 2, 7, 100, 101, 124, 128, 133, 135
Yogananda, Paramahansa, 8, 13, 70, 143

Index

Zen, 2, 8, 13, 20, 72, 85, 96, 102, 145

www.ingramcontent.com/pod-product-compliance
Lightning Source LLC
Chambersburg PA
CBHW030812090426
42736CB00027B/320